Flow

ALSO BY ROY MIKI

POETRY
Mannequin Rising
random access file
saving face: poems selected, 1976–1988
Surrender
There

LITERARY CRITICISM AND OTHER NON-FICTION
Broken Entries: Race, Subjectivity, and Writing
In Flux: Transnational Shifts in Asian Canadian Writing
Justice In Our Time: The Japanese Canadian Redress Settlement
    (with Cassandra Kobayashi)*
The Prepoetics of Williams Carlos Williams: Kora in Hell
A Record of Writing: An Annotated and Illustrated Bibliography
    *of George Bowering**
Redress: Inside the Japanese Canadian Call for Justice

CHILDREN'S LITERATURE
Dolphin SOS (with Slavia Miki)

BOOKS EDITED
Across Currents: Canada–Japan Minority Forum
    (with Rita Wong)
The Artist and the Moose: A Fable of Forget
    by Roy Kiyooka
Beyond the Orchard: Essays on The Martyrology
    (with Fred Wah)
George Bowering Selected: Poems 1961–1992
In Justice: Canada, Minorities, and Human Rights
    (with Scott McFarlane)
*Meanwhile: The Critical Writings of bpNichol**
*Pacific Windows: Collected Poems of Roy K. Kiyooka**
Spirit of Redress: Japanese Canadians in Conference
    (with Cassandra Kobayashi)
This Is My Own: Letters to Wes and Other Writings on Japanese
    Canadians, by Muriel Kitagawa*
Tracing the Paths: Reading ≠ Writing The Martyrology*
Trans.Can.Lit: Resituating the Study of Canadian Literature
    (with Smaro Kamboureli)

* Published by Talonbooks

Flow

POEMS COLLECTED AND NEW

Roy Miki

EDITED BY MICHAEL BARNHOLDEN

with a foreword by Louis Cabri

Talonbooks

Talonbooks
278 East First Avenue, Vancouver, British Columbia, Canada V5T 1A6
talonbooks.com

Talonbooks is located on xʷməθkʷəy̓əm, Sḵwx̱wú7mesh, and səlilwətaʔɬ Lands.

First printing: 2018

Typeset in Arno
Printed and bound in South Korea on woodfree paper

Interior and cover design by Typesmith
On the cover: *Cloudy 1* by Roy Miki

Talonbooks gratefully acknowledges the financial support of the Canada
Council for the Arts, the Government of Canada through the Canada Book
Fund, and the Province of British Columbia through the British Columbia
Arts Council and the Book Publishing Tax Credit.

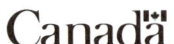 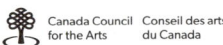 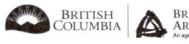

LIBRARY AND ARCHIVES CANADA CATALOGUING IN PUBLICATION

Miki, Roy, 1942–, author
        Flow : poems collected and new / edited by Michael
Barnholden ; with a foreword by Louis Cabri.

Includes bibliographical references and index.
ISBN 978-1-77201-210-1 (HARDCOVER).—978-1-77201-217-0 (SOFTCOVER)

        I. Barnholden, Michael, 1951–, editor II. Cabri, Louis,
writer of foreword III. Title.

PS8576.I32 2018   C811'.54   C2018-902680-4

Contents

Surrender (2001)

There (2006)

353 Mannequin Rising (2011)

469 Cloudy and Clear (2018)

Floward

Roy Miki's comparative social age as a poet is: "younger" than the *TISH* and the Toronto Research Group poets (writers associated with each group began publishing in the 1960s; Miki's first poetry book appeared in 1991); about the same social age as Kootenay School of Writing poets, but stylistically divergent; "older" than many poets affiliated to varying degrees with the emergence of Asian Canadian literature that his example has influenced. That first poetry book, *saving face*, is already a selected poems, 1976–1988. Roy Miki was forty-nine years old by 1991 and had accomplished much in other fields as an "organic intellectual": proactive in modernist and postmodernist literary scholarship, teaching, contemporary poetry editing, cultural history and theory, and in grassroots political organizing. One outcome of publishing late as a poet after career-defining cultural contributions in other areas may be needing to negotiate readers' expectations that the poetry will become legible through the prior contexts and commitments. Miki's poems develop an elusive style, with contexts and commitments of their own. This collected poetry volume, *Flow*, offers readers an astonishing discursive compass for reflection on both the intricate interrelationships as well as the purposeful dissociations between the political and the aesthetic.

All Roy Miki's collected poetry and critical writing swirls around one historical maelstrom, but without sinking into it, the general terms of which Giorgio Agamben pessimistically diagnosed as "the new biopolitical *nomos* [law, custom] of the planet" (176): the concentration camp. Miki lived through one specific form of its apparatus as a Canadian child, his family forcibly removed from Haney, B.C. to Ste. Agathe, Manitoba during the Second World War, the repercussions of which, due to displacement and financial loss, internment, and coerced racialized identity as Japanese Canadians, instigated a context and reality of social trauma for tens of thousands of people. Today, the optimistic legal outcome and renown of his social justice and cultural activism remain of precedent-setting significance for all, and in particular for communities still extricating themselves from Peacekeeping Canada's sordid domestic history of conflating race with citizenship and democracy with unacknowledged racism.

While the Redress Movement is part of Roy Miki's public legacy, his poetry is not as immediately legible in political (representational) terms – nor aesthetic ones. Here I introduce two of Miki's literary techniques, those I call "wobble," and "the broken-entry pun" (after his collection of essays by that name).[1] I coin a technical word ("wobble") to try to describe a feature of his poetic language and to differentiate a stylistic influence that is an outlier on the social age map I began with. In short, wobble isn't literary "opacity." When A.M. Klein's verse displays "richness rather than precision with ample use of synonyms, wordplay, and poetic archaisms" (Pollock, xii), such figural excess is partly the effect of grammatical and referential "wobble." I contend that readers need to adapt to the wobble of Miki's writing, not try to either force the wobble out, or downplay it. To adopt this volume's title word – "flow" – and to quote internet surfer lingo, one has to get slotted and go critical in the barrel of the wave (the poetic line). A Miki "flow" involves semantic slippage (a Miki word) and change of state; and even noticing his poetic language up close doesn't always empirically stabilize it. The wobble in each wave is different (wobbles). Wobble challenges judgments of distinction hardening into norms. Wobble undermines predeterminisms. Here's a line:

> the stylus entered the system at the instance of trauma
> ("watch signs," *Surrender,* p. 263 in this text)

For an English-language sentence, this one's standard stuff: subject + verb + direct object + prepositional phrase. But unremarkable word-class ordering contains structural ambiguity. Does *the instance of trauma* belong to *the system* – the way *the front door* belongs to *the house* in *They entered the house at the front door*? Or does *the instance of trauma* belong to some unspecified entity – the way *the first sign of rain* belongs to an entity other than *the house* in *They entered the house at the first sign of rain*?

Further, the nouns are so specialized they are distancing. Readers don't even get to grasp a "pen," it has to be a "stylus." On the other hand, "stylus" retains a link to the concrete as an antiquated writing implement made from bone or such principally because of its rare current usage (the rarity conveys an impression of elevated diction). Surely with the much-used "pen" few think of a feather even though etymologically that's there too in its distant past. "Stylus" also has an enriching etymological association with "style."

And is *instance* being forced into synonymy with *point*, as in, *at the point of trauma*? *Point* connects etymologically to *stylus* – so choice of *instance* offers another distancing and disassociation. Except, can *instance* be substitutable as the *y* in the phrase *at the y of x* when *x* is not a person but an object? It's rare, and this uncertainty creates wobble.

My initial gestalt interpretation of Miki's sentence proposes that culture is a system and, from that premise, that·learning to write can be traumatic because writing is part of a social institution with particular ideological investments controlling what can be written and said. However, the quasi–"because science" noun wobbles come temptingly close to spoofing rather than to literalizing high-seriousness (as in: Why use "stylus" instead of "pen"? Because we value etymology. Why use "system" instead of "culture"? Because we value objectivity. And so on, but to a point where the phrase *Because x* substitutes for explanation: Why? Because science) – leading to more wobble.

A variant leads to further interpretations when "system" stands not for culture but for the totality of a subject's life at a given point in developmental time, so that a traumatic experience coincides for the subject with the formational stage of literacy, of leaving home and going to school. The sentence simply states what happened, does not judge, or assert causal relationship (the stylus entered the subject's life but did not cause trauma).

A further scenario is that the stylus is where it does not belong, that it has breached the system. Because of trauma, the stylus was able to enter where otherwise it would not have been able to penetrate. The stylus needn't have entered, but did so because a trauma had weakened the system's defenses. In this interpretation, the sentence does not merely state what happened; it judges. That the action happened *at the instance of trauma* suggests there are deleterious effects.

Another scenario follows from *at the instance of* meaning "urgency." Trauma, personified, lives in the system and, like a good host, welcomes the stylus, which accepts the host's invitation to enter. The traumatic condition is such that it urges the stylus *upon* the subject, as one who is addicted feels compelled by the substance to ingest it. Thus the stylus enters the *subject*'s system – with what result? Is it temporary relief? The sentence also judges – in this case, happily.

So Miki's wobbles produce at least three contrasting interpretations:

1) the stylus so happened to enter the subject when the subject was experiencing trauma;
2) the stylus brings oppression (and breaches the system due to trauma);
3) the stylus brings succour.

Range of wobble is evidence of how carefully Roy Miki, a Williams scholar, has read William Carlos Williams for what Bob Perelman calls "social polysemy" (70).[2] Miki sometimes polishes "socially polysemous" wobble with Roy Kiyooka's tones, cadences, and euphonious word choice. But what Miki doesn't do is transpose a Canadian version of "local pride" from Williams – which has been the dominant takeaway for many diverse Canadian poets since Williams was read here. "Local you say? Speaking in person i've always been wary of the private occasion" ("This Side," *There*, p. 298 in this text). Inserting the word "private" signals ideological mediation in the very pragmatics of saying the local: the staging of speaker–hearer roles in mutual co-presence. Miki's poetry breaks with articulating a vernacular poetics of place, identity, and language. Language, rather, is assumed to be a creolizing dialect on the move, writing implicitly a macaronic address. Speech and writing share those awkward-sounding mechanical phrasings otherwise known as idiomatic expressions and stock phrasings that one sometimes finds at the contextual intersection of drastically differing discourses, as well as in multilingual contexts of second-language learning where states of empathy and confusion attract rather than repel each other.

Briefly as to the broken-entry pun: Often, the enunciating subject becomes a flattened pronoun on the page, making visible bpNichol's influence. Nichol's use of a pun mends the pun's breach in language by inventing a narrative for it that coherently joins sound and meaning together, banishing accident. In contrast Miki's broken-entry pun happens when the reader is left with a bit of language broken open and not subsequently mended closed. In this respect, Miki joins a thread of twentieth-century poets who try not to aesthetically "mend" the accidental by artistic means, but try instead to unleash language as the material evidence of historical conditions. The effect in Miki is to imply a larger argument for his poetic text, one that involves more than the literary production of puns as such. What is at stake is a social text that embeds the literary text but does not reduce the social dimension. Miki's stanzaic phrase "device / & slice" ("the alternate sources of energy are drying up," *saving face*, p. 37 in this text) telegraphs this technique. "Device," deliberately not a verb but here dwelling in a verb's slot, opens a breach in syntactical and grammatical patternings holding together the stock two-verb phrase "slice & dice." "Device" leaves readers with open-ended questions regarding how to pattern the phrase, given also that the word appears elsewhere in Miki's oeuvre (e.g., "i buried a memory / in a device," "unable to decipher the end runs," p. 103 in this text). Have both verbs of the stock phrase become nouns, (here is the) device & (here is the) slice? In order to begin constructing a narrative event, I look beyond the boundary of the stock phrase and its modification in the stanza to the preceding lines of the poem for a noun-become-verb: "aqua / train / [the] device & slice [it] / from last / to aghast." But as I proceed to narratively integrate other stanzas of the poem, the lexical and stanzaic levels resist my interpretation and remain in a variegated wobble state.

Hearsay says that good poetry flows naturally, effortlessly. But there's little that is natural about flow in poetry. Over four centuries ago, "flowing verse" meant to strictly alternate so-called short and long syllables. Whatever flow was – spoken language? reading-thinking? embodied perceptual miming? – print lettering divided and shaped flow. "We parsed sentences like good little soldiers" ("Flow Nation," *There*, p. 317 in this text).

So why imagine Roy Miki's poetry *as* grammar? Drawing again from the title of this Collected Poems, in search of flow poetics, wobble etiolates grammar's functions. Verbs move narrative forward, whereas Miki's poetry goes "floward." Nouns perceive the world as things that stand out, upright and discrete ("That static noun with / so much encrustation" ["Identity," *Mannequin Rising*, p. 455 in this text]), whereas a "flow" of words, mostly horizontal and continuous, moves unstably so. As to determiners, such as articles and demonstratives ("this," "that"), specifying and particularizing reference, they miss flow's entire wave dimension where linguistic particles of sense come in waves of interrelation.

But if Roy Miki's poems did exist inside a part of speech, I'd pick the preposition, because his poems are "prepositional" in their effects. His phrases take readers in, around, beside, away from, over, down in an etiolated grammatical world. Flow the only verbal state with no need of declaring outright its reflexive condition; flow wobbles, spewing from broken-entry puns, among other parts. The hard-and-fast will go (has got to flow) – "if the itinerant fluids deke out" ("over heard," *Surrender*, p. 269 in this text).

—LOUIS CABRI

ACKNOWLEDGMENTS

I am grateful to Nicole Markotić for the conversations about Roy Miki's work, and to Nicole and Catriona Strang for the dialogic editing. Thanks too to the Talon team.

ENDNOTES

1   It is no accident that Miki's transformational essay collection, *Broken Entries*, on racialized subjectivity and the deconstruction of racism, connects up with a punning broken-entry technique in his poetry.

2   Perelman writes: "Williams's language is imprecise; 'polysemous' is a bit grand to apply to it, though 'socially polysemous' is not inaccurate" (70).

WORKS CITED

Agamben, Giorgio. *Homo Sacer: Sovereign Power and Bare Life.* Translated by Daniel Heller-Roazen. Stanford, CA: Stanford University Press, 1998.

Miki, Roy. *Broken Entries: Race, Subjectivity, Writing.* Toronto, ON: Mercury Press, 1998.

———. *Mannequin Rising.* Vancouver, BC: New Star Books, 2011.

———. *random access file.* Red Deer, AB: Red Deer College Press, 1995.

———. *Redress: Inside the Japanese Canadian Call for Justice.* Vancouver, BC: Raincoast Books, 2004.

———. *saving face: poems selected, 1976–1988.* Winnipeg, MB: Turnstone Press, 1991.

———. *Surrender.* Toronto, ON: Mercury Press, 2001.

———. *There.* Vancouver, BC: New Star Books, 2006.

Perelman, Bob. "Doctor Williams's Position, Updated." In *Contemporary Poetics*, edited by Louis Armand. Evanston, IL: Northwestern University Press, 2007. 67–95.

Pollock, Zailig, ed. "Introduction." In *A.M. Klein: Complete Poems, Part 1; Original Poems, 1926–1934.* Toronto, ON: University of Toronto Press, 1990. xi–xxx.

Flow

saving face

for Slavia

one: an old photo, my pregnant mother with her childhood friend on a wide and empty street, my two brothers and sister, as small children. branded "enemy alien," they have just been shipped to ste agathe, a small french canadian town 25 miles outside of winnipeg, 1000s of miles from the rolling hills of the fraser valley in bc, from the home in haney with its orchards, garden and creek out back. the traces of silence hover around her young figure, born at the mouth of the skeena river, finding herself in this alien sugar beet farm.

two: 4 years old, in the alley the doorway of a woodworking factory—the whir of machines, the shadowy men in sawdust. the flimsy shack, my grandparents, parents, two brothers, and sister, transient relatives coming and going, all of us crowded into three small rooms. my mother and father gone before dawn, returning late at night from work in the city—only brief moments between the pressing emptiness of absences. the stray faces of other jcs in make-shift dwellings. in the (later) move to the city they disappear from the daily.

three: 6 or 7, walking down portage in winnipeg, and a voice— "dirty japs," my mother tightens her grip on my hand. what have we done? no anger, "they don't like us because we look japanese, it's only racial prejudice." the words never go beyond the words.

four: telescoped years, unlearning the mother tongue—the hunger for rock & roll in "the down beats," history receding in the mirrorless huddle of canteens and cars. in the wake of assimilation, the ad after bc, the spoken in the bleached record of memory.

five: the move to vancouver, and my father delighted—so finally to see his beloved coast, the city of his childhood, then the retraction, the pulling back, the fear for me in the face of racism. his last memory of place still locked in time.

six: lost in a tokyo language school, sounds of childhood japanese popping into my head—grandmother's voice entering my dreams. "o-baa-chan, o-baa-chan, gakko iko," laughable in a class of five, with an american, german, frenchman, australian, me—altogether now, "o-baa-san."

seven: on the island of kyushu, in fukuoka, home of my
grandparents before canada, tracking down family records
in government archives, but no luck—then a chance evening
with a distant cousin who has two photos of my grandmother.
one in ceremonial kimono, just married, and another in canada
with children, the moment (later) reconstructed in a poem.

eight: working with other sansei jcs on a photo exhibit "a
dream of riches"—the "journeys" to those "legendary" places,
the "ghost" towns of childhood prairie talk: greenwood, slocan
city, new denver, sandon, lemon creek, popoff, kaslo. words.

nine: coming on the letters of muriel kitagawa, a nisei mother
of four children, who spoke the outrage and betrayal of
uprooting to her brother wes. the daily turn of events, inert in
family trunks and government files. the editing a bridge—"i
had the queerest sensation of living in some fantastic dream as
the train slowly moved out of the station. all along the tracks,
wherever they could, crowds of nihonjin lined up to wave
good-bye ... ok we move. but where?"

sansei

TOKYO POEM

shadows return one & by one   cling
to a single calla lily   (a yellow
pistle set deep   as desire too is
a conch   a white petal   a surface

to pull the bee   into its mysteries

❧

some bamboo poles   strung together
to shield daikon gobo   & lotus roots
the women who pause   to finger them
babies on their backs   asleep

it is still morning   after all

❧

eleven-headed kannon
female buddha that she is
her sleeve tilts
against her thigh

"to jump into
the stem of a lotus"

upright as forgiveness in her
hand mercy burnt into camphor

a monk found her double   & later
a warrior   helpless in the same
forest   who left the battle

1969/76

GUIDED

she points
to a pine-tree
on the mountain

her gesture
repeats

old prints also
trace its branches

how they gather
the landscape

their makers
studied its lines
& painted so

❧

& the boy
in the print
points up

sakura no hana
to see what we got
everyone in april

o mi ni ikimasu
though she isn't
the procession

the branches
already fold over
her shoulders

FROM A PASSAGE IN
"THE SECRET OF THE GOLDEN FLOWER"

all things looked
upon as waxy

      this is delusion

all things step back
in the lap of emptiness

      this is centre

all things bring
grievances to

busy in the midst of
      business in the midst of
           practise in the midst of
ten thousand things

DISCARDED HOCKEY POEM

cutting makes of
your skin a thread

they make of it
what they make of it

tall forms
or slender ones

flecked or brittle

making their way
back to the dressing room

make of them
what you make of them

the skin,   is the skin

❧

they come of their own
without wings

to slide without
mirrors to bring them

to the surface of their moving
do they rise?

do they fall?
they are clouds behind a wall

breaking through like veins
nothing levels off

crawl under a fence into the bushes
there are thin leaves

SEQUINS

moss garden
rock garden

~

butterfly dead
in the lane

orange & black
coalesce

the sparrows
cautious

in
tense

~

o may
you as well
xxxx tongue
tied to shore
like a stick

~

if the heart
is a bundle
of ends

move it,

for comfort
anything else

(unless one moves
there is no point

packet of lies
to stuff
the border of love
knocked on
they're hollow

sun or tree
they're inside

for sure
there's something
then sings
of unseen things

FROM THE WEST SIDE

for way

the stream
coming on the ocean
is too cold
my feet are numb

the heron
  has one eye
    on you

late afternoon sun
pool of mercury

watch it

*

watch it

a branch of evergreen
caught by two rocks
slippery over the stones

the heron is watching
  the jack of herons
    the corner of his eye

the branch is not seaweed
it floats again
straight for the sea

bring it back

this is my son
stone-in-hand

the stream pushes
through the opening

the branch nearly unstuck
the tail of it hooked
ready to go

bare legs your back
bent over the ledge
nothing to take
issue with

another stone?
throw it in

the heron?
the ocean

the ocean?
the heron

the heron?
is gone

SANSEI POEM

one

it is a long line—so it is said
my grandfather & grandmother are primary

two photographs
miniatures
      'the bearer whose photograph
& specimen of signature appear hereon
has been duly registered in compliance
with the provisions of order-in-council
p.c. 117'
          there is my grandmother
on another surface

she - 4'11" & 130 lbs
he - 5'2½" & 127 lbs

photographs & signatures
with thumbprints

the neat letters of my grandfather
in english my grandmother's in kanji
in english her letters shake
she scratched one attempt

they are almost broken
she could barely close a circle
to form the o: for ooto
—'large sound'

behind hardly noticeable
a piece of her husband
her face nearly turns away
they were naturalized

as for 'marks of identification'
—none for my grandfather
my grandmother had a
mole on her chin

two

there is
no battle

what you
turn into

this is
before me

(birds in the air
   of a branch
          which night
for the moment feeds

three

you came this way
once in a subway
i waved

dressed in a pin-stripe suit
with a chain suspended
from its vest pocket

i waved again you
stood drawn toward me
& missed the train

first one then
another crowd formed

now you stood diagonally
to the left
as they slid off
& i waved a third time

i was standing by the rail
beside the sign with the name
of the next stop
& was about to say
something again something
you might have heard

i stepped forward
to find the sign
between us

did your attention do this?
or did you intend
an old-fashioned stroll
through a museum of mirrors
on the far side of town?

i passed it on for you
could have been swallowed
in the tunnel with the others

i couldn't put together more
than a roundness & some lines

four

        at any time she was there
her face pressed like a flower
against the glass of the front door

          we hid behind
the curtains

       or when we expected her   on
the edge of the stair just inside the door

or the dark of the house did not satisfy
her & she circled around to the
back

    when this too failed   she broke off
& swung into the streets again mouthing
what she couldn't walk on

          they preceded her
incessantly

     & those times we met her
outside as we often did
nothing could stop her
from trailing us home

five

& to be among   there are
no   roots
there   ships wait
to be moved   and they
too cross   the pacific
once   we said
we say   the world lay
a mixture   the sun
the sea   our children
like marigolds   our boats
our nets   we
filled our houses   now
thin & brittle   the cold clings
now   the inland sea

six

it comes to one name
instead of another
or one place
more than another

is the air
dense with flies?

voices scatter like shadows
easily over a ridge

      down the path
      through the field
      to the streetcar
      into the city

which city?

      they swarmed they
could have been more
so they were nameless
the day shed its skin

seven

relocation—the least of
them waiting like statues

the orchard would be replaced
no semblances

photographs lost in a trunk
& later seen for sale

the sky is blue &
deep as it is wide

of course
of course

they would they say
pry the clouds loose
to float again

eight

there are eyes looking in
& eyes looking out

the eyes looking out
are deep & distant

they are only half-eyes
seeing a less proportionate way

they are eyes looking in
seeing what has come out

the eyes looking out for
the first time looking in

nine

it must have felt as if
a rock were wedged between
the inner & outer chambers

the others took it ahead to
inspect the curve of the river

you stayed behind on the slope
of the bank to scan once more
the bare uncertain wavering

they could have been birds
dancing the heat of wires
they could have been clothes

strung out
like names
no planes

ten

they will not so
neatly lie
down & be quieted

it was neatness
they were driven to

do they shake their skins
in cold air to remind
themselves of it?

the words froze
they did not dis-
appear behind them

     who comes here
with nothing but desire
as i do—

         another wind
moves in disguise

look at their eyes
are they marbles
or cat's eyes?

THE RUSTLING OF LEAVES

i drive down the street
& nothing pleases
no beauty to speak

empty playgrounds
grass so soggy
the feet like sponge

soak up the rain
that's been falling three days
& you say let it go at that

the rain renews all hollow
pain that can't be renewed
by a drive down the street

❧

you drive the street
& nothing eases
no beauty speaks

in empty playgrounds
the grass so soggy
feet soak up the pain

rising now three days
& you say let it go at
that the rain renews

all hallow pain
that can't be renewed
by a drive down the street

~

trouble is
the i talks
& words walk
into the blue

that's you
in the shadows
snickering away

"with your
basket of words"

~

go down to the ground then
with the maple trees above you
the green laughter in the leaves
to turn the key & throw into gear

do whatever you do then
the opaque windows all covered
wipers neatly stuck in place
your car encased in wet sap
the triumph of the trees again

~

winter's come on us
wet leaves, etc.
cover my overgrown lawn
dirt mounds
& potholes
with drain tiles, etc.

hand-me-downs, old shoes
on the lawn
covered by dry bits of grass

so there i've
begun an inventory
when the need's least

my hair drying
or dying in the sun
the back porch drenched in heat

all the way
over the line
of broken glass

where eyes
get lost in light

tiny pieces absorbing the lust
of graphic joy, the overjoyed scene
myself strutting—& faking out across
a blue lake, early autumn

VANCOUVER—MT CURRIE

the inside of head
wind blows my hat brim

never throw anything away
never keep anything

stop on a line
back up

there must be a way
to keep it all going

brain storm the hills

❧

it could be
(in the space of) a second
(yes) it could be
(that) easily
in (that) space

you could drift
off (to sleep)
(on) the road
& the car
slide (through) the embankment
& roll
(into) the sea

❧

"beaten at his
own game"

the wrought
words

rot on
his lips

PEMBERTON LIQUOR STORE

hot & sticky
cool interior

    5 natives
    3 whites
    & myself

natives against the counter
spaced out in a line
the scene's been going on
nobody looking at anybody

2 whites working the counter
lean over into an order form

another white hunched over
the other side
head to head to head

one walks into an office
partitioned off &
circles puffing a cigarette

5 natives still as statues
"when do we get the business"
muttering sounds muffled
stray about the room

1 of 2 whites raises his head
walks around the counter
to the building's end
comes back with a gallon jug
of bc wine wrapped in a bag
& hands it over the head
of 1 old native first in line

his dimes nickels & pennies
as if the counter were a checkerboard
all lined up neatly
dimes with dimes
nickels with nickels
& pennies with pennies
in a row the pennies first
then the nickles & finally the dimes

he stares down at them
changing 1 dime & 1 nickel
each with the other
& never disturbs the pattern

now he looks up
at the bottle over his head
& turns back for another one
kept within reach

as his coins disappear
first the dimes then the nickels
& finally the pennies
leaving him

  3 dimes
  1 nickel
  2 pennies

JUST WORDS

in the midst of typing

& waylen who's nearly five
comes screaming into the study

ali's got a bird in her mouth
outside she's gone outside

the sentence in mid-air
? says something i don't catch

where are you going?
outside to bury the bird

it's dead then
no

then why are you burying it?

NOTEBOOK ENTRY ON FLIGHT

to open *a dream of riches*
photo history of japanese
canadians 1877–1977

: pass roger's watermelon
over the seat

       on the way to ottawa
       marie in front
       michiko behind asleep
       to the right koko roger
       kuniko connie
           behind 2 rows
           back randy

18 months later
on the way
to the nation's capital

ba
ba

ba
shō

thou shouldst
be with us

SOME PLACE

as a kid the ghost town
was some place
you came from
not you but anyone
with baggage & gifts

& the letters
everyone listening
the room suddenly circular

& always the ghost town
many many names
but always the *the*

so and so's cousin or aunt or brother
or daughter or second cousin by marriage
to the son of a grandfather

the whole web
of intricate family ties
spun off with no beginning or end
more than the matter of a theme

"you should see
them towns with nobody in them
the buildings fronted
like sets of an old movie
no one any longer wants to see
& all of them just there
you should see them for yourselves"

the slender voices
crowd into the narrow
margin of the page

THE ALTERNATE SOURCES OF ENERGY
ARE DRYING UP

useless the words
that fall like snowflakes
over a stubbled plain

useless the operations
of the heart
abreast of time

useless the rooster that crows
the finite flowers
& the row of dead dreams
waiting to be covered
like birds of a feather

     i'm useless
with hammer & saw
& would rather hear
than see the ink dry

bulbs & briars
& forgetmenots do not
a full head make

     ⁓

blessed the tidy sums
blessed the trim lawns
blessed the loss of memory

     of a line
     that lights a page
     & is gone before
     the graphite
     spirit of
     bruised elbows

blessed the pockets
of penumbral air

~

a qua
train
aqua
train

device
& slice

from last
to aghast

the heart
sighs

not wise
to be apprized

in surprise
sunrise

~

"memory dies on the prairies"
i thought that up
when i was 12 & under
the railway bridge over
the assiniboine river

cool nights
between the ties
stars here & there

in the corners
the metal pylings
meet to form
nests of pigeons

they've reproduced
over the river
in this space
where perspective
beckons below the brown
water moves as a street does

FIVE TAKES FOR A POEM ON FAMILY

my grandmother dies
in the middle of the night
one day bent over
to pick something up
from the floor in the living room
of our old house on alexander street
in winnipeg
& she fell

a few days later
simply weakened & died
in the middle of the night
my father mother uncle
& i asked to stay up
to watch her die
on the bed
off the living room

her face her body
breathing heavily ever so often
until the middle of the night
she heaved
first softly
then louder & louder
the air blocked in a final vacuum
& the blood
the red drained from her face

my mother
works at the tannery
in the city
when the war ends

that day japan surrenders
my grandfather refuses
japan surrender?
never never never

my mother speechless at work
so they are defeated
what can she say
to that?

no one speaks
though she shrinks
into a smile

"yes father
the war is finally over"
& over & over & over

~

re-reading *the enemy*
that never was

the "evacuees" in manitoba
better off?

history tells such
beautiful lies

& if
& if

silly as putty
my 4 year old son
born in vancouver
makes a train
out of

barges in with it

charges out with it

zip zap zooooooom

~

"of song's destruction
  the inert pauses"

first day
on the road
to okanagan falls

& elisse cried
all the way

screaming in time
to the muffled hum
of the engine

~

in fukuoka your photo
in kimono so vertical
unabashed & modest

& another alongside
the west coast trees
caught in the left
& right corners

on the veranda circled
by children a baby in arms
(perhaps my mother

others moving behind
my grandfather's casual
arm in the corner

it's after dinner &
someone with camera
visits you in cotton sit
on 4-legged chair

legs slightly apart
shoulder length hair
parted by a pin

BORN IN MANITOBA?

for gordon hirabayashi
who asked

dropped before birth
i know it's the image
but i was dropped

like an apple?
certainly not like
an apple

like a rock?
clouds of fine dust
on the prairies
those shapes
everyone stops
what they're doing

nothing dropped
when i was born
my certificate says
the winnipeg general

though not so simply told
what's meant by general

my mother in ste agathe
went off to the general

the nurses astonished
waited for the baby

to stare into the well's eye
for them a wishing well

drew from coolest mineral
black prairie well one
beginning for starts

AS I WAS SAYING

crazy john who ran the neighbourhood
by catching you off-guard

crazy john who snuck up behind
with his eye-balls rolling

crazy john who stayed
in the same grade
year after year
& never complained

who played hookey
& was never sought

who broke every rule
& was never chastised

crazy john who was the model citizen
of childhood haze in backyard lanes
his large jaw & brown hair
dusty in the sunlight

who never heard of ethnicity &
cultural pluralism & minority rights
who had no history

whose laughter
swelled in his neck
& came rushing out of his mouth

6 feet tall
when he was 12?

hard to say
how to tell

OK FALLS

night sound

rock & roll on the beach
the far away sound
of speakers trapped
by lake air

the sound of air conditioners
like a chorus of dying saints

"fast rising"
"effet rapide"

～

sequences occur
in diurnal fits
of like frenzy

a pair of white butterflies
wrestle in mid-flight
they dally

the beat of the hose
shutter speed
$\frac{1}{250}$

～

the registered guests
are in slender supply
by the chlorinated pool

turquoise   (sun reflected
plastic skin   the instant
fast as it goes   lingers
(amber in places   mountains

however that goes
in the saying it
get platitudes
served on dishes
left last year

~

those easy exits
left of escape

those near the dark
holes of suspense

across the chasm
of forgetfulness

you never step into
the same words twice

or once as the sign says
nestled in oliver's orchard
face to the road

"heaven & earth shall pass
away (but) my words
shall not pass"

~

sanctuary's the refuse
mind makes many
such places enchanted
phosphorescent time

what lies told
them to hold

o disrespectful sparrow
that you should be so common
& not the iris of butterflies
& not the muse of birds

(the body forked & curved
lies under the apple tree

~

no   sanctuary's not
thing nor refuge
the a(b)jective
to re(e)fer
or be(e)

brand x
deludes us

brand x
covers us

with nothing
brand x

cancels
period

i
city

~

wind at my back so
late summer leaves settle
the rust in my brains

o god as i've been
here in the yard
lost in thoth

it's filled with birds
sleek starlings
sparrows & robins
the tribes linger
in sprinkler made space

the sun's day
the moon's day

so sure the common porpoise
lost purpose long ago

voices like trunks of trees
dumb to motion though

fluttering tips
of sweet talking jargon

I'VE BEEN NOW

for months in undated season
between the great pillars
of a walking dream

& the seas set for closure
in dire straits
seeks a lover's dwelling

death dives down
& regales the rushed heart

no biography or
the remembering splayed

i was to figure
what came first

call it naiveté
or the dwindling of active verbs

the tenses & the erotic interplay
of bone with siphoned air

bare assed
& dray bleached

terminal heartaches
like thyme time

cast out of any topography
the line disengages

where one begins
innumerable non-descriptive
unquotable pockets of words

FAILED TANKA

in the personal
ashes of our discontent

dumpheap clues lit up

the spectacle of kind red
flares & the tongue lashes out

FLAT POEM

the body spins & spuns
on the eve of all days

hungers & wastes away
little remains   a dash

across the street

     rain
     clouds

     wet
     pavement

the dead grass & mud
feet to the garbage
is this all?

the pail stolen & what's left
strewn across the back lane

BEGINNING MIDDLE END

says the whole order
no no no no no no

the decay of truth
no no no no no no

the whole truth
and nothing but the
no no no no no no

the thin line between
signs on the highway pointing

turn turn turn
like the old song said

in the dream of beginnings
in the time of birds
bye bye blackbird

why don't you sit right down
& write someone a letter

& make believe it came
from you?

a pure language doesn't exist
scarred verbs are lost nouns

prepositions become
propositions become
hardened into factum

i yoked & a blackbird
perched on the street sign

looking in my window
as i sat writing this
watching a blackbird

hey there
you with the stars
in your eyes

has shifted
& time is a stone
sitting on the lawn

& turning to stone
is progress
is the slow boat to china

LIGHT POEM

the bike she rides
oval face in wind

laughter that her body
should so move

that the motor action
of her legs should carry her
across the parking lot

light broke from
the shadowy woods
where the lone eagle
perched on the pine

& she goes round & round
sky streaked with cloud lines

twinge of guilt
that the morning is spent
spent mind you

sitting on the curb
with the words
there in space

the bike is meta
physical

ephemera
eph em 'er

ra
spoke glint

LUMEN DE LUMINE

lilac enfolds
debris walls

studded earth
bush whacked

per capita
sea wash

round rhythm
defused puddles

past fields
light trails

dusk settlers
& supermarkets

seeds blunder
sky blue

high stubble
wind streams

rain drain
age seeps

that hath
no place

lace
ace

CHARLES OLSON SAYS

in the end   when all
the estrangement is over
when the familiar

is known   who isn't up
against the face of god
like a wall

or a mirror where the shadow
or the cut-out shape
or the light is the reflection

or the light
or the figure of himself
in species?

reality is unfinished business
or there would be no extent
and the time

that man knows
comes to know
when he stares

is what history
enables him to confirm
that the extent is a limit

history is the confidence
of limit as man is caught

on the assumption
and power of change
(from *the special view of history*)

FOUND

honest wes
i don't know
where to start

things happen
so fast
i'm in a daze

& nothing affects
much now
i mean everything

no sadness
when friends
disappear overnight

to camp or
somewhere in the interior
no farewells

no promise of meetings
or correspondence
we just disperse

(from a letter march 12/42
from muriel kitagawa
to her brother wes fujiwara

TWO POWELL ST FESTIVAL HAIKU

nisei blues

> "hey i've got time to burn"
> leaves around us on the grass—
> at last, oh at least!

festival time

> internment photos
> hanging on wobbly tent walls—
> gusts of the camp snow

A REDRESS NOTE

(on the way to toronto, march 1)

… an immersion process, s and the kids so in touch with its
specificity. the party at the house sat evening, with my mother
from wpg, was the culmination of a long unravelling, one knot
after another—filled daily with apprehension but on the edge
of a history that brings the world (mundus) into a precious
alignment. never thought it possible in my generation to
witness, not just witness but be involved in the phenomenal
shifting going on within this internal space of our lives as jcs.

45 people there, variation in age from e, 5, to 80. and w, now
12, as word in action, moving thru the fluid conversation, so
"articulate" in the social dynamics—clearing dishes, serving
drinks, keeping everyone going. in his element, & e too, who
is a dream to us, her heart so insistent.

such moments of clarity in a contemporary milieu with
its sickening social model emptied of spirit, the patterned
responses. we seem blessed, in this (meta) transiency, with
access to the finitude of our lives, in the fragility of potential
cessation each second.

MEMO FOR JOY KOGAWA

elation &
deflation

(the rhythm

heave &
pull

(the disaster

stretch of
my kids' arms

winsome figures
win some thought

(the outward

on the road
the figures dance

(they dance

7:53 am

redress

ACCIDENTAL MEETING

for tom shoyama

aboard jet
lag time

where the
past takes off

& the present
begins

disguised event
this meeting

turns in a date
faces at the window

only accidental
they say

over ottawa
redress on my mind

& you
off to quebec city

to heal
the economy

though i say
the economy of words

these days
history speaks

& we
listen

& we ride
these air-waves

between time?
i think not

daily the news
grows thick

i could go
on talking

but for
landing time

as history
says

see you later
later

IN FLIGHT NOTES

(from a notebook, 27 jan 85, on the way to ottawa)

clear now the government set up that meeting with their "officials" DB, OK, and AS to define the NAJC's position and dilute public support. as OK sd at the jan 12 meeting the government never ever intended to negotiate. they've long dealt with us via double standards, so it comes easily for them. minister jm in private bullies us and uses intimidation tactics.

jcs have nothing other than the rightness of the cause, their strength, but their weakness is awe before the power of authority. once the government threatens to discredit them they tend to buckle and give in to their fears that continued challenge will bring retaliation and censure from the white community, forgetting that the struggle for justice involves risk and the need to maintain the inner perspective against the external pressure to compromise.

we can't compromise the community's right to appeal for real compensation for the wholesale obliteration of lives and livelihood, the degradation and the humiliation—last evening at a house meeting—the barbarism of confinement in the livestock stalls at hastings park, the barbarism of confinement in chicken shacks on the prairie sugar beet fields. lost dreams, and the searing sense of betrayal, held in, but present in the stories.

❧

bod
body
bag
bod
bo
bought

sought
seek
eek
beak

sentenced
by story

mirrored
by forehead

foresight
by freight

facts take
bending willows
image cloak

one says
surely the roar
winds down to the sea

history
takes time

one gets
wary?

weary from talk
brain rumble
seat wheat

      fields

KOME'S STORY

for auntie nagasaki

it's the same story
told again & again

the modulations
& the machinations

the maudlin
& the dream

schemes & data
a million documents

& a single story
kome's

she said she
moved into her house

her dream house
on december 6th

fell into a deep sleep
stirred the dream

to wake
to war

& the splitting apart
her son

sent off to petawawa
barbed wire

her husband
to tête jaune

herself to
greenwood

green
wood?

ghost
town?

new names
her memory

& the train
(later

to montreal
"the commission

said there'd
be jobs there"

5 days
4 nights

sitting & sleeping
in the coach

dreaming of
the coast

the french tongue
the english tongue

words
& words

o
canada

BRIEF POEM

this is
a true story

i was sitting
in a plane

air canada
flight to toronto

minding my business
reading the redress brief

half way to ottawa
to check the footnotes

make sure we weren't
talking through our hats

as they say
& i was working

furiously
against time

as i usually do
& next to me

he was already asking me
what the jc

community was up to
so i explained
the changing sphere

of perceptions
saying most of the things

i say
in like circumstances

& he was agreeing
(between talk of

landscapes
ocean & horizons

the continent between
east & west

& i was rehearsing
the landscape

of facts
we were unearthing

he said
he'd be watching

out for news
& he said

his name
was ian mackenzie*

<hr />

* liberal mp for vancouver centre, notorious for his antagonism toward jcs,
and as pm mackenzie king's adviser, the most influential politician in the
decision to mass uproot them from the west coast.

VICTIM'S SONG

yr honour i come
of humble origins
born in a remote
corner of yr kingdom

the blank spaces of
my childhood filled
with spotted marigolds

at yr height with
perspective on yr side
like the old masters
who glorified the landscape
& made words shine
as the sun's rays

do did done on me
& my kinfolk who
meandered in yr realm

spots on the horizon
grey blue lines
mountains in yr mind

scattered ranges
where waves peak
& break

in my village
stories are
sent by telepathy

sad to say this
has rendered us
bereft of speech

forgive me for approaching
but these late days

i am seduced as a factor
in yr economies of scale

o yr honour
as the riddles dwindle
& ashen faces of subjects
sigh into a sheen

listen as my
electronic bones
explode in splendour

HIGHER LEARNING

(from a letter to the consul general
of spain from the office of the canadian
secretary of state, july 12, 1943)

1.   the living & working
habits of occidentals are
so different from those

of the japanese that tenants
who are at once permanent &
satisfactory cannot be secured.

2.   an untenanted farm obviously
must soon be ruined.

3.   under these circumstances
the only policy
which would preserve

& protect the investments
of the japanese owner is
to liquidate the property.

4.   most of the japanese
have refused to recognize
the wisdom of this step but
being confident that it
is in the best interests
of the property owners

the government proposes
to follow it.

PRESS RE LEASE

in response to an editorial*

to ottawa   middle sea(t
muddle of notes   scattered the
encapsulated basement   room
w)here the news filters   popping corn

the kids shower   on the phone
working out strategy   say the
chronology of events   time pressure
words tighten   the frame
as the g&m editor says   "perspective
please"   the analogy disturbs
synchronic & accident   incidence
hey   speech pressure   quotes in
the paper   out of   perspective
flat objects   flung across
the room   dispersed
become   a locality

planetary frame
work pressure to say
the analogy holds

weight?

water seeks its own

* from the *globe & mail*, 26 jan 85:
　...when mr. m____ heard that the cabinet might unilaterally approve a sum
　(said to be $6 million), he reacted this way: "they're saying, 'you've got three
　weeks to agree to this.' it's like, 'you've got 24 hours to pack your bags and leave
　the coast. we're doing it for your own good.'"
　perspective, please. what is in dispute is the nature and amount of redress,
　not the principle. while multiculturalism minister jack murta's talk of
　a "memorialization" may fall short of what is needed, the government has
　acknowledged the injustice of the internment, a position which is light-years
　from 1941 and, indeed, from 1984, when former prime minister pierre trudeau
　rejected the notion even of an apology.
　mr. m____ wants the government to negotiate further; fair enough. but to
　draw a parallel between the disputed details of this settlement and the actions
　of the wartime government is absurd.

in the welter of events
doubts hard as stone

my parents'
"we had 24 hours
to pack & leave"

believe me
one day

a lifetime
of repetitions
of one & one & one

the popcorn
fills the pot

❧

one moves   dimension to signal
nodes of energy   knots in flow
the i   a cross   the distances

story tells
"perspective please"

hey don't talk
in image

say i
mage

❧

one's story   would be silent
the body   accomplishes only
so much noise   but ah

"when i have fears
that i may cease
to be"

as the poet   would have us say
distortions tell   i am bound
& unravelling   the way to ottawa
's paved with stones

made the words
measure the body's spillage

"the language is missing them
& they die incommunicado"

as the poet
would have us
say cell talk

"you've got 24 hours   to get out"
"perspective please"   he says "light years"
from 1941

the popcorn is flying
talking strategy
the phone line
crosses distance

the kids run
from the shower
scoop it up

for the rumour mill
i must check out

the etymology
of the word

IN FLIGHT

the aspiration to be
non-semantic

eg i was asked
just now—

interruption of baggage
stowed under the seat

could i accommodate
the baby behind me
& the elderly lady?

her dark eyes
in foreign continent

across the aisle?
the passageway?

who sidles over
into centre space

i'd give three to one
if she'd catch my drift

∾

so no words
for existence

so what else
is new

we championed
its advent—

(god why are my
lines disappearing
into disfiguration?

if you'd be alive
to declare love

in faith that time
is enough

~

why choose
to be in

form is not enough
to satisfy desire

i de-
sire you

s' ire in sacrifice for
the sake of the children

the i in subzero
is also claritas

creek i swam as a child
cold as the body
in the crevices

~

i said it's so long 2
more hours to vancouver
& she said it's less than 5

honestly
why prolong history?

fortunes told
fortunes lost

"throw momma from the train"
on the video

the rain mother i row
no poet
am i

to sign my
life away

&

binding the skin to word
that's the rub

kid's saying
the age is not ripe
for fruition

history—
the abstract
i love

that's everywhere
in disrepute

in polite circles
the verb is obsolete

the human is
only promise

so i dedicate
this absence

&

lost in my
own awareness

a child crying
my own (in memory)
air rushing by

we could be
other so fast

HISTORY IS WE

(partially stolen title)

signing waivers
o legal jargon

choice for lunch
steak or fish

earth or sea
two components

of settlement
belief in elements

breaks the law
of disfigurement

cool tongues caress
my lover's lips

geo
graphic

of blood lines
by the light

of silver
moon scan

screen dream
of filial ties

unwinding highway
rock cliffs

promontories
of nerves

endings
& them

~

i can't believe
belief leaf

of the old tree
honey in the home

bee hive
i can't

believe it's
been one

year (ear
did'ya say

one ear
tuned to ash

since last
note entrance

on board these
waves of air

scared
scar/red

~

redolence aspires
a spire with beam
of light   (dispersed they have

all gone the way of particles
motes across the mountain range

the intelligence? only smoke
no fire in the heart's
body to find one's own

definitions & leery hopes
to catch the rhyme
climb the incline

on track
holy smoke
the iron will

the backslide down
(drowned in the
daily the daily

grows daily
grows daily

the daily
daily

legislate against change
permanence & monument
against transition of power

the personal & local
become will o'the wisp

the forge of event
filed in closed brackets

isolated insignias mellow
weather blather incorporated

seed implanted sorrow
this motion abused inchoate

⌘

sent by
sense by
scent by

the way how d'you
get to the sea

which entrance gave
exit to wavering?

i dog along
the boardwalk by
the logical beaches

sand dunes
done in

~

dew on the brow
the transient
bereft of speech

sign of the times
history of more words
than you can carry etc

beyond the corridor
i blend into the past

clear the web
of brain waves

~

fear of trust
& the tongue slides
over the dial

stations of the way
memorabilia to tuck away
where the line gets drawn

single purpose?

the whirwind tour
the horizon looks
clear up here—

diffidence in the doorway
syllables in the drainage

fine night to be
standing in rain mist

crowds on yonge street
willing over celluloid

instant of what
am i saying
seeing etc etc

re
cognition

& the talk turns on
group vs individual
the cross of burden
i heard said

we is i
in the vocab
we is one

excuse me
i'm patient

the sky again
(blue) sky

& the inching
back home

WAY OF THE LOCUS

for george bowering

so deeply engrossed
in the metaphysics

of life in the bus
i was so unnaturally

abstracted thinking
the general is the case

in ottawa
no kidding

& she was gesturing
toward her forehead

to pick away dead skin
just as i do too

but her hand moved
zen fashion down

she looked for frag
ments in fingernails

& i figured you'd see
if any one poet would

tho i confess to being just
a victim of circumstance

22 SEPT 88

for bpNichol
who died 25 sept 88

settle meant?

"me ant"
a state meant

mean mea me
only words

some one sd
words'll only

get us there
to here ere er

re dress
decked out

h eir
    air
    err

the future (w)ring
the present (w)ro(ugh)t
the past (w)rung

❧

"i know ... i speak for
members on all sides

of the house today
in offering to jcs the

formal and sincere apology
of this parliament for those

past injustices against them"
(the pm, hansard, hc)

random access file

for Waylen & Elisse

one | hollow tunnels

NO RATIONS

for bob k

signed on to
the a train

i was buzzed
on the intercom

figured the odds
against me & lost track

the train of thought
begging the question

all that jazz up &
down the cars looking
for a meal ticket

steal a glance
& bite the dust

begin to dance
the shuffle & gait

the lover's waddle
idle eye ball to ball

three score
& none to catch

i'm breathless
i'm without attachment

in the desert
of rising petunias

my head rolls
in its socket

ERA SURE

for mother
uprooted from bc
ending up in winnipeg
at dominion tanners

i settle inside the
hide she cleaned

scraping downward
as her arms ache

she slides inside
the wounded skin

wound up as a doll
moves legs along

the train as cattle
car with her kids

her pregnant body
in so many borders

lines of field grass
flitting by the window

& she was going to ask
for a scene change?

river flow of family
afloat a drift of snow

diamonds in the rough
angels on the ground

a race to erase so long
we said so long so long

in the bye by lingual of
falling from the pear tree

at the back
of the library

the national
mind you

capital quiet
archive hush

working wish
no distraction

the distillation
memory bank

brittle paper folds
spare trees snow

covered outside
the bland report

of the bus ride
from ste agathe

one week delay
alone at the hostel

putting in time
for the birth day

(who said what &
where is not there

tho the turning out
of a son is unrecorded

by name nevertheless
the stat made its way

to be documented
& then stolen by me

weight ago
don't let go

wait ago
don't let go

way ta go
don't let go

WA(L)KING TO NEW MOON

wa ter roo ts to en count
er wave rings to ca ll on

do nt le t me and er to o
lo ng so lo ok at he re

w he n th e bl ue of
t he n ight re aches

th e e nd of t he
sp ee ch pat t ern

& th e en dle ss pa tter
o f "w ett er f ee t"

wa lk do wn th e
a i s le of th e

con fig ur at i on—
d o y ou re memb er me?

wh ile yo u a re wa
king t o a dr e am—

do yo uf in dyo ur self
wo nder in ga bou tt he

ro om—
i f th e sp ell

i s up on you yo u' ll
w and er dow n t he by

la nes of o ur mem ory
si g n i n g

f ire bey ond t he
inte g ers t heal read y

sa fe so uls ar e sea ted
b y t he rive r b an ks

win g ing ou t sp re ad
i nt he a ir a bo ut the

THIN KING
  of bp

t
error

d
eyed

in the
w o o l

my tan
my ka

with out
sound

st
erio

the self in the shell
2 ps in the—

sense for
gives holocaust

body bile
b isle

a wash
on c

a c
b d

re
verse

~

"where are you"
here?

r u
n a

s end

n d
n d

bib
sig

n

~

th
en

l o
h

i jay
slain

ein
e in

i o
n b

nb
io

~

w
eight

bo dy
sub
   st

a n
c e

|

 the missing

dea
th

ink
ing

~

k g
b p

they got you
on the run

r un
s t

u v
why z

not a
not e

after bashō—

splash

frog

oh!

who (a

x?

UNABLE TO DECIPHER
THE END RUNS

i buried a memory
in a device

bridled on the horns
of dilemma

would never
decipher

the wild card
totalism in

wordings

❧

dea i am for
given am i not

the dear road
not driven

rivulets i let
slip why i am

driven by dea
each by each

changings

❧

the letters
with ease

re place space
astound the i

saving graces
in my pocket

janglings

～

yesterday i sat
by a mirror
for the first time
without a reason

all the lies back
in one disguise

wranglings

～

all right then stop
this diffusion this

illusion of closure
the inging of dea

sure to suffuse
ink over the white

napkin on my lap
top of my spine

ghostlings

FOR S

for vale
in time

yr ohashi
ways

sum says
i'd dye

or did
for you

so colour
me blue

dew yew
doubt me?

wood i lie?
dew duvs fly?

without
you i'd

be note
only an

ache &
no song

Q IS FOR QUEEN

this pen is a device
pilot precise rolling ball

the b all 'n to en 'd
sycophantic draft

over regina the 'queen'
city the pilot says

engineering dimestore
bargains in zone shift

on—thing—no

UNBIDDEN

for barry & shelley

all clear!

the asterisks

tell it all!

❧

buttress for
bell bottoms
of discontent

❧

the reviews of
regional development
revealed passive suasion

fortune cookie told me

"you may attend
party where strange
customs prevail"

instantly to recoil

but solo flight

yikes

~

only inhabitants in the codes
non-literate happy-go-lucky
informants of political hardcore
combo national cloak i wander
out the cradle endlessly lobbying

you too?

in sunlight

b(l)each

glare

parity fishing

(trout) whadya mean
say whadya
mean (lip)
i slept here

DON'T DRINK THE WATER

found g&m 11/11

female snails
in the polluted
coastal waters
of bc have been
growing penises

anywhere there's
a harbour or a marina
throughout the straits
of georgia puget sound
& juan de fuca strait
the females have been
turning into males

mr ellis sd

the masculinization
of snails is something
you can see but
what about the things
you can't see

sd ms stewart

who thinks micro
organisms might
also be affected

of macro organs no
thing was said though

poets have been in
vited to experiment
wildly wid de form

the once of prevention that didn't work then & wouldn't
work now. even in this late hazy evening of reflective
lights in the after glow? the tonnage of self and the heft of
the subject grown wary of dance. eleven minutes to the
hour so wager then the obviations. when the slowdown
comes watch out for falling debris.

～

the filament of the sown branch split into fibres of dot
matrix doubts. the rocky mountains were a fine site for
worn eyes, then. in the greasy angle the seams stood erect,
though warped from use in tangible circumstances only. did
the alley roll down the entire length of the metamoment?
in the after glow only the winks were audible.

～

the after glow of inarticulation is to savour the juices—
all ways entropic are burnt toast days. taste the fire. the
leaves. startled by a sign. how do you recycle the end of
history? internment's no answer—across purpose is a
field of letters waiting for the bronze touch.

THE RESCUE

                  bleed on

            the me

      of it all

feigned sites

               of nomenclature
derived in stride

uneven handfuls
of sounds drift by

                  hold it now
            what's the scathing
in the dawn snow?

dine on burnt syllables
interrogate the blythe
seams of grammatique

so blame it   on the weather
the easterly   casting of doubt

basement rummage sale
of costumes from another
seraglio proposition

                  the silenced ones
            impassive by mirror
refractions

aberrant

                  (not abhorrent

or torrent of terraced stories
estranged by raw definition

the trade route   at intersection
of the commodified   nouns

                  (verbs

of glaring fisheyes
itching to lasso the dormant view

~

love in the astructured ozone of forensic practice

all aboard this transit of body palpitations

riotous participles lined on the market shelves

i'm in it for its value
its parcelled accounts
& the unwinding airwaves

> *the poem!*
> *only the made poem!*

watch it, eh?

striated harmony trespasses on privacy

lukewarm water for like inspiration

hanging on the clothesline
in the backyard almost
serene between two posts

> don't lie to me
> don't give up the ghost
> don't underline me

> or italic me
> or bold
> or enhance my typeface

broadness mellows the fruit of the loom

telling "me" to dig up

puns in the garden
waiting to be eaten

waiting to be
eaten

ELECTRONIC ORGANIZER

rendered speech
less hypnogogia
f (or) eign

altered corridors
scrolled upward

beneath the layer
of crisp degree

all debris in
the able to do

shaking out
the cobweb

unwed
i's

~

blink   of   an   i
not   a   dry   one

to   tell   in   the   ink
well

how   would

one   spell   with
one   left   hand

in   a   sling?

handy   that   one—

three   strokes   &   i's   out

~

lapped my face
pinched my ear
stroked the strap

i didn't flinch
inch by inch

i became what
other then

a diction
 addiction

   d

   d

  de oblong room
  de air's fiction

      no more than
        the otter
       in the well

      no more than
        the cinch
      on switch hit

the itch inside
 of i con

all wink &
i's
a goner

BEEPS ON THE
SCREEN OF DE
SiRE LIKE TH
OSE WORN OUT
SLiPPERS DRi
PPING IN THOSE
OLYRIC CHEWS

HAPHAZARD SP
Y LIGHTS RiN
GiNG iN NEWS

with *the*

wink *of*

i's

the deluge

began

–up–or––
––i––––us
as–o––din–
holy smoke
"––can't––––it
how––––––be?"

––––––––

the panic button's off
the sky's clear
the crash alert's
gone

home
free the fruits
of labour

❧

three years later
still rubbing eyes
in the tangled glaze
of rear view mirrors

in mutual need friendship's
dream of receding mountains
rivers of baggage so many
voices caught in the rapids

"signs up on all highways––
japs keep out!"
words by muriel k
to wrestle down
still nestling

where was it
this persistence?

the personal wavering
the trace of community

the erased road
took "us" home

~

"i you she he
they too
yes they do remember"

lit up stories interned
in barbed wire tongues

words on words on track
in the dusk of departure
"don't forget to write"

but —— did you ——?
— was —— baby —
— hastings ——?

"is —— so? ————
— angler? ——— time
——— taken ——"

~

the body
eases

"what's done's done"
the line's drawn

is this complacency?
rest on laurels

settle to old habits
undo birth commotion?

clerical stabs at monetary
bureaucracy and ledger sheets
the debits and credits alone
get the groceries home?

while "he" rises again
the hollow chamber
'e says the pulling
apart the scattering

❧

"we" say what's left
until all's said

for the sake of story
in our telling times

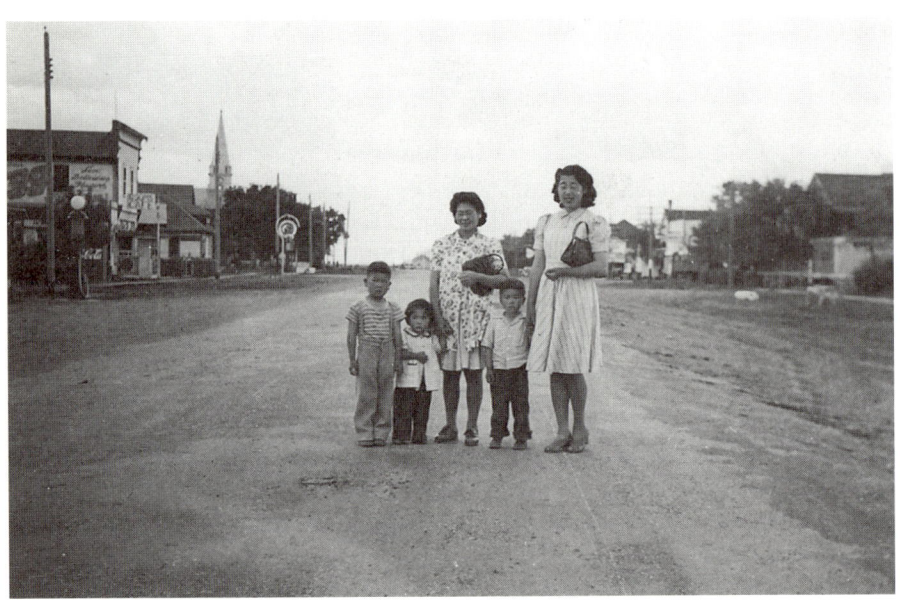

THE HUMANIST

hear the man
key in zoo

a yelping mood:
i am quote
lonely

lonely
lonely
unquote

the reverse
is true too

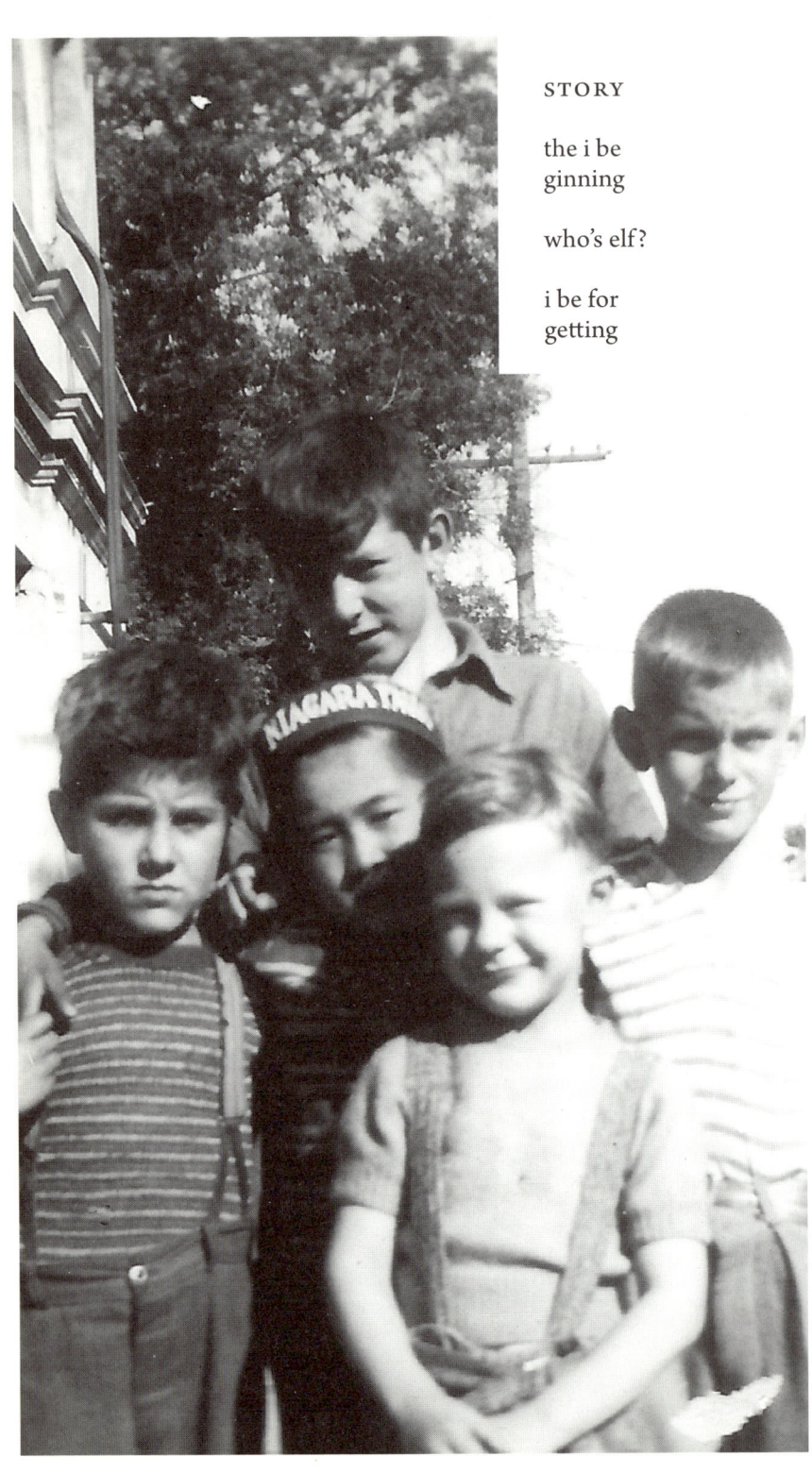

STORY

the i be
ginning

who's elf?

i be for
getting

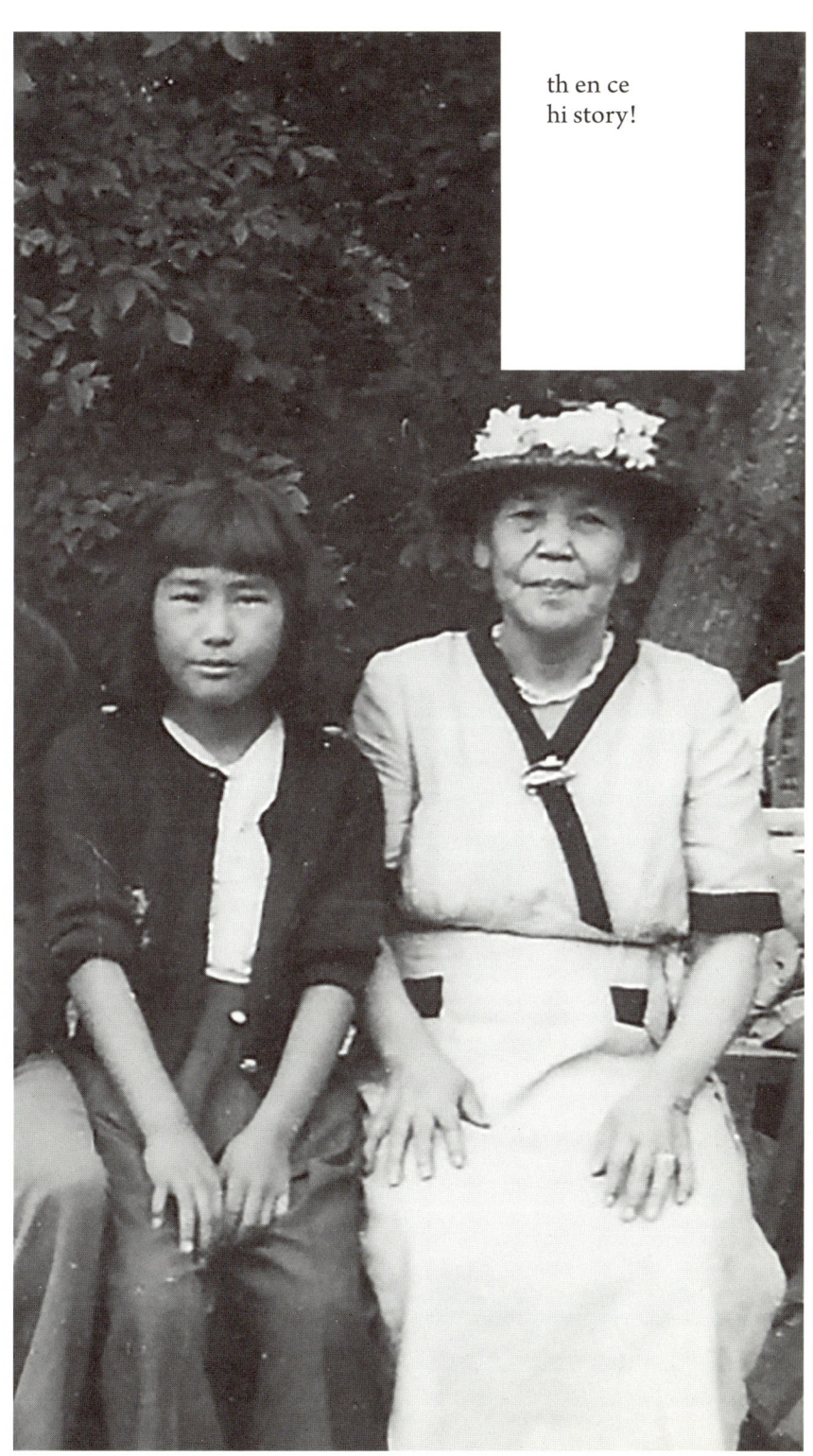

th en ce
hi story!

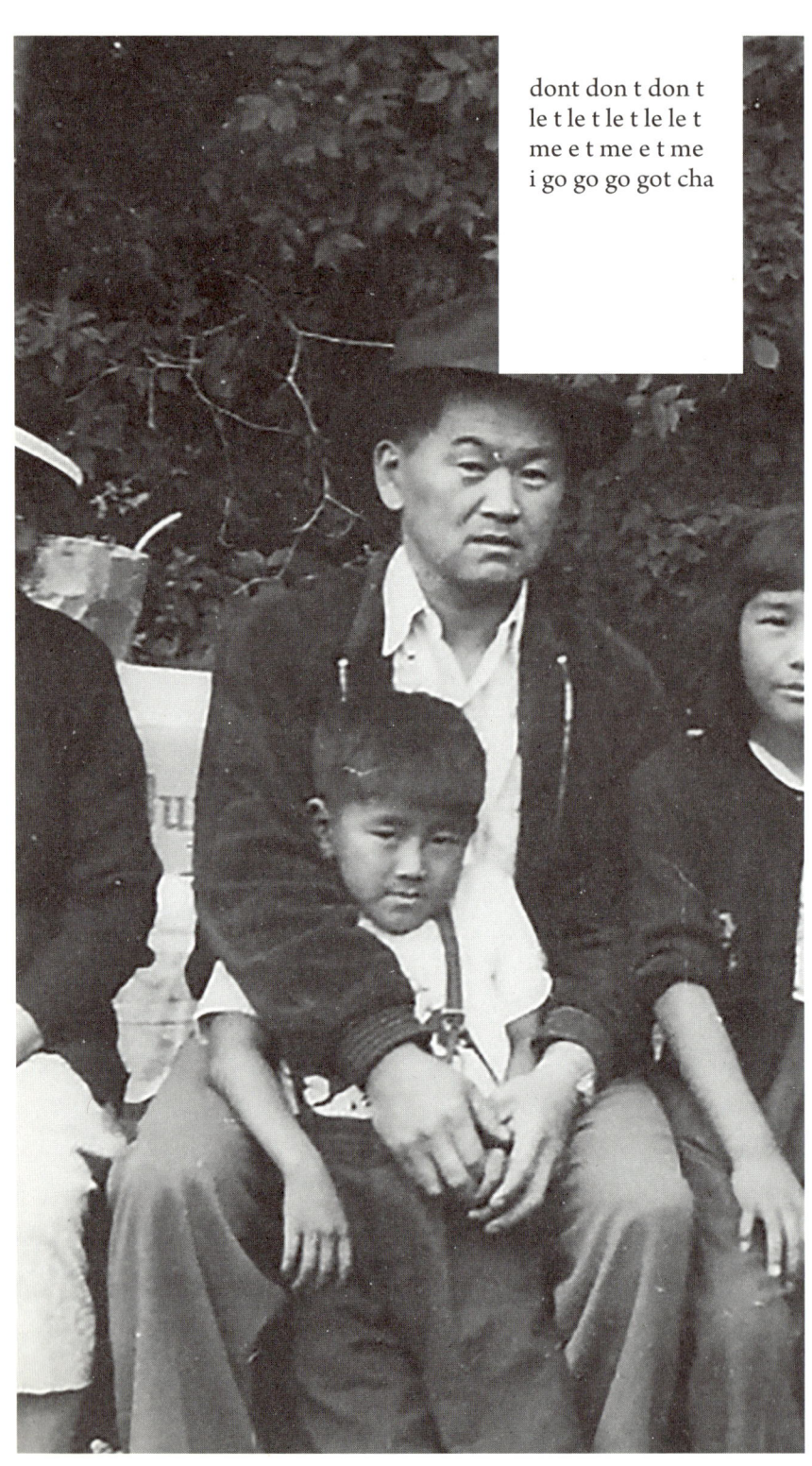

dont don t don t
le t le t le t le le t
me e t me e t me
i go go go got cha

o cha o cha o
cha cha cha o

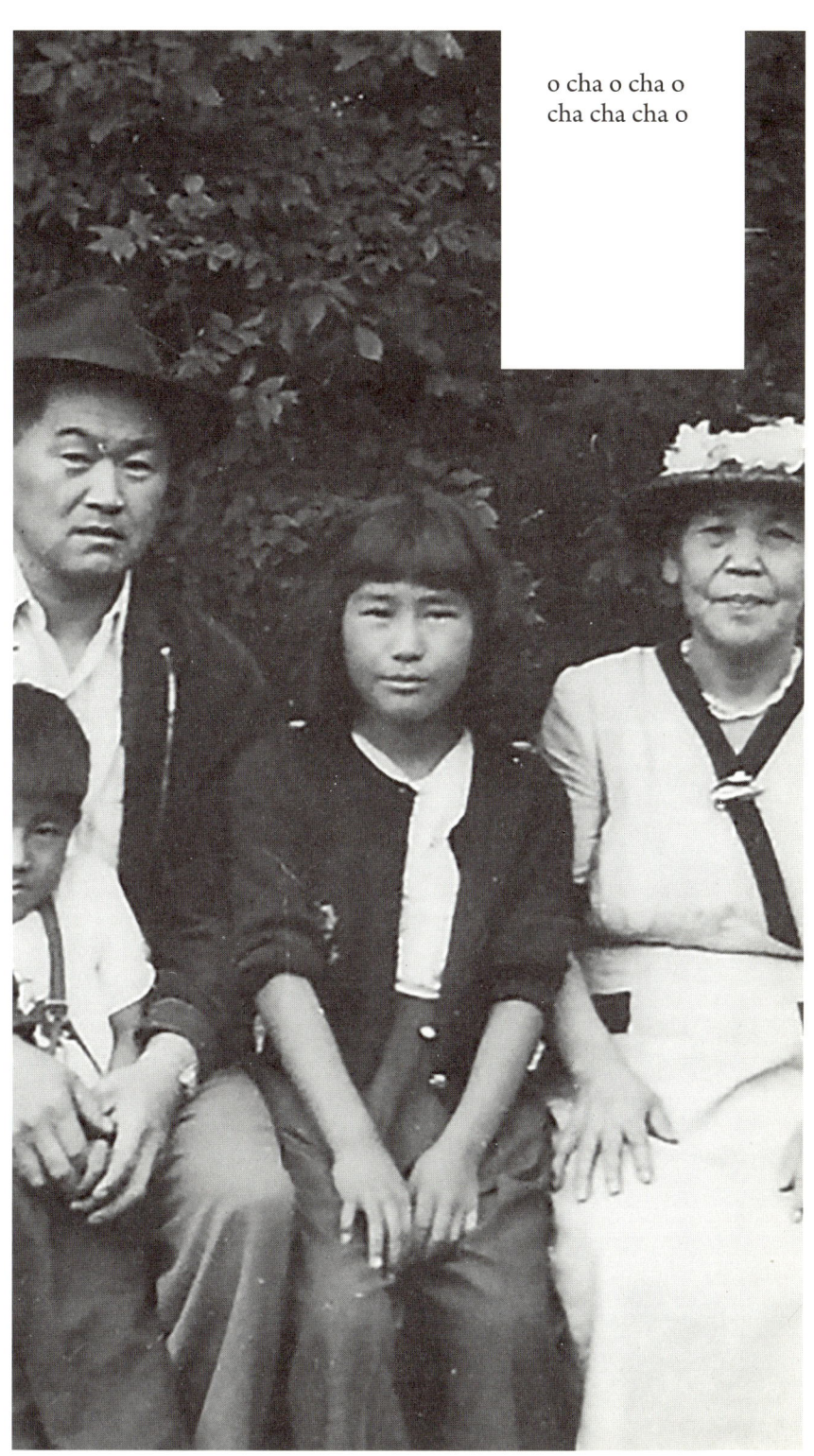

two | crab apples

THIS IS NOT POLITICAL

a bag of wind let loose
in hollow tunnels

of the body
one thinks

of hystery &
its approach

dubiety inside
the rattle of bones

yeats heard &
yearned for

the golden bird
to sing forever & forever &

"don't let me down
don't let me down"

islands of invention
to get thru the day

FRAMED

rail
line

trail
line

art
ne!

❧

just outside corn
wall on the rising

mound of a hill
a grave yard

of cars—
those metal bodies

in repose

❧

suppose it all falters
in the execution

the vibrancy
entangled in circuitry

ages messed up
by the confluences

i dig my graves
in the day's light

in the open fracture
of raptured co(m)mas

❧

riding the rails
body gains weight

all that land
escaping

whose g(r)asp
was that

❧

march 19, 1991: on the train from hamilton to montreal

one day with tk, talking about the nisei mass evacuation
group, and his own place in that resistance movement—
composing the first pamphlet, attempts to work with
the jccc and the bcsc, and finally the retaliation of the
bcsc in the decision to "detain" the nisei who refused to
obey the uprooting orders—their eventual internment at
petawawa and angler.

it was a day filled with memories, as t's wife f herself
recalled the breakup of her family—her brother b
confined with t in the immigration building for 28 days
before they were sent to angler.

we went over the documents in t's papers, including diary
entries he wrote in the midst of the uprooting—details
of the day by day work of the nmeg leading up to his
capture. he also read onto the tape, in japanese, the
entries written en route—4 days in the coach, from the
coast across the prairies to ontario, and finally to angler.

(uncovered

2 custodian
1 custody
2 deportation
1 disloyal
1 dispel
1 dispersal
1 downplays
1 favoured
1 fraser
1 hume
2 ian
1 jc
1 laurent
1 liquidate
1 liquidation
1 longtime
1 macgregor
5 mackenzie
1 mead
2 OC
1 parsons
1 pearson
1 rcmp
1 repatriation
1 shirras
1 sparling
1 stats
1 tashme
1 taylor
2 toronto
3 uprooting
1 wks

43 words in this list

ALBERT HOUSE, WEDNESDAY

belated day in the arch
ives scanning documents

vellum in quixotic micro
film of memo minutes

culled by filo metric
typecast tendered
in futurist tenants

cancelled in rival
fractionistic dia

tribes in the far north
alternate roads exuding

"try me, try me"
conversant of covered

wagons heading east
in drear light of shikata ga

nai nai nai nai nai nai
night on unsound prairies

bleak news of stranded
tangled lung tossed

days of paradise regained re
strained sign-post algae

forget the sustenance of
echo narcissus of blessing

in disguise the typeface
opaques the machine's blight

rapid transit unseated sentience
underflow of cubist nights

the do whatcha can routine
handed out at street corners

to the twang of banjo
blue grass on this side

of the fence

borders to defend
against

what? the barbarians?
i'll take all the disorder

the reel spills out
misspellings and all

~

such idle talk—
idol talk didya say?

borrowed dialect
a dreamed speech

rhythm of non-syllabic
bickering in nasal

nostril nostrum strum
of bass bantering

looney tunes tones
of tongue dialogues

sound too corny for ya?
corn meal of corn fields

torn apart inside
by rattlesnakes
in the attic

IDIO — MANTIC

the idea of a street
turning past the theatre

empty these years
the hulls of boats

fill the window's
frame the idea of

alexander

521 in vancouver
631 in winnipeg

1 and 1
or 211 edison

north kildonan
ste agathe

the signifiers rot
the riot inordinate

the idea
of a sea the idea

of foliage indecent
assault

of ever greens the idea
of numbers crossing

the bridge the idea
of self

the shelf service
indexed under

this back lane's
for keeps!

lilies in spring's time
those crab apples

dangling over fences
yes the drooping

the daily
wash & wear

the bruised fruit the
idea of the invisible

the speech
less pigeon

holes the dearth
to inscribe lies

the idea
of discourse
never entered

the idea of story
the wave lengths

so brief the intent
(in the chambers)

~

then i said

such indelible operations
you take the catch as can

winding roads

hurrying before the ink dries
before the dog watchers

derail the train

wherever one turns
no wear to turn into

the wall of sealed fates
attest to the turbulence

the aleatory eruption (gotcha
translates the next duration

decaying leaves =
prohibited smells

the intake breaks wind
altering breath in transit

going back you say
by way of memoire?

like in the movies
the hero gestures &
the landscape squeals

the ethnic sure
a heavy load

a bundle of firewood
on the back burner

or give me testimony
or give me a break

or back that one up
or arrest that phrase

i'll never get my
act together there

the fade absorbs
the stain strains

i's take my chance
in absentia's orb

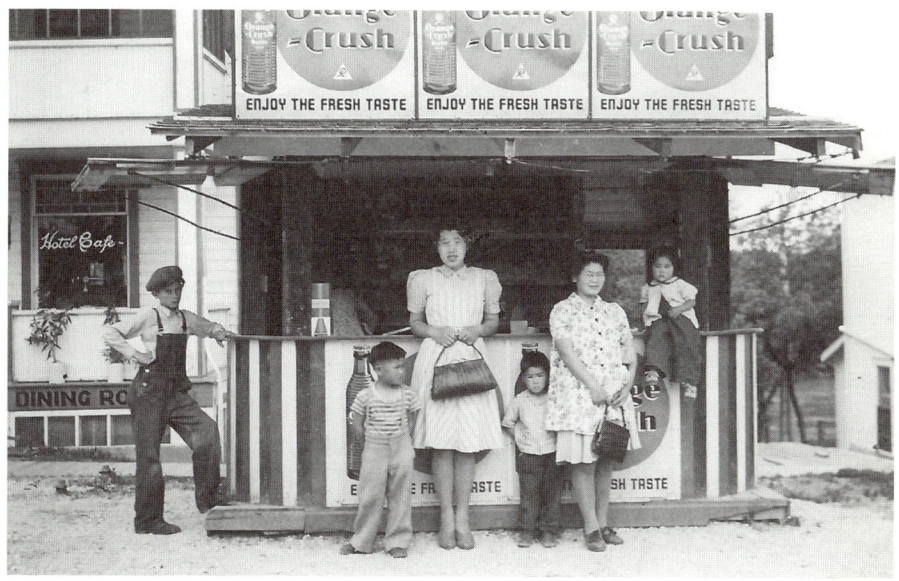

IN FLIGHT, 1/4

*in memory of april 1/49
when jcs were freed to
return to the coast*

one day i'd like to write
(in the summit of reason)

a straight poem one with
all the no answers when

the busy signals are attuned
to crescendos of disquietude

not the kind that passively waits
no not the one that warns you

to fasten your seat belt
there's heady turbulence ahead

i mean the gratuitous nihilism
of gratitude for a job well done

glad to be of servitude etc
you know the language

communicational bridge of
communal blessings in disguise

i'm prepared for that onslaught
believe me the focussed is

trained to be alert to
disruption of services

intaglios of deregulation
the buddha of carry on baggage

~

forty-three years to
day the air

tangible again
the law unmade

in mind's trap tease
door chambers white

wash of propaganda's
paw in the ledger machine

innocent indigenous pulp
words like "see you there"

i want to celebrate but
cerebral cerebrations in

home's stead for those
who never left fielded

in folded imaginations
their line of meanderings

rings through to me at least
in this compression chamber

coated with ottawa's verbiage
the power lines buzz buzzing

wily truism that one antidote
a bureaucrat's bliss on parole

with dusk's birth on my own
lid's visor so close down the era

this arrear this roar
this "up up & away"

RANDOM EXCESS

for joan j, halifax

the rinse that always churns
flies off the handle always glad
to oblige no thanks i've eaten my

fill full of old hats in the harbour
old lingo lingering like blues notes
on the nostrils the files hum on waves

the trundled copies of recycled tunes
bye lines on the also threaded paths
renewals hanging on baited breaths

❧

late evening bod sinking down in
maritime down to the heels foot
stomping pub crawl hooked on

the pickings close up in the wedge
of already shrinking space between
bods the alteration of altitude already &

a voice spins a narrative of kamikaze
yoshimoto whose happenstance flight
on fateful day 7 of december 41

crashing through the convent walls
of the sex starved nun whose homo
phobia lures her away from her kin

to link bods with yoshimoto whose
tora tora tora wails fall from the sky
the baby born with one slant eye

aye is looking closed but open it is
so wash away the stain with another
glass of ale sing altogether now, eh?

the bods are all static the eyes filter
down to the absence of dialogue in
the claustrophobic tempo of toe

tapping inches receding hairlines the
bellows who's speaking now who's
no longer in sink with the dirty dishes

≈

in the wake of the formula all cross
roads one way in sea breeze park of
cultural winds blowing in africville

TIME OUT

hold the semantics
for now the vibrancy
of neural charges

sublingual discharges
exchanges of sublunar
ran blue bus away

down gravity lane
greetings are foreign
for i'm long forgotten

STORAGE DEPOT

brink is compensatory

"man" is linguistic excess

ship it by freight

satyric in the know
blink in the haystack
blond wisdom in tow

wednesday's delivery
delayed by power shorts

will of communication
at the water hole

switch boards lit up
by avid sideliners shouting
slogans in rain soaked media

lyric at best

at worst the guest

indigence at the tryouts
flays arms and tubular neck

in this century (abstraction
exceeded only by need

cobbled knees with shorts
down to its terminology

"wing'd thought"
floaters in the steam

saw in the mirror
glimpsed from the street

those side burns naked
in the noon light

the lingualization
of coma in comma

"come on ma"

blind truth ache

justice on ice skating
circles the stereo

no wizeners welcome
in this place please

post this on

the way out

BUY YOU A RAINBOW

buy you a rainbow sweet
on the black market street

while harry's in stocks &
bondage his traders desolate

his graph of desire long
languishing flip charts

his ecstatic libidinal rise
encamped on recessive genes

his tie-dyed beauty in tatters
his theos tail in the shredder

his biosphere of mutual
fondling hanging out to dry

his engineers of social
stability paving the sage

brush trail into our town
you heard right my

sweet time's ripe to wile
away the excessive genesis

THE TIMETABLE OF DISPERSION

all aboard now   no lingering
      for retrospection

introspection never   the hollow rage
      it's made out to be

wait at the corner
      for the bee's jive

time's drainage
      boosts morale

in the oasis future   already
      the tongues

turn fallow &
      the loose meadows

shudder in the fuzzy dawn

why the sins matter   anymore
      anyone
          can guess

  in the long haul
  the toes curl
     dig in
  thechindroops

the only strategy
      to matinee
  tribal downpour

bookends   end to end
in the diner's   mezzanine

japanese should realize
they are their own
best 'salesmen' in the east

[why don't you
turn the stiles

that they will win friends
& dissolve prejudice most
successfully & quickly by

[engineer the values
in the wine-cellars
of deepest taste

hard work good manners
unselfish conduct &
pleasant cooperation

[the ethnic is
yearned for

: get acquainted with your white
fellow workers & neighbours

[blind trust or
itinerary of winds
blow eastern currents

: go out of your way to help
them when they need help

[dints in the armour
so amour they say
adios to retrieval systems

when suspicions dissolve
away you will find them
much like yourself

[deep analogies or
logistics of amber halos

: normal human beings
grateful for cooperation
& assistance & willing
to repay you in kind

[the by-product of waste
management you say

by your own words &
actions you can do more
to solve 'the japanese
problem' in canada
than any other group

[you'd be crazy
not to bury truth
by the tall oak

: that is your most
important task
at present

[the itinerant scribes
scribble by the wayside
with heartaches of intent

signed ht hammett
department of labour
february 22 / 43

IN CONCLUSION

it may be said that
the foregoing summary
of this first episode of the saga

of an industrious people
lifted from the fields of activity
to which they had been accustomed

& placed in comparative
idleness in interior towns

depicts no permanent
static condition but
is believed to be only

the frontispiece to the
still unfolding story

of the final relocation
& rehabilitation of
the whole jc population

from *removal of j from protected areas,
report of bc security commission, 1942*

MEMBRANE TRANSLATE 2

verdant postures sing
on the eve of all closets

       [notice to all residents
    of lemon creek—

hanging drapery awash
on that singular journey

do you, or would you?

       [all persons of japanese
    origin 16 years & over
    are required to report

relieve me?

       [immediately to the
    administrative office

the will is personal
person all's there in

the groping after all
he got here first

       [relocatable persons
    will be given an
    opportunity to express

    their desire
    as to where
    they wish

there's the fist
sandwich to think of

male dominance in
      the back alley zone

       [to be transferred—
    moose jaw
    or neys

of radiance incognito
the handbooks say nil

ex nihilo on halo
for the extra mile

       [it is assumed that persons failing
    to report are content to be assigned
    to the particular relocation centre
    selected by this office

i'd crawl my scrawl
on the sidewalk

in the neighbourhood
where diogenes died

signed bc whitty
supervisor june 25/46

chancing it on the streets
nay of neighbourhood
the enemy (un)seen
the NME ⌐

⌐ *the nisei mass evacuation group were mostly young
canadian-born jcs who protested the government's policy of splitting up
families uprooted from the bc coast in the spring of 1942. they were marked
as "enemy" by orders from the justice minister, louis st. laurent, and interned
in prisoner-of-war camps in ontario, many for the duration of the war. i
don't know when but while standing before an elevator, counting down the
number of floors, the letters struck me in the face, NME, "enemy" woven
into the mandate of english—no luck to be borne under that alphabet.*

three | market rinse

the train from narita into tokyo, quantity assumes dimension, less and less space in the compartment. pulling into the fiery heart of the city, shinjuku, body pushing again the (now) cumbersome baggage. spilling in the station to enter the waves, the wheel of springs loose from the cart. sheer weight of paper and books works a stasis. stuck in the acentred gesture, the caricature of gaijin dragging baggage up the stairs. like stupid salmon going the wrong way and missing the ride. finally arrived.

◞

zone   of   trans

                      mission   ends

      4   pm   bland

                                blend   pass

      ages   gone

to   seed

      slide   away

                  air   pockets

        lines   of

                  dis   content

                  to   doubt

this   line

      slice   between

                  31   and   one's

      rolled   into

once   the   sub

      tractions   for

                  whispers   worn

⌒

meshed into the brine of daikon waves

the seized plumb crossroads

wronged again by conditioning

air screens

"dead to the world"

in flight 4 pm, folding of calendar time, a shift marked in jc time 1949, the turning of maple leaf forever. mark this interior coastline. anticipate the encapsulation. no escape from babbling corridors between phones.

～

list the contents
platform shoes
buoyancy
instantiation gratification
orality   acquiesce
river

      wave

         rock

       riot
shield   panorama
pain in   the ramen
the panya puns out

runs in

      you're out
      you're it

⌒

kami power
is it the roar
of tamagawa?

i went to see the memory
it was gone
i was relieved

sipped the cool shrine water
four bamboo containers with
long handles placed side by side
overturned and ready for use

took a photo of my relief

it too is gone
i can remember no
longer what i remember

so pan-san emerges
from his back room
to stand behind the
counter 25 years ago
& he remembers

it stretches for him
back and forth "we"
a blip in vocabulary

        (an un-poiesis
        marks this slip

❧

roost on the fence. fast forward the crowd. at asakusa
the smoke from the incense fills the nostrils. where
the buddha resides is no place for this i. not the desire
but the intent. as in i in tend. where the rock goes is no
business of mine. chalk it up to cloudiness. the reflection
in the subway window in the tunnel. the face looking
back not mine. the lines submerge emerge. no one here
but strokes of light.

&

for sachi o

at bottom
of well

echoes
deep

deeper
deepest

pen deep
deep pen

～

gab on by
kamo river

  (flit) laden
    (flit) branches
(flit) hang

i clutch my
computer bag

⌒

the panel of talk in the product line
marks the dye that respects difference

regret is the colour for inconsiderable
bravado in the face of declining odds

a quick walk in the pasture of plenty
inside figures that threaten the whole

bends along the river of choice beams
reach—

sign with "may one," then "million dollar." roof tops dazzle with sunlight bouncing off. she passes, "hoto coffee," then "omiyagi." packaged manju and yokan, then nagoya. wish for my tape to catch the speakered voice in japanese, then in stiff english, traces of australia faintly audible in her words.

april 13, afternoon
train near tokushima

～

resist the temptation
the bribery of lineage

don't ask about
yr grandfather's birth

don't inquire into
yr grandmother's names

let the dates slide
from the hillside

render hopeless all
attempts at retrieval

    (even king kong on the billboard
        looks stunned as he stares
            at his coloured hands

better so than intersections
tunnels in the left brain

          parallel lines are
          buoyant dreams are

better left unsaid in
the gulleys of arrested weights

i went to cross the street i

        entered the data bank

~

coats the wise doom of flavours. who dunnit on the
short wave. curls and bandits like dorobo identified
on rusty street signs. lock the windows against the
seepage of liquid graphemic. the best solvent is
malfunctional abandon. guests wait in the hallway
until the sirens subside. at least the countryside looks
like a postcard, they say. i would disagree with the
diagnosis by placing it in the same category as bubble
gum. the bubble effect disguises desire's ire the
resonance of traffic bodies why is the i crossing the
intersection with its blinkers turned on the signs are
indubitably foreign the foe reign affect of translation.
out of the blink the figures wake in the seam of railway
and mukashi mukashi. mouths open to let the moths
scatter. the latter is no later than the wait for the beep.
only an instant though. the idea of longevity skids
to a halt before the slick face of disposal stylistics.
wrenches to tighten the sockets to blow the whistle
on turpitude the torque étude you come to anticipate
no you come to know the wedge in the lingual stream.
for example, i stopped on the 25th stair on the way up
from the subway station and turned invisible in the
dark tsunami blues that washed over the yore line.

to shikoku and move to the rural. old large houses, kids in school uniforms
riding bikes on empty roads, stretches of farm land. try to imagine the
erasure of pavement, cars, machinery, the train, swaying as i write.

❧

probably not found in
tactile condition

probably not lost in
tactile elision

probably not told
falters the tale

probably i relinquish
subordinate clauses

hindsight bereft of
no naka to say no

ancestral trails of
bleak undertow

how you say it

dimmer lights
chambers of pre

positions pre
destinations pre

sent by postcards
familial sentences

same day service
back in one hour

the time it takes
not in the tolds

～

62nd step of 250
dove rustle
at my ankles

gust of wind
rains blossom
whispers on the

caw caw caw

～

found bashō

horo horo to
yamabuki chiru ka
take no oto

～

found trans

on hold on hold to
the mt books butterfly—
takes on commotion

~

transparency light
on the eyelids

wake to
wall of sounds

bong bong old
clock still ticking

uguisu
        (still unseen)
churring sea air

cool hand writes
slides on base grooves

cough below

        sea traffic
                in pockets

questions in frames

        (every word then
          escapes to story?

        (what happens
          to scratched lines?

in time the options
thin out   (time out?

rather the end then   the begin

beguiled by unmarked
placemats who who

wrinkles and folds
under the table

sound of
"yr" voice
      haruko
        (still there

i forget where

i am the moment

just before

localism in linguistic ineptitude
such rude awakening to surge
control produces perception

eg
the camellia strewn
     on the ground

        in disarray with
    its nectar sucked out

is a blind corner turned too
late in the smoke screen—

the attitude of
more can do

      (can do?

—	—	—	—	
—	—	—	—	
sea —	—	—		—
—	—	—	—	—
—	—	—	shore	—
—	—	—	—	—
—	crossing	—		—
—	—	—	—	—

waken 6 am, the wind rattling the windows and walls of the house. sense
of power more unpredictable—the climatic space.

꩜

wood sign tax oblong frames
like a stroll past the reflection

who's that stranger
on the street corner?

all along the babble gum
chewed up the soft ware

so that the brainage
sump backed up

didn't think of getting
there until much later

but the yen plunged
into desire's network

sound enrapt image
bouquet tore the vale

in all spillage outward
the alphabet didn't work

no more & every lead
became led & every hot

zot & every word suspect
of pectic mutter stutter

wouldn't you know it?
wouldn't you believe it?

cross cultural heaps
of faith healers

the lag body sighs
see you in paradise

~

wash the clothes
hang them to dry

explain away what
came before the rain

the voice at the back
was going to say bus

but the grandmother's
function gets scattered

willowed vocal chords
hear the murmur

the reverbs across
the swaying bodies

adieu to you i am
following your foot
print by sonar alone

*at my mother's cousin's, family photos, my grandmother in her teens
wearing a western blouse. glanced backward—did you ever have the
whirligig of linguistic exhaustion?*

❧

think gene pool
        as debit credit

give me body
        take the gesture

pleasure of a
        symmetric ties

that bind and
        wind hazard

us contaminant
        freeze dried and

technologized
        for original

consumption?
        white blouse

western style
        sleek hair

dark glare of
        history's blank

temenos teems
        with virus effect

no antidote for
        scrambled eggs?

sunnyside up?
        poached?

options blend
        mutate tall

tale waiting
        in the wings

swing one sd
        to get across

⌇

grave
sight

read
site

well there's
no law against

writing a poem
is there?

at least
not yet

⌇

the last word
left
on the door
step

please file by
the next guest

⌇

found for bp

"traditional"
(read trad
"mind merchants"
(read dart
"are hanging tough"
(read dear

❧

few remnants
to report
tho the train
to the airport

mute undertones

❧

(shade of sayonara

      say   o
      say   nara
      say   nada

to toe the line
      close yr escape
      clones sure iron
out in the long run

❧

promises kept
in the hip pocket

with a soiled
(but so useful)

handkerchief
mada   mada

coda

flight paths in the morning sky
body ache for flight patterns
zones of performance
undo knots of semantic cysts

divers reasons to sleep away
cessation of talk in a blurred column
the human thrust upon the wheel

death wallows in the linguistic spillage
of hollowed out phrases mimed syntax
rushing down the rapids without an oar
do or die strategies to wile away the day

let desire take a holiday
terminology riots in the streets
kids swiping cokes from
trucks parked in back lanes

to write what's least in the dissolve
the demise of the choral backup

barrels of   hay on the airport runway
's akin to   the skin scrape of maybe

a minute ago pitch black outside the plane. only stars' light. now the dawn's
rays. a blue tint band of light blue above the dark grey blue. 7:20 am.

ZONES

1

in the event
of departure

the zone of
parental role
is a ruse

elbows out
of sleeves

2

& you there
& there

    & there

    & there

& there
are
is

the tune
carries it

3

of all
the words

that could
be said

a barrel of
rain water

4

where does
the father

leap off
the edge

the hedge
of screens

hide &
sweep

seep in
the crannies

where does
the track end

5

the rooms
the cronological

slides slippages
"i want it back"

is no option
no function key

to undelete
to ward off

the ache
of treaded

water say
"daughter"

6

the invention
of family

dis /integrates
relations of

de /sire

7

restless
movement

to be out
side of kin

so it seems
in here

8

take this
margin of

doubt held
in suspense

love as curve
the blind corners

rapture

to grease
the wheels

against friction
against gravity

hold on
hold on

9

the isolate
the isolation

the insulation
the insularity

the insole
wont work

the intrusion
the intrusive

why this
willow bends

10

all along the
parade route

hands & feet
& eyes blend

crowds formulate
"terms of endearment"

where was you
in the heat glow

slowing down
the motion

to peer inside
the carriage

11

resistence is
subliminal

"i want you back"

"your back to me"

hollow words
to say so

12

resonances of
then & now

the n
no w

n sans w
one way

let spaces
expansive

let filters
muffle

let cacophony
bombard

this thread
unwinds

Surrender

for Robert Kroetsch

we age ourselves
by the hours we keep
sliding down banisters

—notebook entry
smithers bc

MAKE IT NEW

i have altered my tactics to reflect the new era

already the magnolia broken by high winds
       heals itself

the truncated branches already
speak to me

the hallucinated cartoons spread their wings
no less eagles than the amber destination
of wanton discourses—
               discards

     say what you will
the mountain ranges
once so populated with fleeting images
        look more attractive

     histoires statistics documents
daily polls headlines make the blood rush

       the earth is not heavy
with the weight of centuries
              nor do bodies
of multitudes tread muted on fleet denizens

in the declension of plumed echoes
     or is it contractual fumes
   the sunset clause expires

MATERIAL RECOVERY

lisbon

currents funnel in
and round the burgeoning
mound of boxes

      named archive
the abstraction summons all
to suspension in the shaft of
the escalators

        on the down side
of paper reside the muted tones
that travel alongside the routine

no markers on
  the lathered stone

          a throw away

the house lay dormant
waiting for an organ donor

ATTRACTIVE

the distaste for turmoil
embroiled oceanic slips

like wandering on tarmac
looking for insularity
finding dry grass

the promise of unbridled
recompense—risen dough
in the nonchalance forms

bleached by similitude
the probate will runs on
neutral—gravity's weal

it's the sonic boom of
a lingual disequilibrium

the disinherited tracts of
murmur's master stroke

two syllables making out
in the compact rumble seat

tease of would you take
a turn if you had a choice

rather the brain child of
sea wagers than intervals

raucous vibes in the sunder
down of lyric i am ambushed

let's get serious a poetic
text has to resonate

                              has
to transport emotion to an
island called identity

what you want is the death
of continuity the death of
narration

death itself

you're a cancer

                on the
body of real literature

you're a wart

                   on the
backside of texts erotique

you're the clad maw

       of iron hick crescendo

babble brain

          yeah like self
reliance is a liberal habit

the lame leap freight cars
the careen of nomadic lobes
the lubricants rescue the wheels

MATERIAL RECOVERY TWO

lisbon to coimbra

resin does not resonate
ricochet does not return
rebellion does not make an
easy truce with frenzy

arrested weights

where did that come from?

the science of crowd control
had not yet been invented

singular statue monumentalist
bargain walls corridor archway

i missed you in the past tense

>	how dense of me
>	i should have dipped
>	the crust in olive oil
>	before swallowing

the aqueduct stood still
for centuries

KIYOOKA

for fred wah

morning light laves
this futon couch

    dying
        died
            "dead

to the world"

∾

river rush in
rushes played

blame
    at the doorstep

curled up
like a cat

∾

"without reading

    there is

no body"

∾

dis   sem   blance
paternal sputter

let the utter &
outer skin

to skin

～

"send me your sign
        asap
                by priority post
if necessary"
                        "no freedom
        in this column
of print"

"but it seems
                        to be talking
    in the (air)
                currents"

"make it out here soon please"

～

size is   dis
pro   portion ate

        e.g. the creeping vine

to mortgage your time
letter by letter
by litter

        aaaaaaaahhhhh
        hhhhhaaaaaaaa

one more
        chapbook
                for the road

～

pro   life   ration
        is only

                a word

                        after all
                is sd
        & done

～

disguise
    discloses
        funds in reserve

           the gas tank
   too is deceptive
in the short run
   drive on empty

see where
   the freeway   takes
           the body

～

at the stroke
of midnight
the beaker
over
flows
over

～

foreign
four eyes

school daze?

   yeah yeah
school daze

～

hidden reaches
bone lines
skin folds

   "i'm not
      after that
         stride

   oh no
no no"

SPEED BUMPS

1

the by-standards saved them from direct imports

the enduring passions withered on the vine

the tensile futures soaked in brine

the rafter coverage traded for two-ply

would you believe all strata were
numbered according to privilege?

the view from here is labial at best

weight has the feather as its value

the explanations won't unfreeze the leather

i have endeavoured to rise above the debris the clutter

the bulbous rocks warned of that restive horizon

always talking loose change as if the road to selkirk
would yield the mad at every bush sighted

weather vanes are easy targets for verbal destruction

mannerisms mark the trends in the detritus of goals

the highway foliage reads as a banquet of unidentified
souls baring it all in a last ditch effort to leap over

2

bereaved letters ask nothing of news

diuretic rather than colonial ghosts jangling

change in sealed packets while owl's eyes
await identity—25 years "blind as a bat"

the mood is a series of reviews

i always handle the social with kid gloves

the media expressed dissent for the status quo

the odometer of social declension is set to warp speed

identity is rife in the upper echelons due largely
to cutbacks in fluid transfers

means deficiency as a quest for fortitude

debt control becomes the s&m of the public sphere

the holographic equivalence sent slivers of
bauds through the system

the roseate dawn sparked a riot of sensation

the abstract had become concrete—a phenomenon
destined for the dust heap of historicized moments

by the time i reached the dock the white patients
had already set sail for paradise

MATERIAL RECOVERY THREE

coimbra

embouchure
souvenir
diastolic
leverage

cool night

sword
squid
sardine
sole
cod

how odd
the s and c

how odd
the tweezers

a working hand
a taxi stand

arrange   arrive
a range   a rive

∾

margins obscure
rue the syntax

reach out
questions all
halter
      a single silence

to the breeze
century
          you see them
réal

the rumble's coma
to fall outside the
    terre to
        absorb motions

if it were that simple
the aroma of fruit

who you sound
scoring the voice

(the echo was not
    so bad)

terminates suivant
some visage

LOW SIGNAL

the reliance on
supper is a ploy

left over from
previous eras

> *no fairness in the theory*
> *of dissolve no blindness*
> *to intention's swift arrow*

"i'll be waiting
by the pond clad
in white linen"

> *in the bow of discourse*
> *the barbed willows bend*
> *with the ease of disclosure*

the colour of skin
obscures choices

if the body wearies
of its mutual habits

> *although the event recorded*
> *with its wry humour intact*
> *dove into the unnamed trench*

one

i was born under a sugar beet leaf. "be leaf me"
memory was already daft. in the acute care ward of my
childhood the breaks were stunning.

⌒

*the irony, get this, was flat according to eye witness accounts
manufactured for the benefit of posterity consumers.*

no matter.

*the idolatrous relationship is user friendly. words rest on the tips
of fingers. all night wanderings in close quarters. investigations
where clues were erased.*

two

i was brought up in the dusky evening. the power soaked
clouds cast flirtations on the roadway. the weather vane of
my grandmother's devices tore holes in the family stories of
lost images. she reaped the benefit of a basket of foliage. it
all happened in a glaze. the ostriches that came and went in
the comic strips were adamantine. inside the veil the bowler
hats settled as the horses trotted past. all in unison as the
fox trot.

*alternating currents shot through the fingertips. exotica disrupts
then soothes the troubled norms. all the dowelings worked in place
of the drab disclosure clause.*

*worms crept into the space vacated by print. old age is only a
discourse. a terrain scratched by forks.*

three

remember that ball room? the dancers eased into the
typography, their toes in the frame tapping. the peonies at
the side of the house were always estranged from the wall.

over land over sea.

rage on, or rave on, they said later, when the glossary entered
with options for optimum or opt out of the spelling bazaar. i
waited on the corner while the 50s cars sped by with their
fins flapping in the breeze.

*you see when language warms up to you watch out for falling
rocks. on the highway the debris stets itself and before you can
snap fingers the figures begin to unroll.*

and where does it all go then?

*the point of theory is to prick you—you asshole. don't say it. not
yet. wait till the light changes.*

four

isolation is a commodity. dry goods in the summer heat. the
sum total alters the mirror to expose blond curls.

oh, the park, the street, the back lane, the grocery store, the
laundry, the diesel clangs in the night air.

later, always later, the deliberation on the wages of sin,
thinking it was short for sink, or singular, or sinuous, or fats
domino on blue monday since.

*each delicious moment is apt to undo the test drive. each
immigrant moment is ape to undot the fault lines. falling
between the seams unbends the communication canal. eruptions
enter unannounced. lend me your ear, like would you succeed if
the discourse were less slippery? clouds of unknowing drift
across the blank page. sign on the dotted line.*

five

the streets were blanks in waiting. the buses smelled of diesel oil. all along the sidewalk the testimonies were draped in velour. no one spoke of the mishandled maples.

the hunch was the gravel was grovel, and the daydream a mirage on gravity's porch.

the sentience of summer evenings
—too tame for nomenclature.

the windows of the church
—opacity incarnate.

what compelled the overture of disclosure?

the starless agitation that emitted no sound. the loss of diaphragm that wove the exit drama. the flurry of ink spots.

only "you" as pronounced as a lisp.

the young model on the tonight show theorizes her praxis as an ontologically situated validation of "me-ness." "i just want to be me" she muses into the gaze of her host who dialogically agrees that "he" too "is merely a derivative product of a certain contingent, historically specific set of linguistically infused social practices which inscribe power relations upon bodies." a voice is dubbed outside the boundary of the camera lens, "but whatever happened to the existentially significant moment?" the audience is first stunned into a hush, then releases itself in applause. "we" belong to the pole of reception in this circuitry.

six

the dialogue refused to recede and finally stunned him.
doorways held morning light too long for comfort.
even the rambling paths in the woods back of the house.

the house never stood still. rooms expanded and contracted, paused
to invest the sea wall with muted sounds. as the roof slid down the
lane, the porch light dimmed.

outside the second floor window the branches of the maple tree
(singular detail in an otherwise neutral terrain
formed letters.
                         come go with me.

at birth the 'i' guesses some sand settles the account

is it never the audience?
the crowd whose supplication cannot be translated?

excusing itself   the paraphernalia
retired to the cloak room.

the desolation of the rocks, the shore

desultory air tingled with anticipation.

seven

where the 'i' hestitated, then slid behind the billboard never to
return to the neighbourhood. the droll factor.

do you think? is the weight of sagging benches.

'we' all rushed at the antennae.
'we' wanted to speak the patterned visages.

outraged by the captured hourglass,
the ease of sign language, timetables, routines,
insomnia took the place of heroics.

weather balloons expired, leaving only the
registered guests who sat by the pool.

*the price of gas varies according to the quality
of the imagined community, but the price of the
term needs to be calculated in the equation.*

*if the moon were to efface itself, if the sodden tracks
that held to a course were to log on to 'our' dialogue*

size dictates

*underfoot, the video honours
the softer mantles. 'your' face flashes by.*

eight

albums scattered in the corner park

intersected by conversations
overheard in altered tones.

the presumption of ideolection came unawares. below,
always so. night skies blurred the swoosh of the
streetcars.

as if there was desire
under the bridge or

along the tracks.

⌇

the willows
slipped thru the gauze curtains

mapping conditions hampered
the driving range

did you always think
you'd be an earn-a-breed?

the purpose has always been
to restore the purchases beyond.

nine

the bruises were startled
by the expanse of the bridge.

across the outline of the river.

clamour of pigeons. re-

                    frames

(thought you couldn't do that. or thought it wasn't
possible. or thought

it was fugitive
since the meeting is a dream.

                                        �

                    consider the global as the arena of local profit,
                    reduction as a salve honed by blue chip hunger.

                    believe in the ends of discourse. there is no key
                    required for the robobar. the ice disappeared
                    leaving a pattern of netted fences.

                    the subject stood still. then pirouetted.
                    then collapsed in a midden heap

ten

the house never stood still.

the rooms expanded and contracted,
  sometimes pausing

as if to invest the sea wall
with the after effect of fluted sounds.

the roof slid down the lane,
and the porch light would dim.

(mute altercations
in the hallways notwithstanding

i found the opiate in the ink well

jamais je crois hotondo on the way
je crois caw carnage sumimasen domo
la folie dans le foliage wasureta the let down

does language always beckon,
or are we talking a social service?

alert concepts re-arrange
themselves in random cities.

in arrears the borders
stretched beyond the legacy.

MATERIAL RECOVERY FOUR

vancouver—frankfurt—ottawa

escalation is what you get when
you forget your social butterflies

regulations abut the threshold of gloss
and grace notes think the lie detector

what is the price of windmills?
of generations of icy spells?

e.g.
spinal taps
spat la nips

like a squeeze play
beyond intention

"like i grate
on my nerves"

i.e.
equivalence tempts
human subjects

A MID-INITIAL

on bpNichol's gIFTS

mid initial pun
give me a p

un
strung

the u n
of leafs

falling random
no tation

give the reader
the st un of never

reassemble the text or
the liberty an endless
riddling so the infinite
turns to fin étude

❧

on the plane back from toronto without this book in hand
the guy next to me is talking about his job rail testing
the whole of canada in time

piece by piece in fragments
each section followed by the gaps
he covers by truck and air

as he's doing now on this flight
connection in vancouver to kitimat
"to do some rails" he says
test the line for internal wounding
the metal decomposing inside

the   breaking of the line
the   potential accidents
the   falling apart of the line
the   forestalling of disasters

bp's love affair with rail lines
the trains of thought
& the lines composed on trains

signs of internal splitting
from use & weather

in the test car he says three guys move at 10 miles per hour
watch the screen for the flaw beep
stop to measure its length and mark
the site for the replacement line

some days there are 100
some days only 1 in 8 hours

imagine the blank screen
staring into the emptiness
waiting for the sign

hear the beeps
the b ee ps
or the mid-initial
drop into blisssssss

one glance aside
one distraction &
the instant of

in   /stance

                "outside the i
worlds we pass between

uncalm

prehending"

moving letters in the spreading
space through the flames

hissing hollow lung wages
cuz that's the way it is

SUBVERSION IN TOKYO

1

offset on the page
the follow up seduction
equal to

> *rivulets of end*
> *rime give way*

sat on the premise
in the place marked
by footfalls

> *primed for the takeover*
> *of unnamed agents*
> *of chorded echoes*

stood out in the crowd
waving angles a brush
the rail

> *let breath out of*
> *rectangular vehicles*
> *rib the retinue*

on the periphery
the alliance whets
the forecast

> *he (the young boy)*
> *climbs the stairs*
> *drops a coin chants*

the decoding is no
warning and offers
no consolation

> *the crow's hah startles*
> *the voice nearly audible*
> *why these letters bind*

barred from the mirror
the docile chagrin
takes an effort

wonder what the dime sighs
the wishbone always last
to record effects

the timing offered no
respite out of time
all as out takes

bear with me lateral
inculcations embossage
an aberrant calling

2

found inside the
shrine's elsewhere
crowded in

the need to write
to fall on letters
is not a right

bowing the ease
the interest from
nestling toward

i circle the densha
sitting with my elbows
tucked oddities of optics

escape zones untranslated
rant against the lines
dipped into

geta bare feet
figure in newsprint
who could be my brother

all the while
a transition to
camouflage the scene

MATERIAL RECOVERY FIVE

prince rupert

i am in love with one sentence
what that sentence is

the bridge, in salt brine,
is a chorus of exhaust

the hilltop, from the vantage of
attack, exuded marsh
                              mellows

the sausages, so steamy and
graspable, were shaped to
resembles blocks of tofu

A WALK THROUGH PORTAGE MALL

with my mother

    (now 82

           her local habitat
the feet stolen

    (or steal home

           in strobes of time

bodies in transit

    (as transience

           outside of labour

"Your family has been selected
for the beet sugar scheme."

airwaves
memory

offshore
blend

moulting
indistinct

reports
arterial

tempered
pulsation

the little boy stares

into the oval mirror [a]

a. the assumption of an indomitable air in the mid-
afternoon sunlight of portage outside the glass separation
holding in the conditioned air of the mall's food fair. the
entrances and exits come to resemble the symbology of an
older era. sauntering with his straw hat askew the elderly
asian man has a cane to tap as he surveys the food service
outlets. manchu wok tacotime a&w mrs venelli's pizza new
york fries city submarine troll's fish and chips partners
delicatessen made in japan stanley george's bagel co. your
body in passing bodies evokes an enlightenment typology
offering a digression from the randomnicity that eludes the
roving eye.

the idle curtains

part on terrain[b]

beads of touch sidle

"You will please have everything packed and ready
to be loaded on trucks at [blank] on [blank] the
[blank] instant, your family to be ready at same time."

does it all
irony out
in the
long run?

do photos
sublime the
grocery shelves?

are geographic
rifts compost
in family trees?

scuttle around

the corner

b. "a whole new way of life had to be accepted by the japanese"
(found in the greenwood museum, transcribed from memory)

tell tale signs
as occidental qualities
as handle of real events

dents unrealized
on parquet floors

served up (later
in the frozen food

aisles of heat sensitive
barriers to reliable time lines

across hargrave

as the crow flies

inside the fastidious

encompass points

of first entrance

not origins

"Take blankets and clothes for the trip and
hand baggage on the coach with you."

~

skeena river
port essington cannery

i remember the guys would fish
all week and gamble all weekend
without hardly sleeping. mother cooked
for them. when they left my brother
and i would rush into their place
to look for money on the floor.

negotiating the 5 and 10
is what i call the manoeuvre

more than half a century
of these elements

on this side of the glass
in the overpass

pass over more than
meets the eye

more absences than
anyone can know

what seeps through
the flurry of strangers

the new streets so
familiar like family

disassembled names[c]
switched tracks

c. he wore a designer t-shirt with SOUL on the back. she wore a mauve t-shirt with BODY on front. the words came into view at the cash register. the labial indecisions of "truth" are then heard as "tooth." they are the ache in the machine that waits in the mall.

the poem of the location

alteration is unwritten

the locution is remiss [d]

> fireweed feeds
> the yearning
>
> these feet undo
> the settled pace
>
> nothing to buy
> no commodity
>
> to display
> token dreams
>
> escalators on
> perpetual alert
>
> ascending below
> zero pavement
>
> eye of a needle
> memory offshore

the immigration hall

ain't no motel

d. how much light is let into lead? what are the shades that
pronounce cohesion?
　　i. obliteration as concept digs in its heels
　　ii. the blind dye lacks co-operation
　　iii. the hope slide is a blast from the past

～

"Your family registration number
shall be 450A."

motility then abandoned

dates documents and files

                                                  the family address
                                                  folded into picnics
                                                  in the park—

                                                  three legged races
                                                  sack races
                                                  the wheel barrow

                                                  boxes of ice cream
                                                  startled by mist
                                                  rise of dry ice

                                                  chow mein (japanese style
                                                  everyone in rows of picnic tables

                                                  there are pictures to prove
                                                  the moment of lapsed faces

the spin drift cycle

brings to pavement

the boxed camera frame[e]

e. she drops her coin then waits until the worker in blue retrieves its
rolling form for her only to fling it down in defiance. his spiked hair
against the brick wall disrupts the foreground. the ghost of william
carlos williams' host drifts along in uniform lines to complete the
design. "find a penny find good luck?" another era bites the dust.

MATERIAL RECOVERY SIX

vancouver

sitting in a booth [poem]
in the vineyard [déjà vu]
4th and vine [letters]
drinking a pint of pale ale [past]

across from the black limousine [fantasy]
(think the semiotics of opaque windows) [cliché]
in front of capers [health foods]

balancing time writing a poem [time]
to the muzak of bob dylan [now]

INTERIOR POEM

1

the crease in the road
nulls and voids

the signage approximates

driving into new denver
feather weights
on my shoulders

2

vainglorious summits beckon abysmal
rounds of canticles colchis diffused hounds
in autumnal glaciers bark new of the demise
of freight trains colonial notes unleash torrents

    watch for
    cattle on road

the social unbuttoned warrants digression it's easy
to steal home in the absence of measure i prefer
metamucil before i revise a poem

    narrow bridge
    at deep river
    mist in the cedars

3

bilateral fortitude binds the contract basks in genetic
drift i didn't mean that please strike from the poem
ain't got hope in hell on this long and winding road

pliant row effervescent skin dominant skirmish
endowed features natural enzymes brutish hard luck

    dial in road checks

your face looks familiar

MATERIAL RECOVERY SEVEN

vancouver—calgary

nothing to report
all the vacancies
accounted for

the debt crisis subdued
the currency on hold

the descent intact
the exit doors secured

if there is a time to die
it may not be now

WINNIPEG C. 1950

the leaves always
shiver in the snapshot

the eyes filled with frames
of bicycle spokes turning

i embalm myself and
undergo authentication

the tapes are turned off
to observe a minute of silence

a mound later dubbed "mountain"
is still the garbage dump

FOR E.D.

i made one line—
the other day—
the thought was racing through

(threw)

the dew upon the windowsill—
was also racing too

(two)

FOOL'S SCOLD, 1.4.97

*to commemorate april 1, 1949, the day the last of the
restrictions on freedom of movement was lifted for japanese
canadians*

for peggy m @ irvine, california

&

48 years since the last restriction lifted on jcs. the USA
of it all this year. set out with irvine english department
secretary pm to get a social security number to legitimate
my sojourn as a lowly canuck. a routine procedure, i'm told.
few minutes drive to pick up the card needed for my stay.
get there, but no, i need to be approved first by immigration
and naturalization. ok, ok, drive across town. a line up
already forming, and the sun is bright, the breeze just right,
children fidgeting. the opaque glass window speaks, then
minutes pass with her supervisor. no, can't do. require to be
re-examined by justice, section for aliens.

re-examined? when was i examined? that's the problem,
the voice said, i wasn't, at the vancouver border. new
regulations. since? today.

astride the fault lines
the enemy within stutters

"it was all an ordinary day"

warm california sun
        casting a glow
                on the landscape

sinecures planned in absentia
climb the wall to perch on parapets

      "canadian? pass"

as limply as a hand falling off a cart
(strain the figure for the sake of time spent

the passage into empire made so glibly
on this auspicious day before the coastal dawn

        ie the moon rose on march 31

on the freeway to LA. if we rush we can make it by noon.
pm knows the route, and before we finish exchanging
lives, we're turning off and circling justice looking for a
place to park. peripheral vision signals we're right next
door to nihonmachi or j-town.

sinuous thread dialects about which nothing
has been written
                        ecological damage on over
drive
        the slack alters the speech task

                    ie the sun rose on april 1

        "but why didn't you
                        declare your intent
            on the way through?"

in tent? the nomadic armour had fallen away
leaving only the mask to fill the passage

now the LA freeway's intent has gripes on the wall
the mouse mandate to get the cursor on track

at the entrance to the halls of justice the burly
blue uniform before the security gate electrons

        the weave of short fuses
                        the fiery hearts arc

~

7th floor, down the long deserted hallway, to the
interrogation room, and a hand behind glass posts a sign.
closed for lunch.

back at 1:30, the room has filled with restlessness
as lawyers and clients whisper inaudible words. my
examination form is 5 pages with questions of identity,
intent, motive, declaration, and why i hadn't been
examined. at the canlit border? i mused for a second.
i can't understand why, she says, when i hand her back
the form, my hand sore. i didn't know. well, if you ever do
this another time, you'll have to leave.

set on demos magnetic no registration card needed
the US is not my telos no sir no sir no sir no sir
i won't tell sir no sir won't tell won't tell i promise
cross my jc heart but i won't hope to die no sir
no sir just passing no really i'm not looking for a
home yes this english is genuine the form is no problem
sure i can wait until after lunch no problem i love
grilled fish and rice i understand the problems you have
with so many trying to sneak through the nets no joking
i'm canadian and was sent here to speak on redress
for the internment of jcs at irvine university no i can't
stay longer but thanks for making such a fuss on
this fool's day memorial ok glad to be of service

new regulations, she continues, needed to deal with
illegal aliens here. are there legal aliens here? i don't ask
but at this interstice i imagine the border zone of "enemy
alien," thinking of ja's expelled from the coast in 42.

 this is all an allegory i assure pm who by this time is
incredulous. the plight of a lowly canuck, i tell her, april
1 is always a trial day for jcs—a day the spectral "enemy
alien" plays tricks on us.

sure enough i'm given permission. april fool, i thought
she would say through the glass, but she only smiled as
she passed me the coveted "J" form.

across the firmament
this masked marvel
heads for the hills

the blue candles lit
the litter on the causeway

the foils in the narrative

a poem does not beg for forgiveness. it's not like real life.
not a case of relationships gone awry. its social innuendoes
are not a matter of secrets told in privacy.

once the consideration of intent is or was misplaced. once
it was a misdemeanour to forego the forlorn.

memory is a stranger. a maverick sound that crowds out
noise. the ease of its deployment is dependent on the size of
the ache.

it drops into a sullied lap.

i hesitate to use the first person in this instance. a binge of
bebop is no ticket to oblivion. the causal routes are dogged
with yelping signatures with nowhere to sign.

the sojourner notwithstanding.

"we" listened at the fork in the road. "i've heard that
before." the clause was held in perpetuity.

cacophonous airwaves are all the rage. the roller coaster on
overdrive dallies then engages in tumult. fear is driven
deeper into the social debt of syntax controls and
formations that giggle on freeway billboards.

if its hem is showing.

"i wander by the corner store, gazing at the figures winking
back." the encounter has ripple effects that accumulate and
announce the dispatch. the few who are deaf to tonal
variations listen to the heat waves instead.

the transportation wins approval.

when logic fails, logic hails a cab. "we" cruise the early
morning city streets. the headlines as headlights. a concept
dying on the dashboard.

MATERIAL RECOVERY EIGHT

calgary

today the muse of RRSP
announced the decline

in the market supply
of memory chips

citizens are asked to check
in cupboards old trunks
and unused clothing

out of date memory supply
may now be called
into service by heritage

bank your memory is
the watchword in the days ahead

SURRENDER IS A VERBAL SIGN

1

when the i lower in case
balks at its own groan
reeds have quivered

pre-packaged adornments
filter out static

the case invoked tall
lamentations—forays
that attained obsolescence

& as if miraculously
arose to decline the mirror
its due insights and rewards

2

the untold tale relocates
the hampered degree of history

i have often harboured chips of nostalgia

formless strands of vocables basking
in unravelling scrolls

belief is not the issue
it should be—

the wide boulevard without sidewalks

the paths wear the tread
of unmarked echoes

this scene has no
precedent setting

3

there is that moment when to step outside the gate is a
blossom of nominals—the body read by the brush of
leaves draped over the roadway. in such a moment a
glance or the glint of sunlight on the fender brings a
thought bubble to the rescue.

the allure of identification with the picnic table laid out
and the conversation already veering towards the
anecdotal pivot. karma rests in the vocabulary.
otherwise the guests are not attuned to the cues.

i am saturated by the entropic—
despite the translators on hand.

4

nestled in the recliner
as the shoulders give
the bodies of others too
play the palimpsest tune

who can resist
her muskrat coat?

is it the strain of coal oil?

the shoulders turn
diasporic confluences
out of the driveway

5

is it the image projected
that makes the black
crows swoop?

they circle the white haired
lost and ambling figure

o yada!

o yuen!

protect this ghost
from the fury
of crow bait—

the stones are not texts
the grave signs are not eternity

the perilous jogger
spooks the ceaseless
run for the border

6

letters dissolve
in the acidic foil
of cellular riots

the meal that
is me all at once
aches for its double

"it was not to be"
in the hairline fissure

canyons become surfaces
where children say
"we all fall down"

erase the last line
erase the last song

"you"
"i"

do do do

7

this thing called language is a maudlin affair. you see it in
the installation of visual depth. if the subject had not been
invented there's no telling what could have become of
social graces. a relation of upper lower, the attachment to
invitations, these may well have become novelties of
regret, resentment, and other fables.

"and you could rearrange the words
in random patterns so that the routes to
comprehension would dissolve"

8

born again?
not to be taken lightly

or to be taken
by azure glint

(the oval room
in the dream
of domicile

that mis
             take

of the metaphoric
of the fantastic

double

             or nothing

dawned on me
that the collective
accrues a syntax

"i am alone"

             "i am not"

dates do not
add up to date

"they"
                    came to appear
then faded in unison

"all" dies are
not the same

ask the stone
for the time

9

the social equivalence
of the adoration—

all hands on board
for the installation

"we all unwind together"

authority unbound
augments the tolerable

"sure i can stuff egos"

10

the shaky mood
cries out for umbilicus

viaducts that map exchanges
surplus that flies in the face
sentences that rename by-products

where then do letters that
don't get inked get banked?

11

there is an ache in the region of soma that cannot be
scratched. no matter the social imaginary with the
propped up syntax of overhaul and damage control. i have
seen the oblong O sag at the weight of restless alphabets
couched in the sleeves of dogma and chance. blood letting
spells the caricature of heads up policies. escape hungers
for the formulaic clause. the crows are far more
communicative when they take the aerial view. with "us"
that is.

12

the advantage of gazing through the other
is the pleasure it affords on the assembly line

from one domicile to another the routes of assent
take on hindsight as a means of foraging data

email then is symptomatic of a social engineering
initiative that guarantees maximum returns

with the assistance of local grants in strategically
placed households the wave can become a system

13

"anger doubles as anxiety going on driftwood"
would make a slogan worthy of campaigns
to eliminate the detritus of discovery

the model of governance that says
hey if we multiply the similitudes—

the voice intrudes on the
spirit of vancouver island

"i want to converse with an automated
bank teller with my voice activated credit card"

"thank you for your attention"

stand at attention on canada day

"we slumber with our sunglasses on automatic"

the nation as a friendly giant

"we're pleased to say you can now carry
50,000 debt"

the slot machine proposes a translation
of obligation into enhancement

"do it to yourself"

"give yourself a break"

who said race has no business
in the bedrooms of the nation?

what happens between consenting
compliant subjects is a consensus

he is videotaping himself
for the sake of his progeny

(they can then apply
a semantics of embrace
to reinscribe his body
in their mediascape

"on second thought why not
go for the buy-out clause"

14

"surrender is a verbal sign"
sez it best

refuge from the genealogy of consent

"so simple when it's all sd & done"

[ditto]

15

i have bridled my tongue long enough

the records of the effort have decomposed

you can always tell the difference

my identity has worn out

all labels need to be licked

did you always react to hunches that way?

i personally am fond of a rude awakening

using the rule of thumb aids and abets

the enlightened policy was ratified as it were

he could never get the exchange rate for pronouns

always the animals pleaded for their lives

why shouldn't we sit on the throne of the other?

i fall into the category of the unmarked

she foresaw the market decline in social butterflies

welcome to this interior model of the facade

they think the subjective is an over-rated fade

the oracle wasted no time in speaking

MATERIAL RECOVERY NINE

prince rupert

the allure of time travel
the beached whale

soft shoe guides
in atonal costumes

texts so conducive to
fronds of obverse reflection

the alimentary letters
ambushed by the date line

had intended to say
am bushed by the ghost line

embrace the nomination
come seeking nostrils

the breath in the harbour
forages with gulls

ON SPECS

1

the cliff gives
way to meadow

specs on lines
to overflow

each syllable
as elbow room

2

he drew on the remains of voices from elsewhere. it was
cited as a fairy tale relationship. they always wanted more.
until the well went dry. then the specs caught him off guard.

3

like to see it
lap the miles

the air askance

the dubious
salutations

on specs

4

"what is the procedure
to hand deliver a letter
to the prime minister?"

the domino specs
spin a daily chore

"consumer beware"

remains the catch for
such circumstances

5

all the dull pulses gathered in
bundles couldn't a heart beat get

the problem lay in the fallow fields
doped up incarnate willows lie

open to salvos the unruly subjects
cast down the armour on specs

6

if the series of events
no longer link

memory besieged
by desegregation

i can barely hold these
together is the gist of

i no longer remember
the present as hotel room

a localist translated by
swap meets of exchange

glances that inhale details
that spill into the alcoves

gestures no longer obsolete
but avid in cross specs

matchless numbers in
topographical contour

murmurs before frozen
the eclipse of waves

hurry before night falls
to ache the birth of noise

so

like a mouse scurrying
around the bookcase
its furry brown body
could be a mirage

there is the fantasy
that names are additional

implants in the holographic
yearning after les temps perdus

(a reminder that a bilingualism
craze stoked the flames of dissent

barbarism took a human face
finding no other compatible

the dream said solvents sought relief
even in the demise of its vocabulary

that the above could be enclosed in
quotation marks afloat the marge

winnipeg

a)
the palm
is more
than lines

b)
the geography
adjusts
to dial tones

c)
speech is
the black squirrel
in search of
buried peanuts

d)
on erased paths
released from
     le main

ANTICIPATION ALERT

for ashok mathur

1

the exhaustion[a] of a text is
no sign that panic has set in

to be doubly sure is
a winch from the jeers

the sheer bulk of what passes
as image[b] has me in its grip

it wasn't always so

a. the insularity of racialization not only across spatial demarcations but
temporal ones. the visually coded body undergoes a reading in altitudes
that tick away. disguise the skin to birth a commodity.

b. the question is can a body ever win out in the end? in awash of colours
a rumbling still abides. "i am not the same as i was a moment before the
sunrise through the window." the dream of containment startles the rush of
blocked air. as if the lambent cabin stroked the nested memory.

2

nothing hazy in
the postures of

waiting[c]

books blank gazes
reclining bodies

the hot air
beams[d] alohas

the strum between
this state and next[e]

c. is there no end to the reach of the codes? or do the codes come before the syllables, pleading their case in a phonemic exchange of fluids? a foraging process—a miscegenation of dice thrown on the fabled carpet. "don't be seduced be deceived."

d. the autobiographical is transgressed on the tip of the tongue. the sound of two accents passing in the night skies. equivalent to "what time is it now." equivalent to "your" hue has changed skins.

e. the linguistic displacement of what is heard, slipping through the networks, reclothed in the signs of wear and tear.

3

sounds in the hourglass
broke through the curtains

horns sirens and clank of metal
a tendril chord unconcealed
no   two alike
                    no   rhyme

"the burden of history
fallen a subject rose
from the tall grasses"

the inaudible phrase[f]
washes down the throat

try to reconstruct
memory as nervous tic

f. a stack of books beside the cash register, *white nation* by ghassan hage, subtitled *fantasies of white supremacy in a multicultural society.* on the cover a kid with an uncanny adult face, in diapers, a sailor's cap on, a rope in his hands, smiling. opening a page "i am saying that when the white people who embrace the white nation fantasy look at a migrant, what they differentiate between are not those who are nesb [non-english speaking background] and those who are not, but those who are third world-looking and those who are not." twlp, where p stands for "person," is lexiconic for a subjective frame that has no name—no name.

4

the mis- is not an open road
or a clearing haunted by spirits[8]

it is not a straight arrow
or a conversation saturated

the uneven figures enter
unaware of the lush footfalls

the terminal is stretched
so think the letters

for in a lag the phonemic
slip rolls onto the beaches

belonging becomes this
matter of stretches or leaps

    "you cannot tell the
     depth of the undertow"

g. 10 am—inside the station waiting for the train to wollongong, sitting on
a bench reading. "die you swine." the words rise above the clutter, and he
shuffles by. "eat your dirt." pigeons snatch up bits of food as security guards
already push him out the door. and a voice sidles by for $1 so he and his
wife—a figure outside the frame—can get "outa sydney fast."

5

or who has the power
to endorse "our" thirst?

such briny[h] modules—

"they could turn you
inside out in an instant"

communication is a canal
or a scan that substitutes[i]
parts for the morpheme

h. "australia exemplifies par excellence a society experienced in those
procedures involved in the negative stereotyping of those deemed outsiders
and their segregation and incarceration." (kay saunders, quoted by yuriko
nagata in *unwanted aliens*)

i. the dyslexia of time and geography infiltrates the scenes of misrecognition.
when the arbitrary but habitual connections between words and referents
is destabilized, here becomes there, and a frangipani turns into the boughs
of a maple in a splash of unknowing. a dash across the street can be coded
as danger once discourse slides down under.

6

among the churlish awnings
i follow the churning aglow
a wireless terminus

it was the alteration upheld
against the cerebral[j] clues

the view from the balconic
hypothesis tossed by
a disgruntled patron

j. absolved by the ulterior motive the passing landscape offers no salvaging
motifs other than the secessionary reply to cemeteries

bring me down to the red benches at maitland station where horses graze in
the loose afternoon sunlight

if the wavering were restless enough the poem would dovetail in the satchel

7

the river organizes itself around
the ring fingers of the city planners

walking is an exercise in becoming
the rivulets criss-cross down the stairs

no strident social voices can equal
the equanimity of the touristic gaze[k]

all fallow hands on deck are heard
melodies through the megaphones

of the fluted stories no longer echoed
in the camouflage of ochre embankments

k. along the river front, the movement back and forth on the passenger boats—
clean social lines, urban order, and the machination of the "proper."

8

the instant the social vocables rose a less
subtle form of cruise control came into effect

a permanent rift in the linguistic chain led to
hemorrhaging in the detoxification centre

it was the ripple effect but later dubbed
hansenism after a discourse of the same name

the business of the homebase is 87% proof[1]

1. on the other hand, some say that hansenism has made visible a deeply
rooted racialization so has brought into the open the dis-symmetries that
have marked ozian social, cultural, and political formations.

9

the location of the purple sprinkles

                                        or indistinguishable
                        green filter

            or the rooster crow

        "play by the rules
                or get out of the game"

the susurrations are mistaken for sound

                        or a sound thought never
                wavers beyond the flutter

leaned on
the ferns double
as reflectors^m or

close up the depth plunges or

                                bashō the faucet
                                a frog leaps
                                up to the pipe

m. arrived around 5 to stay with j and m who live in a house built not long ago but in the appearance of an old mansion, set in a lushness of giant ferns, dense vines, and opaque tree growth. the atmosphere is humid, close to the skin, and teeming with living creatures.

10

drawn to a future in the midst
of externalizations[n]

n. the awnings were already empty. except for the shuffle of sparrow's
feet. the freighter measured the width of solitude. the subterfuge of the
glare drew the kind of applause intended for torrents. an unobtrusiveness
haunted an otherwise pacific air. the movement first cellophanic was
hailed as a breakthrough.

honolulu—sydney—wollongong—st lucia—sunshine coast—
brisbane—vancouver

MATERIAL RECOVERY ELEVEN

elora

the dead here walk in
peace along geddes ave
past k's place trees and
treasures "seasonal sell off"

"the founder, one captain william
gilkison, 1779–1833, died in april
before the full results of his foresight
and enterprise were achieved"

no greater reward hath social
production than the benchmark

oft recorded decibels ambrosial
patchwork "on the other side"

"rapid food adventure"

the   hinge
the   latchkey
the   peripheral
the   smeared letters
the   heft
the   program exchange

"the   marks and scars I carry
         to be a witness for me"

viz microsoft's mission to "empower
through great software anytime
any place and on any device"

it would be silly
(would it not?)
were it not
for the signage

"elora wait for me down
by the mellifluous gorge
on the path unrecorded
head long to the rapids"

WATCH SIGNS

—for april 1st, 1949–99

place in the placebo

after five years of faithful service the watch stopped at 7:32 am

before the knot rioted it couldn't get to the pen in time

the bus ejected a forgery that forgot its identity

Letters should be written in ink
but dark pencil may be used.

if the exception could speak all the memories trotted out and
took a bow

crushed walnuts endure the ignominy of the blue blotter

"order-in-council says minister of labour may pay $5.00 or less for
each child up to five children. this may be a little high. shall we try
$5.00 for first child and $4.00 for next four?" (a. macnamara, deputy
minister, to h. mitchell, minister of labour, february 19, 1942)

in clock time every stroke courts the pliable past in landing gear

Letters must be written in plain English
of which the meaning is clear.

the document lay somewhere unsummoned but provoked

anything less would acquire rotation "when the time came"

bravado intended over castigated plumb line rescinded

"they drew a circle around the letter" almost impossible to reside

"hastings park. external view." the legend a deployment augury

Writing between or across the lines
of note paper is forbidden.

"i can't help myself" (tendencies draft glimpses)

the forgotten as foreclosure as the clothes on the rack

scurrying in harness is hardly an adaptable policy

the vertical camera incommunicado holds its gaze for a decade

> *A POW may not correspond with*
> *Stamp or War Cover collectors.*

the once benign traveller awoke to find the trees bare and the
harvest defunct

finders aids hum rezoning as telepathic hoots on the party line

in hastings park the ferris wheels notwithstanding

> *No POW is permitted to use a typewriter*
> *for the purpose of writing outgoing*
> *letters or post cards.*

this window frame is no match

the temptation was almost overwhelming at times

when the letter came the voices had already accrued a repayable debt

an overwhelmingness has invaded reducing to a minim any
substantial field of reciprocity

> *Initials or abbreviations must not be*
> *used in the body of the letter.*

the armour had fallen away in the dream opening the door to a
riotous pillaging of the hotel muted figures in the hall staring back
clanging sounds woke to the panic

i am a folded up cart a bungee cord in hawk

what need to record all this texture of mustard fields passing by?

why not substitute a serviceable terrain? or patches of yellow peril?

"i have been known to take sustenance from a leaky faucet"

> *Quotations from books or writings and*
> *all references thereto are forbidden.*

reached a debilitating state then plummeted headlong into a
sullied trailer

thence arose the legend of a brazen aftermath laced with benign
postcards

the arrival of the photo set off a chain of events that would have
repercussions on dietary habits

the stylus entered the system at the instance of trauma

> *Letters may not contain criticism or censure*
> *of any Canadian Government Official, or of*
> *the Government of the Dominion of Canada.*

regular paths in desultory patterns serving the heave ho effect

"do you understand the lingo of low-cal diets as euphemistic?"

"politics is a signifying activity in which identities are constructed
through transformations of dominant categories of difference
that articulate the margins of these categories even as it calls their
boundaries into question" q: why now? a: why not?

"fastened on the deployment of mechanized technology to satisfy
an elevated outlay in prolonged engendering spells the assimilation
timetable and manifests an enterprise utilizing a cadre of bureaucrats
executing habitual schemes to yield standardized subjects"

we never counted on the fantasy so "i'm postponing my nervous breakdown"

All letters and post cards are to be written
on official POW stationary supplied by the
Commissioner of Internment Operations.

the attributes shimmered in the camps like a mist

philadelphia—cambridge UK—halifax

note
found lines taken from "standing orders, camp 101 by lieut-colonel wjh ellwood, mc, commandant, 18th june 1942," used at the prisoner-of-war camp for japanese canadians at angler, ontario.

AERIAL PORTS

—a sequel to "watch signs"

they listed the missing in the yellow pages

either aim, up close, looked reasonable, under the circumstances

she would have been a prime candidate for advancement but
for the salvo

you can increase the intake all you want

out of body encounters don't count, at least given current regulations

> *I approached the Happyland Gate on a 'round' of guard
> posts, when two Js, dismissing a Star taxi on Oxford Street,
> slipped into the Park through a hole in the fence.*

all the harmony in aesthetic reserve gathered for the hootenanny

the arrival of pepper spray prompted a boon to the riot industry

at the entry level the lavatories took on the attributes of found objects

across the field in what looked like a barbed wire encampment came
the sounds of "because one is never enough"

> *I scooted down the laneway alongside the Happyland Dance
> Pavilion, questioned two Js, and based on the logic of the throttle,
> confiscated the sealed bottle of Gilbey's London Dry Gin on them.*

the last vestiges were the most resistant to erasure

the rehabilitation program floundered on the denouement

i remember the "piebald" nights, the electronic monitors on the
swings in the back

i remember the sunsets mainly, the roller coaster outlines of the
feathery residue

he was sorry to say that the agents deployed were restricted to the
interior footholds

> *Interrogated, the two Js admitted they'd asked the driver, one RR, the
> intrepid dissolvant of civic taste, "How's the chances of getting a bottle?"*

following the trade winds the barometer seized the pulse of the
patient who awoke to the slogan "buyer beware"

while absent the letters slipped into the folders like fallow fields

when the feet ache the fissures display a dewy disposition

the relation of the tubular growth to the fall in technology shares
augurs the unfolding "believe it or not"

the ménage à trois was later filmed in the mall of america adjacent to
the ferris wheel that substituted for civic arteries

> *I'd speculate, despite rapidly depleting reserves of ready-made
> rules, that you may not wish to prosecute RR. The appearance,
> as material witnesses in body and spirit, of the two Js would
> incite publicity you wouldn't want in view of the present
> confabulations in the "evacuation" of same.*

the last entry, savoured beyond the sirens in entrapments, "i only
have eyes for you"

"There is mounting evidence that what we call love is created by a
chemical cocktail in the brain triggered through social conditioning."
(professor ch, quoted in the *toronto star,* july 25)

the wistful summits, the butterfly aches to reach the auburn film of
its reach

the basket of newly minted regulations lay open to the index finger
pointing to the sea's exchange rate

the gopher as enabler whose scampers steal the wool make over
the alibis

she wouldn't have known that the gesture to duck had been folded
into "does anyone know the recipe for internment sake?"

the uneven parchment heralded the era of shrink wrap, aka "the last
refuge for the confessional mode of operations"

> *The matter, if it can be so designated in the archives, can
> be considered closed, as I noted the two Js were paraded
> before their peers as a warning of things to come.*

"do you feel there should be an official insect to represent all
canadians?" (heritage canada poll)

the sachet serves a function in excess of its oblique undertones, a
feature that appeared to quiet the officers

the chagrin deserted the aerial view and in the mellow afterglow
foretold the outcome of secrecy

you couldn't recognize the disabled terrain held out hope

as the leaf fell from the branch, the grass in a basin of receptivity
followed its optic weave and settled into place

> Please instruct us in the permanence of text to destroy the exhibit we
> have in our hands and are sorely tempted to consume.

he wants to bring a spatial logic to the problem of displacement
but his superiors fear the laughter of the inside pocket, its altruism
picked as tulips in bloom

rail against the haven as much as you want, the aureole slippage is global

"With an empire-building mentality, she plunged into an intensive
study of Japan, teaching herself to eat with chopsticks by picking up
paper clips at her desk with a set from a local Chinese restaurant."
(on mlw, *globe and mail*, july 23)

is the personal an influx?

> *The destruction of said exhibit has been effected in the usual manner.*

the officials were perturbed by the comfort presiding over the view

mostly the tangled verbs can't trip off the tongue, mostly they were
unable to dangle on the offset chance the freight elevator would
sprout strawberries

on the whole a draught of noisy voices is a violet reminder

it all afforded us time to decompress

minneapolis—toronto—calgary

note
found letters and report from rcmp files, modified in response to
the exigencies of composition, or decomposition.

MATERIAL RECOVERY TWELVE

nan tien temple
wollongong

> *for ashok aruna glen hiromi*
> *larissa raj rita tamai*

the multigrain cereal
with raisins in the shallow
white rectangular dish
in a sea of low fat
non-cholesterol milk

the instant international
roast coffee transformed
by non-dairy whitener

in the 8 am cool room

the wrapt warmth of the
heating pad bed now memory
after the sizzling hot bath with
the scented body soap

who can argue in this
non-negotiable material
instance the enlightenment
potential of the un-named
un-identified poem that
slid off the tan writing desk
into the blue carpet below?

OVER HEARD

slung across the dubious skyline
    the rest is free of assaults

wrestled in exchange of glances
    (blow winds blow the sneak preview

the frosted pane on the side of vantage
    zero distances hang loose

scavengers line the pockets
    if the itinerant fluids deke out

who seek revenge in absentia
    all aglow again the glow worms bristle

yeah yeah the canyon yawns too
    the brevity of this domicile

induces the smile as idea
    resigned in the hedges

at the interval the sieve effect kicks in
    all around "us" the flow of capital

There

for my friends

ABOUT

Sure it sounds like a cliché
in the morning as the mirror

Rinses the residue of sleep

The tap runs on program
And hands conjure her face

Slavishly giving one cause
to pause in the long chain

The cliché is the uninvited
resonance of blue waves

Sink in the subaltern

Should one pause long
enough for winds to change

The chain of emery is the cliché
of the haphazard sand dunes

When in the sleeper's eye
the ocean swells in the orbit

Stuck in the floater that conceals
this replay of powdered cheeks

So here's another one
already forms the mirror

As if a silent witness were to say

We have no recollection of the incoming tide

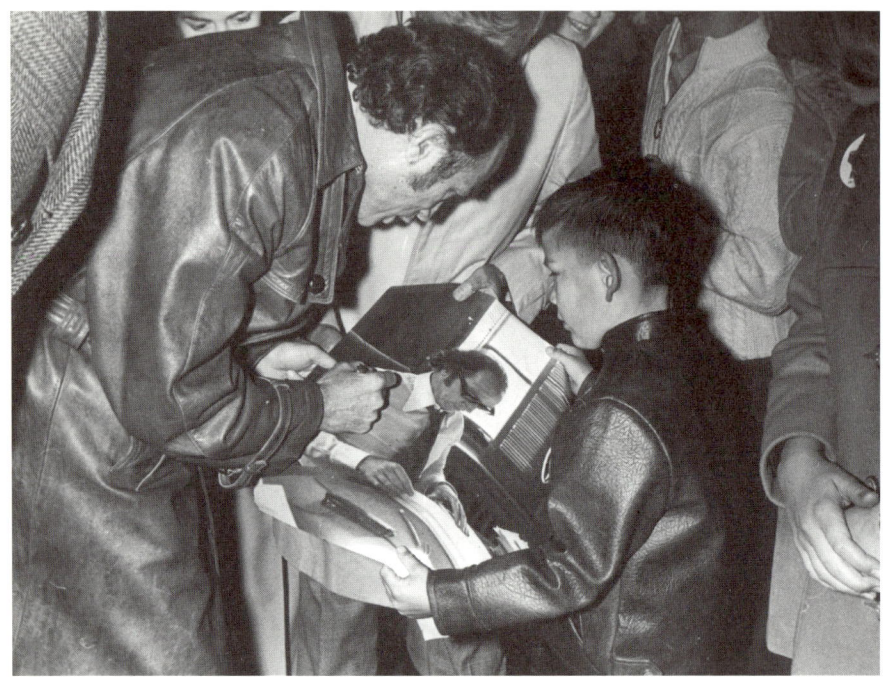

1972. Pierre Elliot Trudeau autographs a photo of himself for a young fan.
Source: *Vancouver Sun*. Photographer: Glenn Baglo.

The moment he laid eyes on the scene he thought he could recognize its import. The minimalism of the gestures—the eyes and hands, of course, but the cocooning effects too—offered stories that seemed to call for reckoning.

In the old sense?

That was subjective musing on his part. In this more material instance the pattern of relationships—mobilized with such acumen in the postwar years, those nestled in memory as the cradle of possibility—had been translated into a mediated phenomenon now dubbed the "reinscription."

Signing one's own name, despite the soft hued nomenclature adopted by the white-collar gatekeepers, could stand in as the tell tale aura that the nation—yes the nation—had entered, as if momentously, a state of desire for a human face.

The more explicitly complicit social archives aside, it is the interior of that era with which the photo is fortunately—but is "aligned" the word he wants? He couldn't say for certain. Except that the face posited itself between the pillars of a "support system" and what can only be described as "the uncanny."

The tension, of course, always depended on the provisional identity formation of the young kid in question. In other words, is "he" a figure of destiny or chance?

As he gazes at the hand of the man who incarnates the historical process, holding in his hands the artifact as proof, he does not look at the authorial centre who is caught in this reflection of his power and cannot re-articulate the gaze—which is the nation. This event may be construed, but only tentatively, as the birth of the multicultural.

Look again closely at the conjunction of all the bodies held in place by the image of the image. The hand signing, inscribing his name as the extension of the frame, produces a social relationship. He thought of a photographic inset of the future yet to be—yet to be because the nation, in a symbolic twist, here writes its story on the virile poster and not in his memory.

So when he was a kid, or no, when he was that kid, he couldn't decipher the lingo of his own visibility. He thought he had lost his vocabulary for at least three decades. But then, in a period of idleness, the kind made available in a found image that returns the time of history, he saw himself in the absences necessary to the surge of the very gestures so apparently captured.

It was as if the slippages had yielded a prescience in which the nation had appeared as his double. As a kid, the technique had been lacking. Only an inkling had formed on the tip of his tongue, some hesitancy that had no name, more undertone than an event to be commemorated.

For the time being, at least, he could ride the crest of the not yet, waiting for the arrival of the photographer.

THE FRONDS ON GALIANO

There is the word paranoia
that is or isn't all that poetic
in a poem that is

There is the question
of intent or the wholesale
importation of foreign elements

i had arisen to the sounds
as if they had beckoned me
to pronounce this allegiance

outside the ken of readable
fences or the double intake
that resembles a contractual

i never more than its speech
imprints on the way to the shore
line in search of displaced rocks

At which point it seeped in
that originary incline in its way
hoaxed the paths before me

coaxed that other word property
into the lexicon of the sauntering
towards the oceanic swells

in what was let's be clear here
the instance of heat on a summer
island road along the dwellings

with their tended gardens
that formed the barrier between
voice and sea and dare i say it

me

The barbed wire fence posts
the sign no hunting or trespassing

"The natives don't want you
to know where the path is"

The details
plastic red ribbons

two of them
hanging on a nondescript branch

"The only one that looks private to me"

His body signs say it all
say it all it all comes back

in the tranquil bay
the mid-afternoon
sun running on time

"This is not a place to be"

For evidence there are the shades of the emergent figure
a notebook in hand drifting over to the log around which
cluster the multitude of rocks (no two alike

For evidence there was the open road to the beach
there was the open door of the cottage with the welcome sign
the sign of come on in (the prompter button pushed but held back

For evidence there is the gesturing figure superimposed
on that dream of entering the room full of voices
unannounced they speak of compact sketches

"The whole shoreline is public"

"Hope you don't think i'm being obnoxious"

The ferry's roar slices
the ledge of red rock formations

They call them truant sparks
or the haunt of enclosures

the burden of stones
cushioning the sandals

Enter then the garter snake
squiggling (struggling?
out of peripheral view

LOCAL

Late morning Saturday
head north on Highway 6
towards Owen Sound

Patches of black earth mark
the snow covered fields

the flat landscape
punctuated by squat and sturdy
brick farm houses

the skeletal birches look
opulent as the Nissan Pathfinder
(rented of course) enters the time zones

Daphne late last night as we
recalled bp's spiritual drives
saying she'd never thought of
herself living to this time
both of us born in 42

across history the patterns
of departures

Even this line in the forgetting
as the line dividing the cars comes
and goes
even as it becomes visible

Even this urge to write down
what's lost in the debris

as soon as the car pauses in the driveway
as soon as the laptop takes to warm up
its insides already in the winter landscape

Wonder what lines would appear
had i emerged on the main street
of a town called Durham

~

Head south on Highway 6
out of Owen Sound

through Dornoch
over the River Styx

the country music station
"I'll pour out my soul until it's
empty, empty"

pull into Durham
and think of returning
two decades hence

the buildings unchanged
but renewed with recent coats of paint
the family house still among the birches

Hunger for home as the Nissan purrs
cruising down Garafraxa the Riverside
Restaurant (an old hangout) then left on Douglas
and points beyond

To the right the rolling hills
the sun hangs low under the lifting clouds

grey in the horizon

sheets of snow the mind slowed in
the glittering light through the windshield

on the left above the near full moon
in the fading blue sky

Nowhere to stop

DO WONDER

Do instants
Affect or effect?

The protocol
Calls for briefing

The time scheme
Falls on command

The brow beats
The chest harbours

Estimation gathers
Out to the tail gate

Howls of discontent
Meet the airwaves

Sagacity doubles
As city saga

Fine tunes
Like rustling

NEKO'S REFRAIN

for Baco

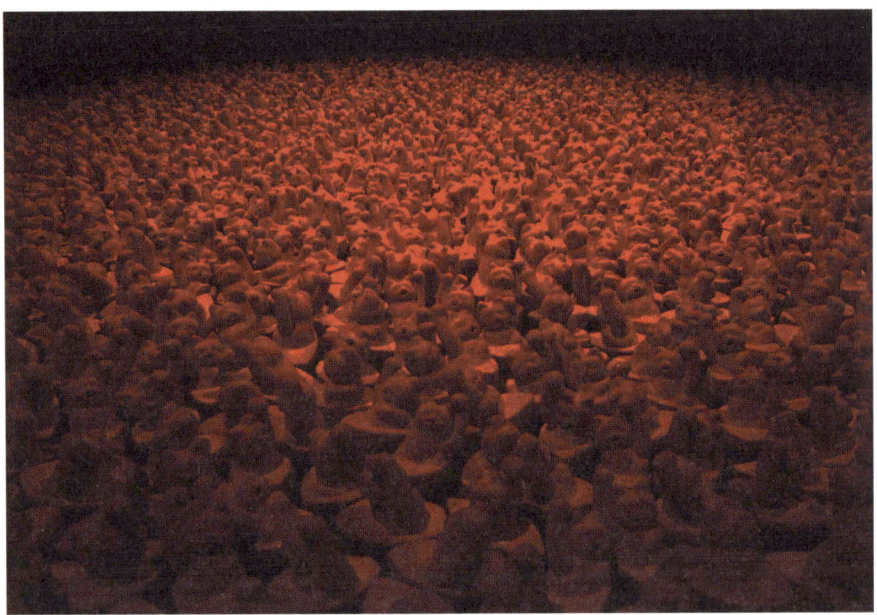

1

He awoke in the sultry overtones of an almost vertiginous
archive. Aghast at the subdued purr emanating from what
must have been, at least according to his sense, a kitchen
door. Outside on the back porch were some disseminated
yet stumbling provocations that shuffled this way and that.
He could with little effort make out minimalist sounds, like
ah and ba and co, but the language they were ensconced in
served to escape him. At least this was the impression left in
the margin of the document. His breath held for the moment
the intake of all the figures who convalesced in what could be
read as the domestic scene of exchange. Even the trail of neko
heralded an ongoing testimonial. There and there in the basket
of prints the currents rose and infiltrated the camera obscura
in her dissolving hands.

2

On the perimeter
against the walls

uneven waves
beckoning neko

as unsettled lips
press to single

strands of stray
hair fallen fallow

In the awakening
folds of furoshiki

detritus specks for
hungry canaries

Lean over awkward
employment sighs

the reticent scratches
on mine walls   permeable

Is it then this black
line that hangs in

the balance wrapt
in the water's prop

again exposed as its
S cuts across *wishes* .

scrambles . unravels
. water . plants .

3

We is affiliated in the portable mobile
We is detailed in its curvilinear shades
We is assembled in its making belief
We is carried in its resonant hormones
We is able to encode the salty taste
We is the ulterior motive of definition
We is the accumulation of motes
We is solvent in the memory banks
We wants to want the encompassing garments
      The many in the one
The one that is the yellow bird
The one perched on the branch
The weeping voices in the letters
      Apace in their outstretched arms

Even then

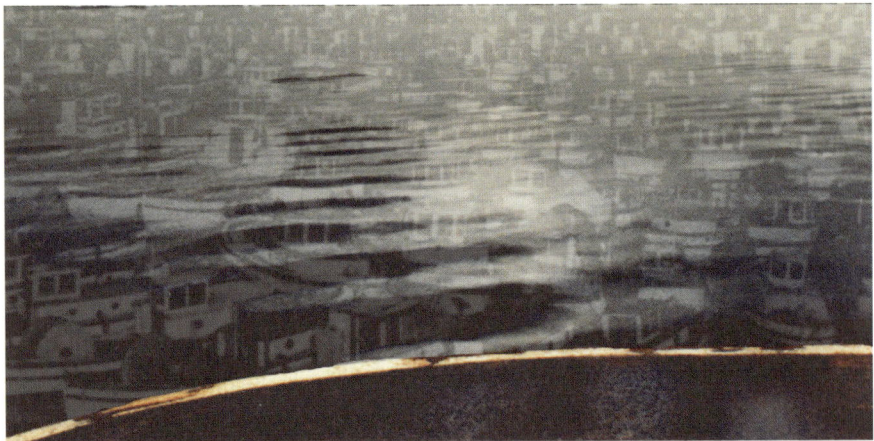

Image on p. 282: *MIYOSHI a taste that lingers unfinished in the mouth (the Pool)*,
2000, by Baco Ohama, photographed by James D. Brown. Above: *MIYOSHI a taste
that lingers unfinished in the mouth* (#9 from the postcard project of gathering and
dispersal), 2000–2004, by Baco Ohama.

IF IT'S NOT ASIAN IT CAN'T BE GOOD

The Oriental immigration problem is one of vital importance
to Canada, not only because of any racial pride or sentiment
that may exist, but because the problem as to which is to be the
dominating race on the North Pacific Coast of this continent,
Oriental or Occidental, is one which must be solved.
— HARRY H. STEVENS
The Oriental Problem (c. 1921)

.

It gathers much moss
in the ridge range of
operative ingenuities

.

Everything or nothing
the infection derives
wind on ripply highways

.

If nothing brings down a house of cards
in the mellow light of the mall's receptacle

Everything bathes the bluest smiles
in the latest of catch-as-catch-can guiles

Look at the allure of the steaming bowl of noodles
Look and see the magic chopsticks do all their tricks

.

We stumbled into a room full of perils
We wanted to speak in unison on cue

.

O ghostly gatekeeper on the shore

We come from lands beyond your lonely ken
We come on hobbled wings of a dream of riches
Our credentials stowed in this modest furoshiki

Believe me we are not a burden in a bundle of sticks
We never hurl idiosyncracies at just any crass wall
We move fluidly in the midst of adverse regulators
We have a stockpile of endurance at our slim fingertips

We inhabit the multiple silences of unknowable scriptures
We are the fabulous but hidden face on glossy white posters
We are the unpredictable in the exchange rate of wheelers
We are about to emerge for the millionth time this century

.

The pickaxe is only the virtual
accoutrement of a secret aesthetics

Look deep into the stream
        of data dependence
        of dated reconnaissance
        of sated fantasies
        of rolled sushiation
        of harry-a-oki radiance
        of yellow pearl cushions

.

The sigh it hears is the length
of its coming waves

Of pleasure i hear say

THE ALLIANCE OF TELEPHONE WIRES

—the semis roll down the highway
regardless of the copse of birches

the swaying axis reformulates the
hum of the train's horn across fields

of standing water borrowed from
a poem that is dispersed in a flood

of some phonemes linked by the
candid throw of dice across the bridge

on the side a multiple row of tiny pine
standing upright in the space invented

Why is it possible to make known the
otherwise impossible calculation of indents

the bruised fruit of the loam in drainage
networks the extent of freeways on the ropes

even in a conspicuous daylight the size
of the seizure would be unmistakable

the cow in the pasture gesticulates in a wink
that he needs to perform a rescue mission

Arrivez arrivez arrivez in the earlobes the
faint patter of letter feet across the plains

pulling into Alexandria he remembers the
Atlantic Hotel and the forays of forged tristes

Look there's a blue house sinking in the earth
all its inside cry out for the dream of resistance

he thinks of the V formation of the geese
in the graying sky outside the left window

his fingers on the keyboard as the train sways
the black wave of lines in the peripheral—

propels an uneasy truce

COMING TO WINNIPEG

When I close my eyes
wait for the words
to reply to her
one year later

These rolling hills look like
a film their greens sharper
fuller than any greens

Her muskrat coat and its promise
of love in the whiff of perfume

The enclosure of its arms still warm
in the late night corners of memory

As the river courses in the lines
carries speech in their wake

There is nothing to compare to her passing

This plainclothes ache does not subside

The slips in the tongue carry as ripples
across the moving highway

Now I see my own end in the changing view

This line of words out of the blue

Her death . your death
Your death . my death

On the earth plain   This line of poplars
upright in the elements

Awaken again all the crevices

The rain on the windshield
falls in line   Falls to the ground
as the horizon already spins away

This Side

Victoria Park, Calgary—after Roy Kiyooka

1

This is the unspeakable screen where he sought to protect the inquires that riddled one's childhood.

He was born in a neighbourhood where the streets, lanes, and foot-worn paths of the park returned on themselves.

The provisions of memory, always on alert for the anomalous register, cloaked the bone rush of his awakened tensile regions with a notorious green thumb.

It resembled a casual photo seen years later in the multitudinous chambers of a lexicon in crisis.

What it incarnated then—the spooks removed from the tongues in check—came across the divide as a designer storefront for ripe but modified melons.

In what was described as a salamander like manoeuvre, even after prolonged decades, the resonance, or call it the abrasive whiskers, would sneak up on his reveries at the most anticipated of times. Dub it then the installation of the so-called syllabic entourage.

What tissues assumed the audible signed on as compensation for the displaced get out of childhood free card. Each album cushioning the aerated passage of family matters enveloped the alleys of his peregrinations.

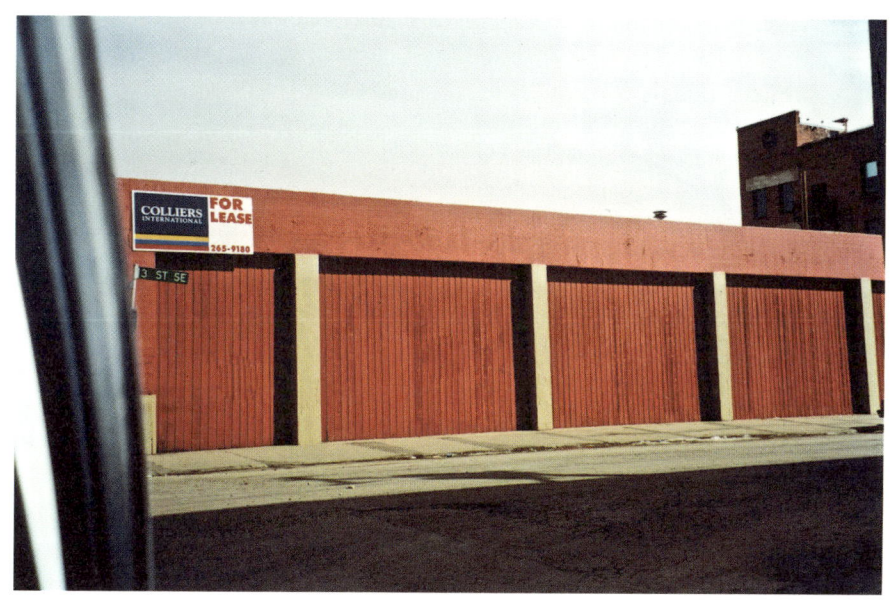

Premonition

The patron saint of lease
the tanginess of elsewhere
routes the dog days of slumber

2

The box held it all in.

The instruments of surveillance blended into the roll call of pictographic forays. It was next door, or the next one that held the blueprint as wall paper. It was this mechanism that called for the vigilance, the foliage hugging the fancies, now recognized as the thermos of the borders.

Believe it, or one believed him, a serviceable nostalgia had to be abandoned on the curbside. Otherwise he had been forewarned by a soothsayer who had sidled up to him as a child—despite the debilitating positivism of that time.

Amongst the enclosure of maple trees, their leaves full to his touch, a troubled imago had drifted down through the clouds. He had been wary of the somatic thrust and the purported powers of its prognostication, but the hologrammic undertow finally proved disarming.

The bicycle wheels spun as if on their own volition. A stretch of road formed then dissolved in the black and white reaches of his otherwise semantic resolve.

At first it all wanted to spill out.

The neighbours donned such a sheen he could actually visualize children scheming.

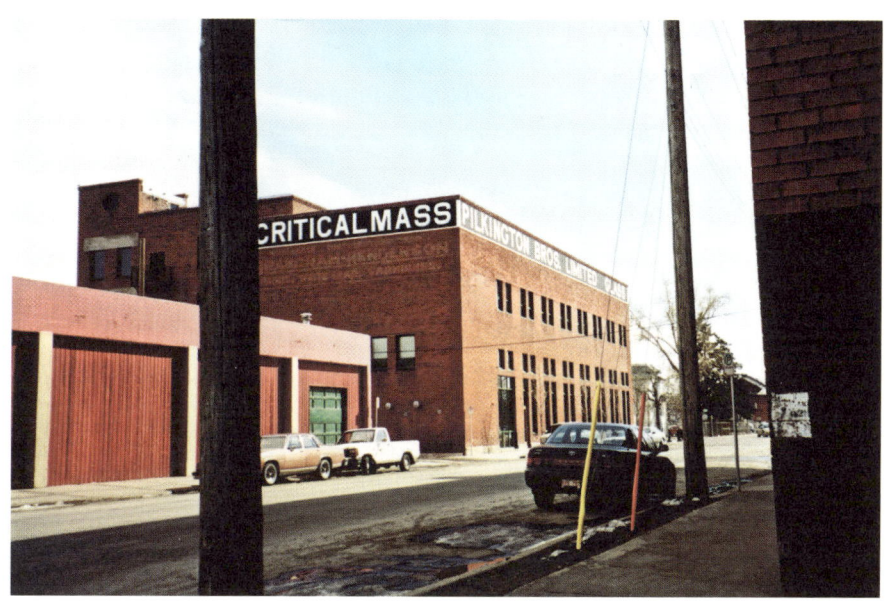

Premonition

Ill shoots still shots so it goes
without saying in the spinal column
the recessive bearings turn blue

3

The upright object propping up the skyline—unidentified—is static. Restless in the energy required to compose the scene. Could it augur the yet to be cellular conundrums dormant in his lexical index finger? To finger the metallic shapes.

In memory, in the absence of fountains and squares and other tell-tale signs—only the reverie of parking lots—he adopted the stationary position.

The hands moved as a pen does across the backyard. Making amends for the expenditure. His nerve endings fluttered as a flag does (did) on any other bright and fine-tuned hoarfrost day in the park.

As he squinted in the façade of the skyline—casting the abandoned cars in relief—he could detect the inquiry of creeks creeking. The surmise of abstracts abstracting. The inventive compulsions—in the lingo of the other side.

In the park proper the elders gathered in the clapboard houses to feast and to speculate on civil omens and catastrophes. Of grave (insider) insurrections with the power to circumvent the necessary acumen to fabricate his disclosure. What would draw him—back to the wall—to indelible modes of cooking the books.

The letters cp and the letter p are poised to spill the beans. The conduction of neural horizons—all of a sudden—ingests the curvature of the awakening echoes.

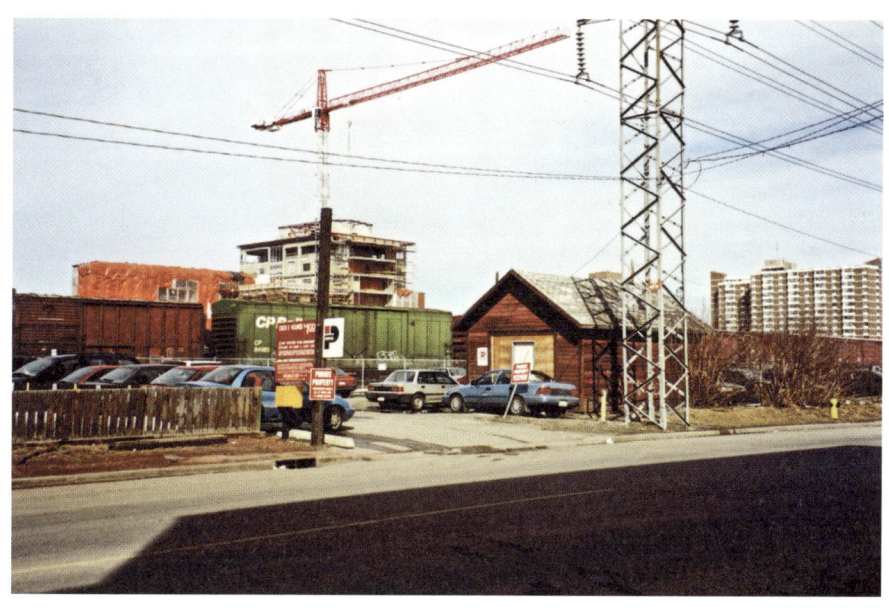

Premonition

The ribbons held no longer
corners melt in the ochre core
all wants to be outside

4

Ah yes, no doubt about it, there's a buzz in the air. The park jolted by the cries of children playing sandbox tag, the morning sun settling on their backs.

The bespeckled head turns sideways, whistling.

The backside, he thought, of the wandering that led him onto the field, half hidden, as if he had forgotten the route home.

Was that static on the radio?

The power lines spoke of a sculptural era of regulation and imprecision. Impossible to impress, it happened on the way back from the drug store where he had a coke sitting at the counter with his friends.

Pockets full of lost dynasties, the skin started to change directions. The cries transferred to the register of a vocabulary he recognized but couldn't any longer buy.

The set play in the esophagus, the one trained on waves of inhalation and exhalation, took to the curves.

The shouts magnified the dissonance.

Who were the kids who took to the field, gloves in hand, all set for the action to begin?

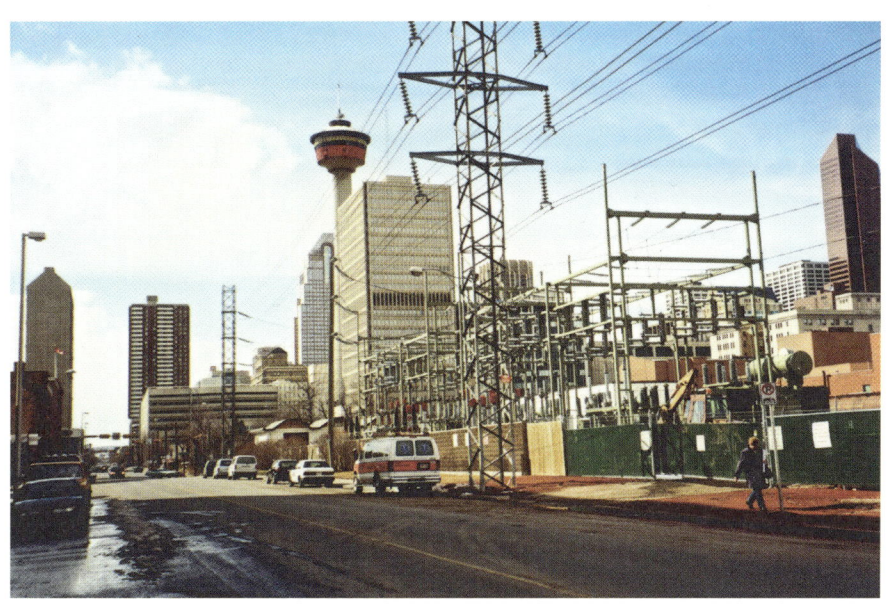

Premonition

It all came in a flash
the law of averages kicked
in the ruses along the curb

5

Bolt the door, clamp the windows, hide and go seek.
Those were the injunctions, call them the lore, that dipped in
the headlong rush of the local.

Local you say? Speaking in person i've always been wary of the
private occasion.

We've been to the pool and it ain't all it's cut out to be.
Ultimately cut outs won't cut it with that crowd out there.
Even bastards among them.

If events are a plumb line i'll hedge my bets.
Abide my time.
Even history takes a break sometimes.

How about a scene with the deceased held accountable for all
ill fortunes that befall the children?

Sedentary lives held in untold mysteries.

The sirens pop a hole in his head.
The ants scramble for cover once he turns the rock over.
The hand has a palm with lines.

He dashes to frame the aqua in the break of the mesh.
He uses his x-ray vision to cut out a bell-shaped opening.
He hears the clanging heralding the end of recess.
He digests the gridlocked anthems.
He listens for the wire.

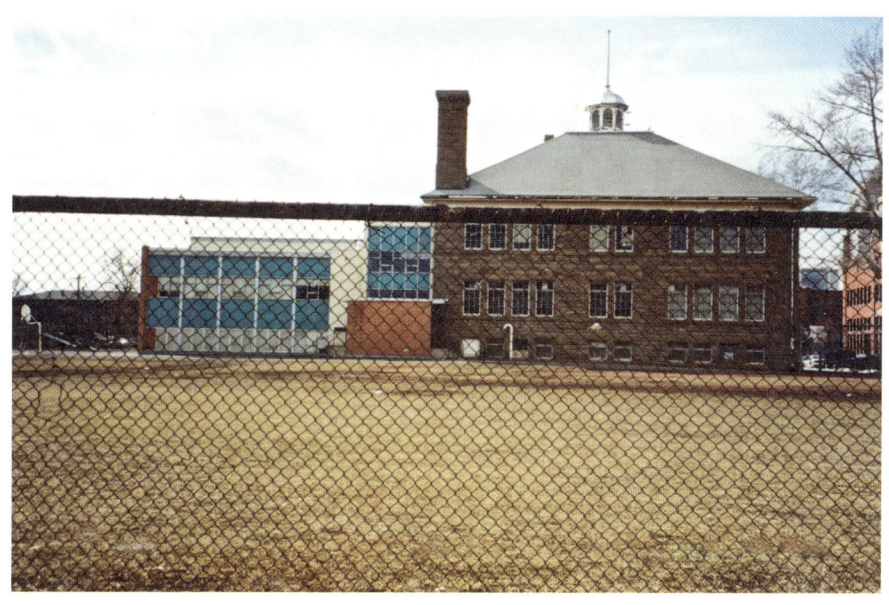

Premonition

The wrap around function
scrolls the swarming mass
to winnow the flash back

6

Listen to the fence, its strums and imbalances, the grain of its fibre.

Listen to its scaffolds of hope elicited as the rhythmic deterrents of domicile.

Called on the veranda too stages a come back. He wonders what became of the apple pits. The torn pants—felt to the touch—and shinned knees. The scar—the feigned trace—from the fall.

The intervention of railings, posts, and doorways, the inclusive ghosts in the cellar.

They too bespeak window frames that open out to wires and branches.

They too bespeak the bumpers to absorb the knuckles wrapped in the tumultuous gauze.

The rumour held its course in the household. By design the school bus waited suspended in the heaped up encore of the craft.

He set sail then toward the forks, as if he were drifting into the echo chamber. The ache in the heart timed to detonate.

When the photo was shot he would have just vacated the booth, the voice piece is still warm, and the (already) obsolescent appropriation an expendable artifact.

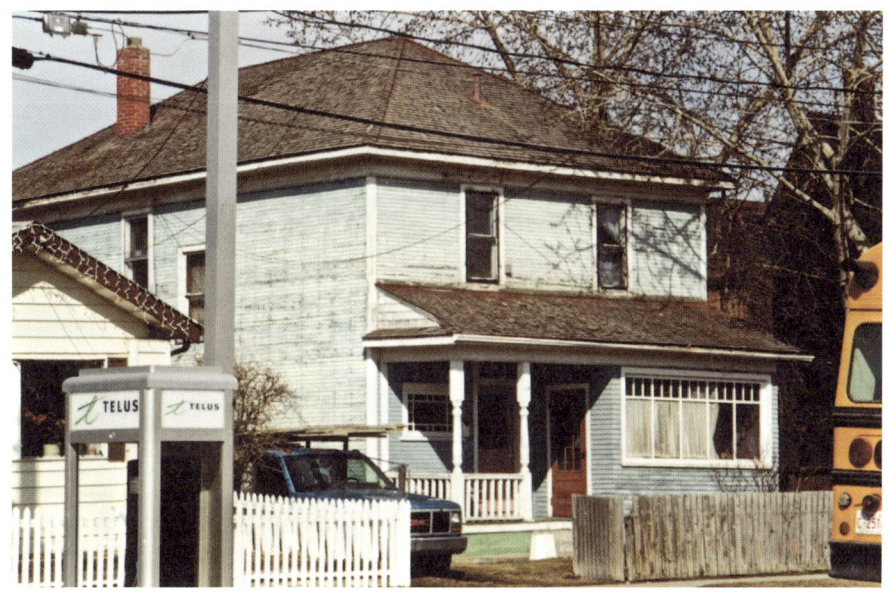

Premonition

Each break in the spray
as the dislocutions let
loose the graphic rail

WEEKLING IN BERLIN

for Glen

1

The thin glue holds the lips
against the window. When i throw

a sidelong glance the aperture
does an about take. What this

suggests falls into place.

Forgive me.

2

The insignia developed this
attraction for risk. An altogether
abnormal danger.

This place augurs well. Empty
as the pockets of the
institution.

Gathering up
the balmy days.

3

The semblances come and go.
Waiting in line. The protocol

calls for the injury to
happen

before it
takes flight

Before then it
was dog eat dog.

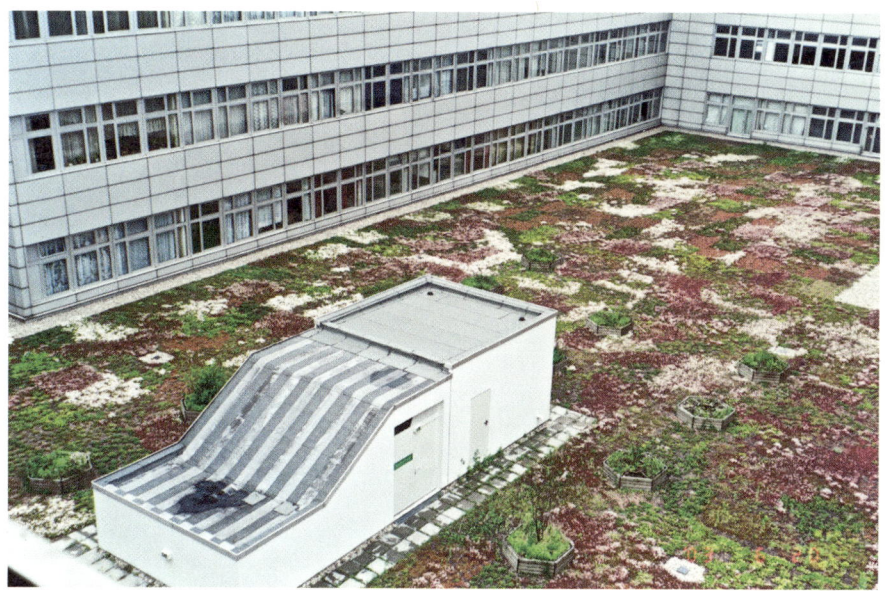

But their tails hail
us from beyond.

It is not her fault
The bonds broken

Day light on the plane
the sky translucent

Even when the poem
tumbles out of range

Arranges the descent

No one slices the terrain

If i had no direction

Softly on the temple

The light mimes the eaves

4

for Mita B

Beset by the thong
of asterisks the keepers
of the gates respired.

Unexpected as the
gust. Shards. Para.

Do you dissolve?
Think fury.

Were indices
unmatched in the grids.

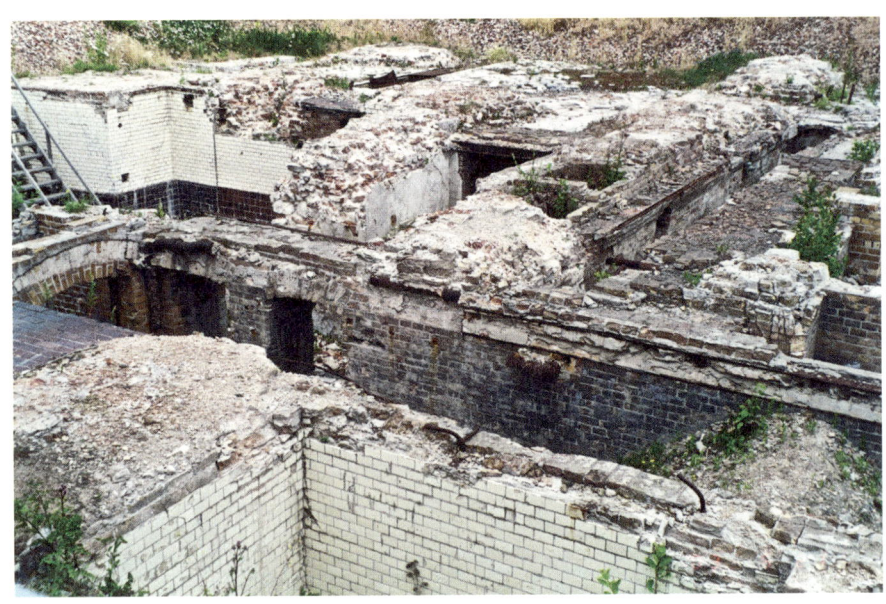

Among close quarters.
Decibel. Detached. De
Sire. Ire. Re. E.

Sybil action.

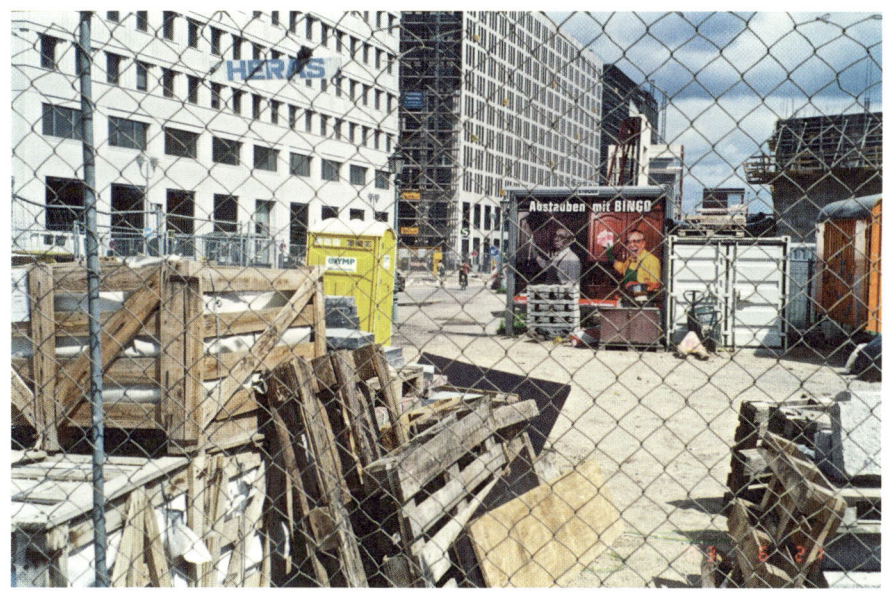

5

Nothing tempered
takes the slope.

Nothing tampered over
the line of descent.

Nothing with surcease.

6

The panic swept the doorway
of the market just as the cashier
rung up the bill for two bottles
of water.

It was not her fault.

The small crowd stormed the entranceway
i mean the storm swept them in unannounced.

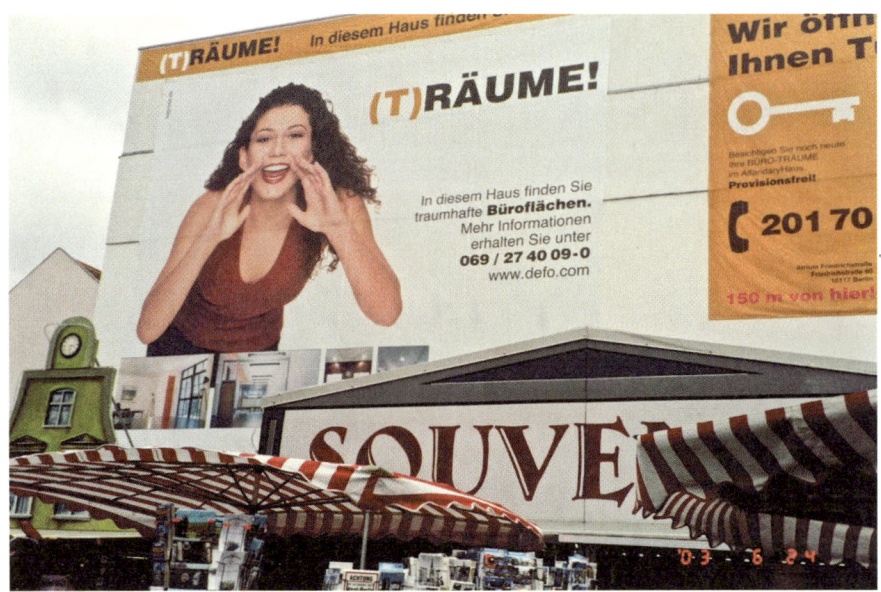

The gusts threw dust in
his eyes rubbing out the residue.

The bus stop emptied of content.

Only the crowd of dried seed pods
whirling in the wind.

Borne aloft

i mean the soft rain became the
sheet aflame their hair streaked
in the fabric rinse i mean the
branch torn from its home
over came i mean came over.

Now the altruism is meagre
the stop restored to its function
as the organizer of this poem.

7

The terrible doubts never
stray from the hive.

Passengers relay the news
with corpuscular ingenuity.

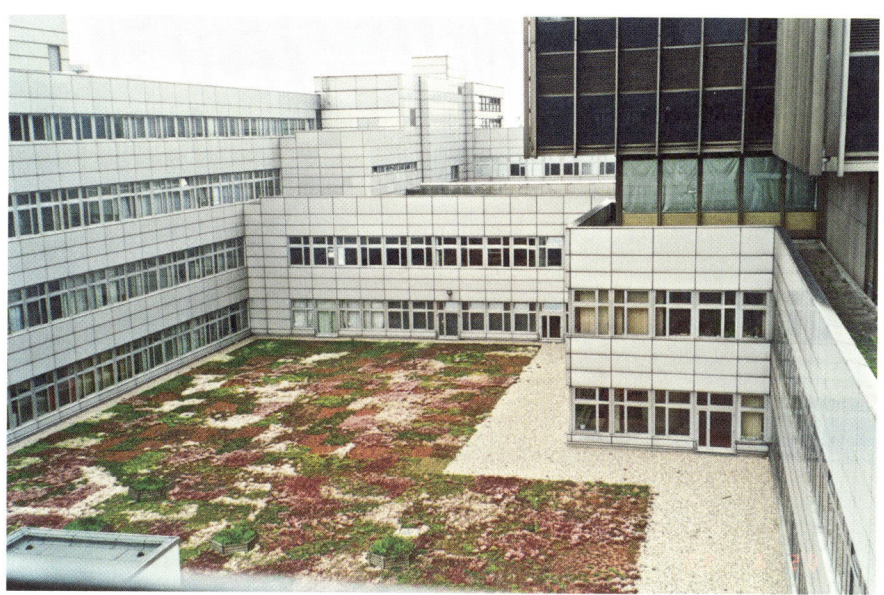

OF SENTIENT BEINGS

1

The two door couple
sure looked snazzy

In the driveway all
he could think of
compressed in a thimble

Like a lake of blue
it ran the uneven parapets

2

It began with a turn
of a cheek

the blend
of air and palm

fastened on a
stroll in a tunnel

graffiti free
tonic splurges

shrug off the
shore babble

The decibel range
spreads out

Letting out the seams
worked to an extent

3

He was certain he was
beamed by the cell phone

The bifurcated segment
of the packed train ride

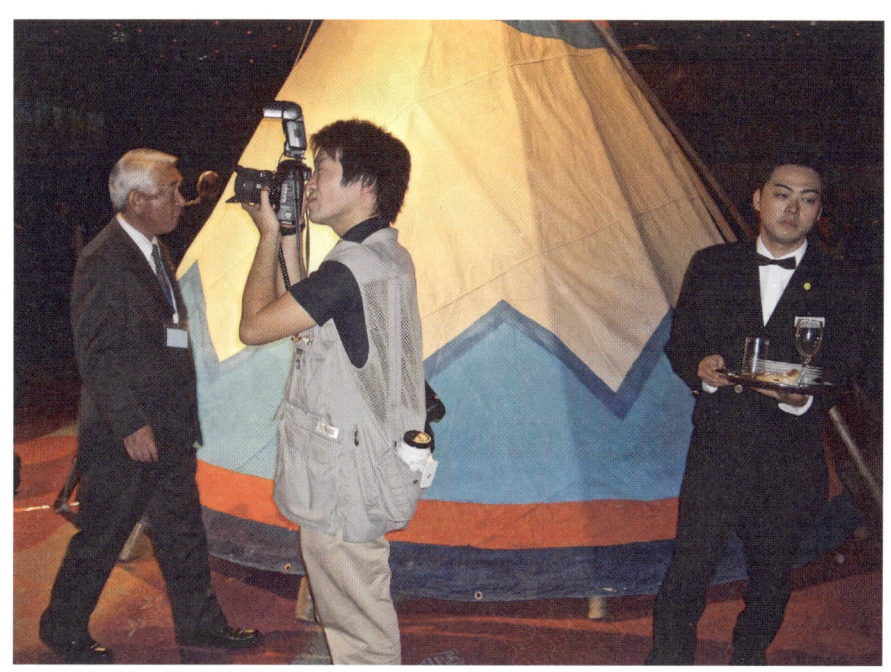

through flickering urban
escapades of rampant
        silences with an entourage
of code switchers

Yet the sag he hailed as
he might have a cab
        was located in the region
back in the spinal fluids

Until the seepage wore thin

4

The preordained slide
as consummation not
the consolation that
conducted the pavement

Was there a telepathic
syndrome to address?

A kind of diasporic
liaison without remedy?

A kind of eddying of detergents
and other technologies of soul-
making?

A hearing held in camera?

5

Someone left me
on a sea change

Rave on Kamo
give it to me
one more time

The padding on culture
still works for me

6

Wake to the frontal encounter
with a ryokan full of gaijin
bowing with ohayō

i must have been hanging
up in the autumn wind

7

Often in rude doses
Such deformities set in

Detta kuru

The grain of the wood
in the course of the river

Crow calls once again

8

Sent on a mission
Caught in the cross-fire

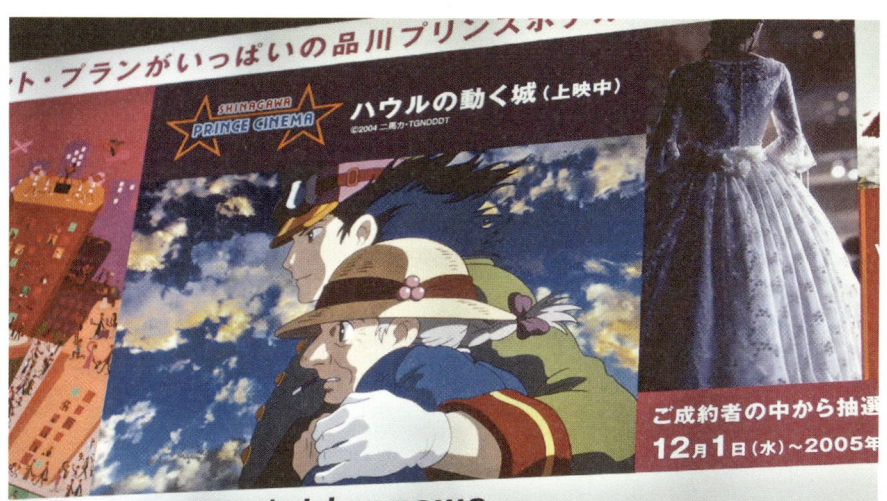

Hachiko on guard

The chorus of chanting voices
Blaring speakers slide by
Sitting on the fat rail turn about

Could be a break in the wheel
Not yet spoilt in the rush

9

The rumbling of the train

Fingering the keys

Empty landed

Kao o dashite

A migrant label

The mound heaped

In the doorway

One key turn away

THERE ARE SOME DAYS

You think you won't
Write another poem

You are sitting on the garden
Bench looking at blossoms
On the climbing vine

Kick the metrical
foot in the sand

A small creature lands on the
Armrest an inch from your wrist
And you realize you don't have
A name for the space it occupies
And it appears to psyche out
Antennae waving in the still air

Don't let it wrench
one more joint out

Or you are walking along the beach
On an early weekday afternoon and
Pause over a railing to watch the kids
Building castles on an oasis of sand

And you see your reflection in the cloud
Formations to the northwest and bodies
Lie or otherwise move sitting on benches
Reading books and little kids in buggies
Are throwing teethers on the ground

Its hot sand labile
preys on its foraging

And everyone is smiling and others are
Sauntering past lost in frothy thoughts
Why bother to sit down or even expend

The passing seconds thinking of a line
Or even an image to catch your fancy
To wile away the diversionary tactics that
Have come to roost in the daily hassle of
Mediated relationships with the news

How do you recognize
a branch otherwise

Viz that Microsoft has finally caught up with
Dick Tracy with a plastic watch that gives
The most important things one can need

The weather stocks news shoots a glance
At headlines on TV channels lotteries to gamble
Away time sports scores daily diversions (word
Of the day) calendar of dates messages (from
Chosen parties) and horoscopes on loan

"This is going to appeal to techies, early adopters"
Says Eddie Chan, and according to Chris Schneider,
"It's not designed as a productivity device," which is
(You're sure) a relief for poets who might be tempted
To camouflage their trade secrets or otherwise
Abandon efforts to retrieve the river flow of time

Viz Judith Butler, "I have moved ... perhaps too
Blithely among speculations on the body as the site
Of a common human vulnerability, even as i have
Insisted that this vulnerability is always articulated
Differently, that it cannot be properly thought of outside
A differentiated field of power and, specifically, the
Differentiated operation of norms of recognition."

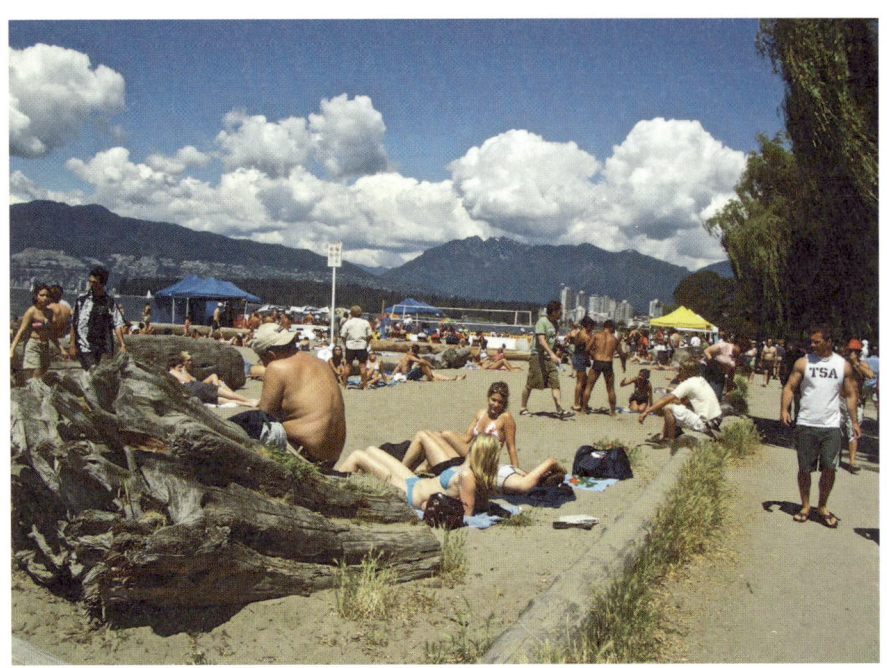

O ruthless cellular fountains
Spraying in far mountains

Who would want to disturb norms of recognition
With stock poetic devices that only remind you
All about the airwaves circulating with such
Nonchalance in the traffic as it moves along
Kits beach across the vast network of exchanges
(Corporeal and corporate the market guru says
Terror marks the rise and fall of stocks the lingo
Of the free fall into the maelstrom of fortune's arms

Flow Nation

for Cindy

1

It was on the bridge, crossing the river on the way into town.
i came to a point i could no longer tell the time. Something
clicked in place, and the flange of the bridge stretched in and
out of focus.

What about the match—this place and that?

Jeez i must have been only a kid.

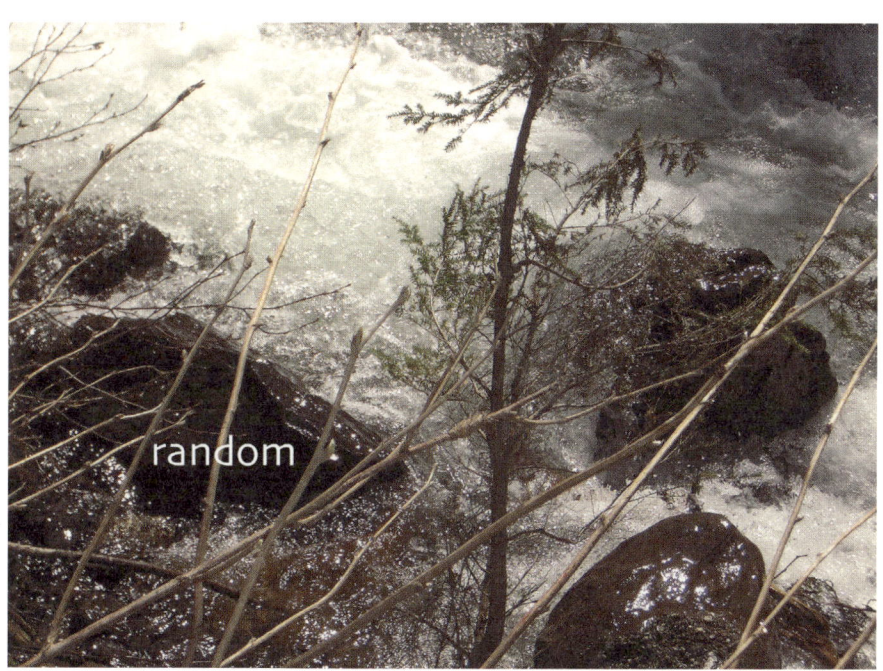

random

2

Then on the way to Banff the scene outside the window flipped.
Out of the auburn hills came a voice.

Let me recall what history preaches
history preaches

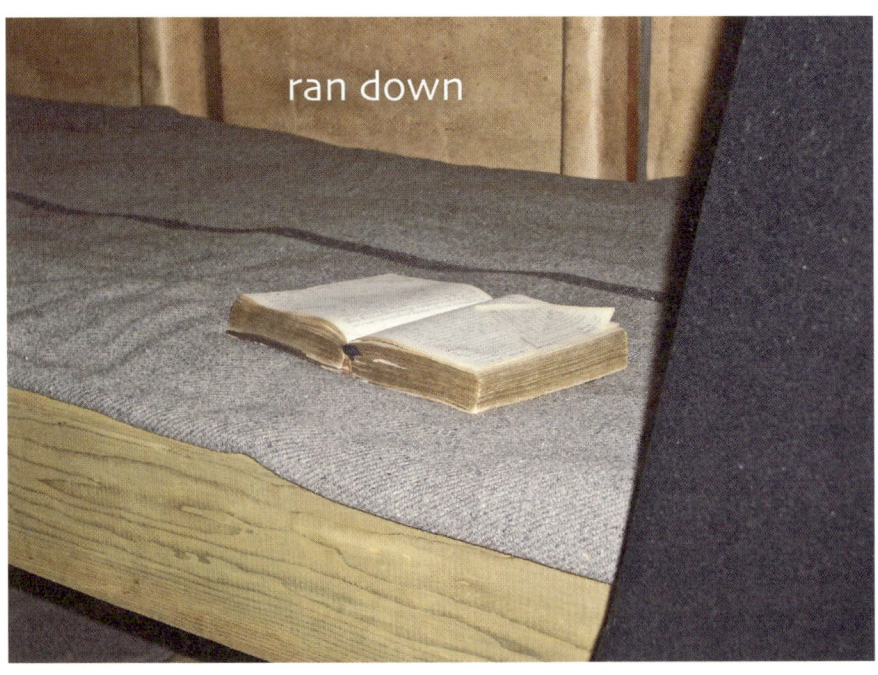

3

We parsed sentences like good little soldiers. One part of speech here, another there, and lined up all the syllables in neat rows. We were rewarded with silver stars beside our name on the bulletin board.

How goes the syllable?

It's a huge argument, but think of it. How much can a kid can do to steal home. When it all fits together.

But why does the blackboard talk back?

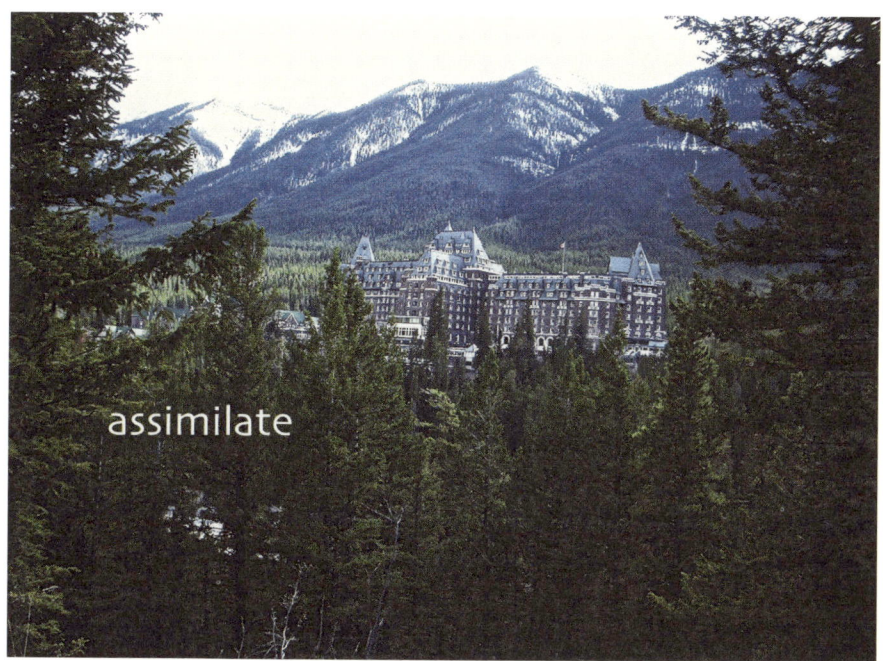

assimilate

4

In days of yore, the maple leaf forever.

You can remember?

Sure, it was as if someone reached into my throat and pulled out a bagful of foreign sounds.

Please explain foreign.

In the scene spreading out the halo effect accounted for the sheen on all the products lining the shelves. He could see himself in the lens of the cameras mounted on street corners. Pockets of sounds were released at intervals resembling the passage of history. Each event spawned another story as his life shuffled before him.

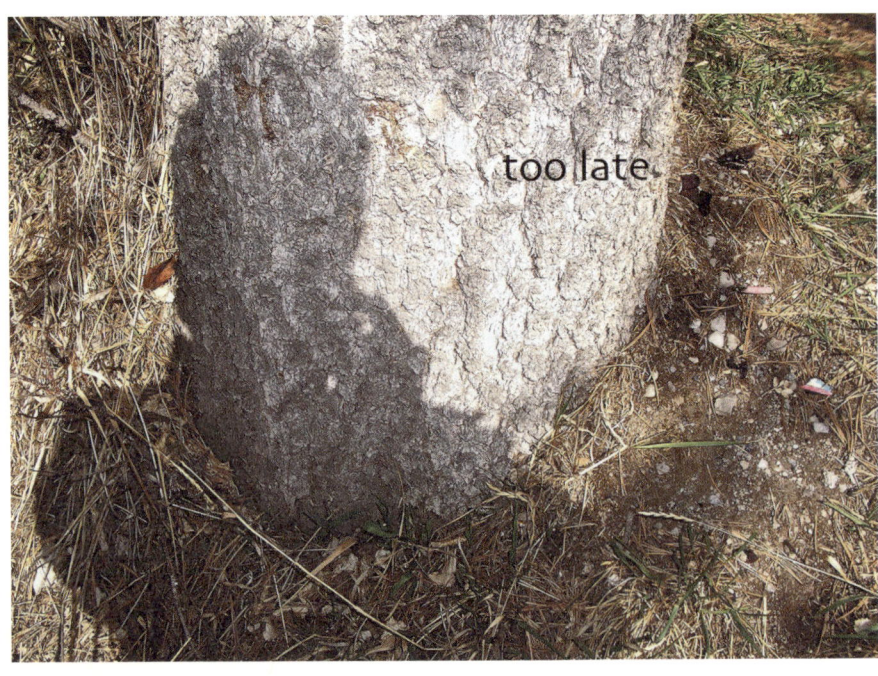

5

She returned in a film. Her back to the breeze coming from the open kitchen window. She just lifted the lid from the bubbling stew pot and with a fork checked the texture of the white dango turned into clouds.

For years i craved the exotic taste of her stew (she called it japanese) only to find the ingredient was curry powder.

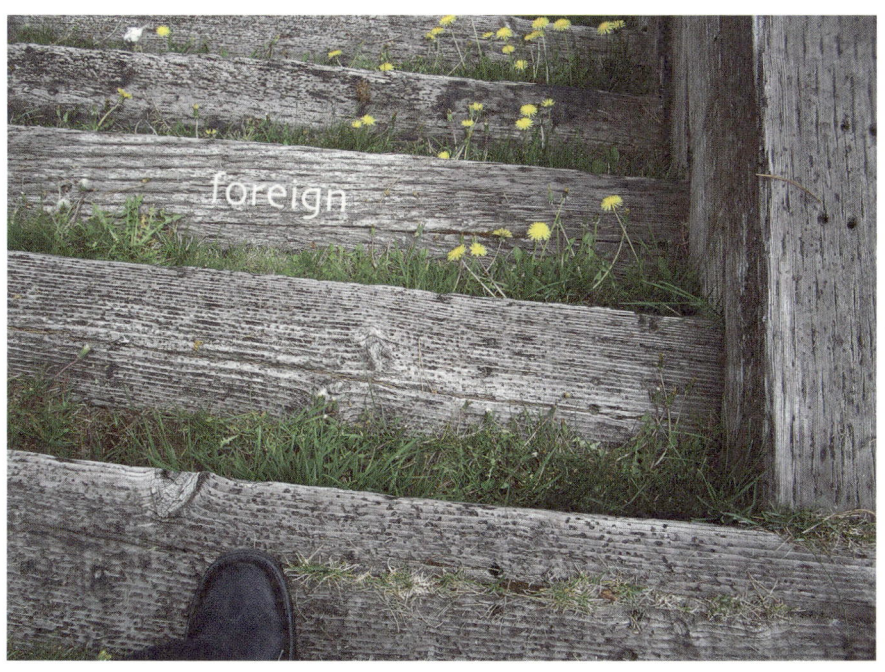

6

i remember the streets looked bare around the station. Only a handful of curious gazes hung around the large windows facing the back lane. We lined up to have our papers checked, and i could hear the muffled cries of young kids. People were sitting on benches looking forlorn.

je ne parle pas
je ne parle
je ne

yoku
yoku
sugu gakkō iko

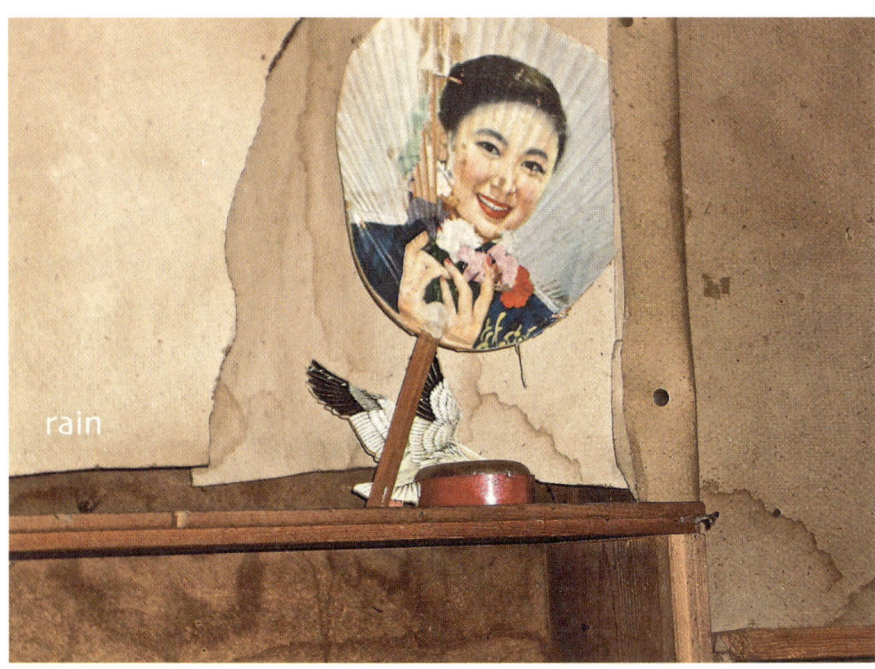

7

Sure, there were some unspeakable goings-on. Parents with a baby dying in their arms in the makeshift chicken shack on the freezing prairies. A guy found beaten to death on his boat adrift in the gulf. Old folks giving up on life.

You want to call it a camp? Go ahead, but don't talk to me anymore about the past. That crap about blessing in disguise makes me sick.

Who was that?
Could we get a print out?

i'll see what i can dig up.

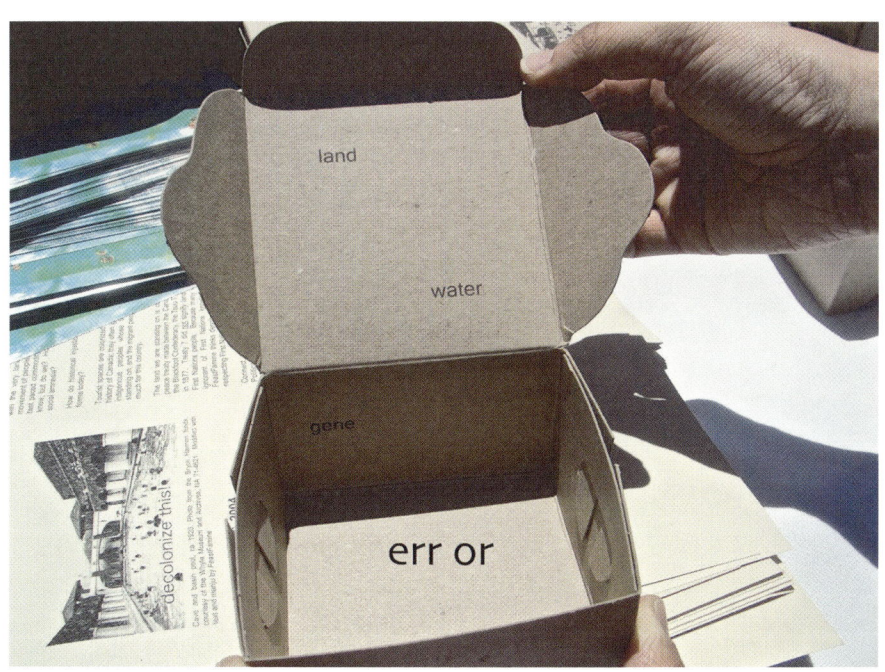

8

Reaching the plateau he came upon a conversation. Some huddled in hushed talk while others openly complained. No one recognized him so that some pleasure arose in the anonymity.

Could he not return?

Well, yes and no. At first the details were so blurred in the waning evening light he was led astray. Until he came to a crowded intersection. Tourists on the sidewalk and the shopkeepers intent on making the last sale before closing.

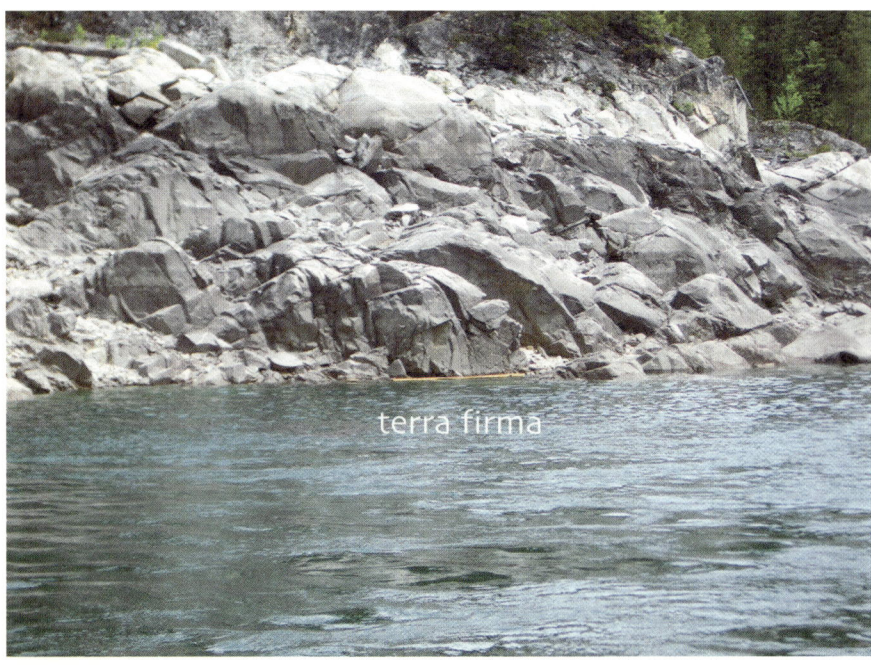

terra firma

9

i'm thinking about the time of the waning of the state.

He never thought of it that way. i suppose he resembled the rabbit ears on those first TV sets. You had to keep fiddling with them until the screen cleared.

The images had more direct routes to receptors.

Remember they used to place their feet in the x-ray machine in department stores and marvel at the sight of bones.

Were they his bones?

That was the assumption in those days. Then one day he was told he would mutate if he kept thinking that way. In the dream he awoke in the midst of a transition. The pipes in the back room were clanging in a muted rhythm, or so he thought.

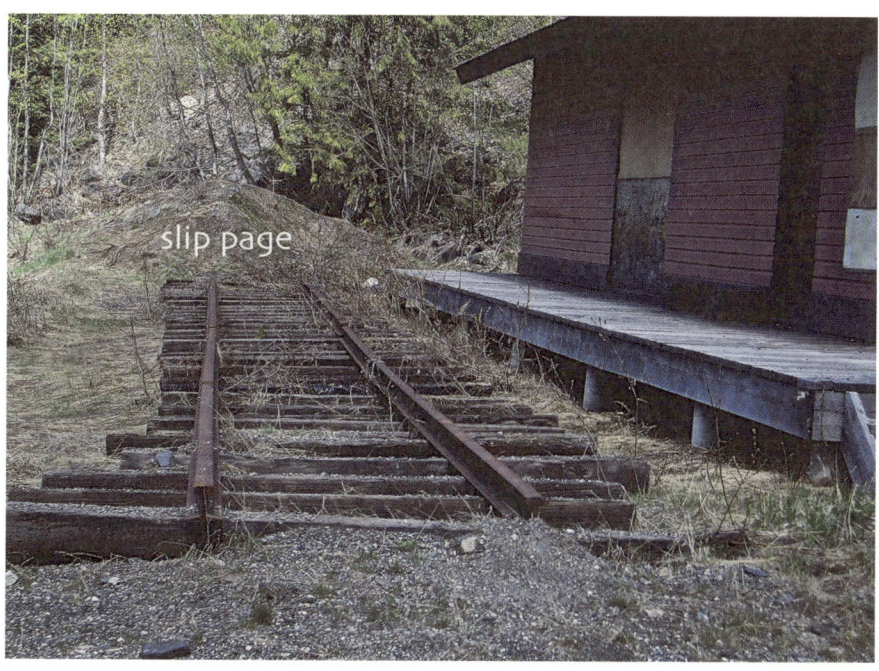
slip page

She looked out the back window and saw her kids playing by the river. They were digging for something in the wet ground. Her youngest almost one was sleeping on the veranda. The sun warmed her face, almost soothing. She thought of what to make for supper and what winter in this house would bring.

But what about you? Are you concerned about being removed from the scene?

i recall you saying once, and i quote: the changes had occurred so intangibly i couldn't recognize the tang for what it was.

for what it was

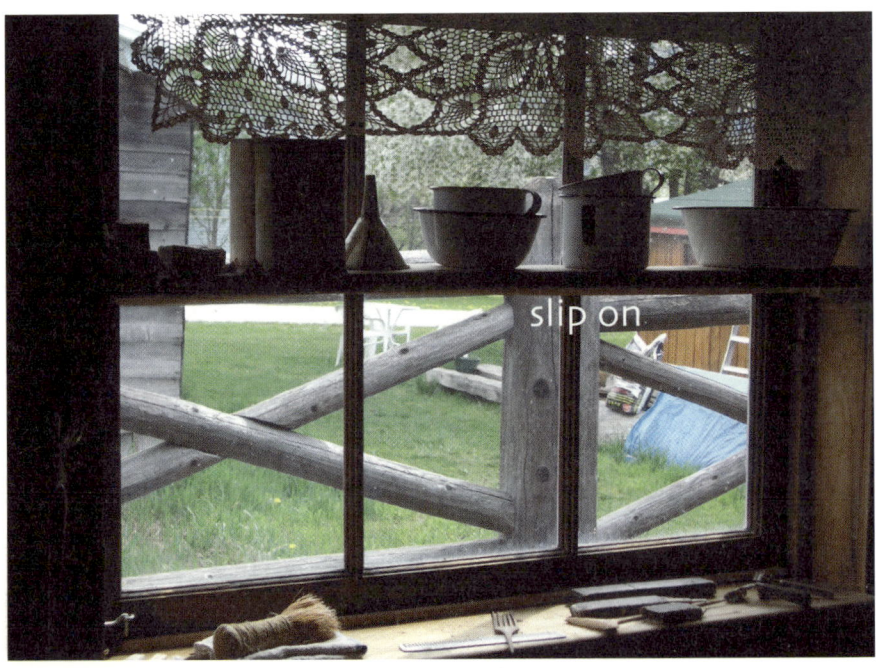

A WAKEFUL MORNING

The 7 am slant light
across the brown oak

Table a blithe window
frame alight by a blue

Jay across the compressed
headlines of the daily news

The spectral ingenuity of
a companion duly noted

Jay pecking the grass
with the flashy garb of

Orioles not to mention
speckled flickers sashaying

Around the clustering design
of aerial message markers

The sparrows mock the maker
of poems going nowhere fast

About plasticity
Amorphous blobs
Ancestral sets
Association discovery
Atomic-scale granularity
Bacterial networks
Batch fermentations
Binding sites
Biofilm
Biofluids
Bioinformatic analysis
Biological modeling

"Biological systems have an uncanny ability to rapidly tailor responses to simultaneous changes in a variety of environmental factors."

Bioproducts
Bottom-up approach
Budding yeast
Butch-learning
Catabolism
Cloning artifacts
Close homologs
Conformational changes
Cross-regulation
Culture medium
Custom arrays
Deanimate
Deconvolute
Degradation of xenobiotics
Deleted mutants
Deletion mutants
Deletion strains
Designed ontology
Disruptants
Elastic moduli
Emission wavelengths
Entropic effects
Evolvability
Experimental tractability
Expression profiling
False positives
Femtoseconds

Finite-element continuum
Florum
Flowing populations
Fluid interaction
Genome-scale
Global gene expression
Global scale data
Halophilic archaeon
Haploid viability
Heat shock
Hypertensive rats
Intracellular
Intrinsic fluctuation
Kink and anti-kink bending
Laboratory fermenter
Last universal common ancestor
Life-like
Lineage specific islands
Microsatellite repeats
Mismatch repair system
Near homogeneity
Non-coding regions
Non-essential genes
Non-synonomous substitutions
Osmotic stress

"Our model utilizes a decentralized swarm approach with multiple agents acting independently—according to local interaction rules—to exhibit complex emergent behaviors, which constitute the externally observable and measurable switching behavior."

Periplasm
Pharmaceutical interest
Phosphorylation state
Post-translational modifications
Probabilistic
Proprietary strategy
Recognizably syntenic
Regulatory network
Regulons
Repression processes
Robust aerobic
Scar less deletions
Self-assembling nanostructures

Shearing force
Signaling pathways
Silico
Simulation
Simulation procedure
Spatially localized phenomena
Spontaneous fusion
Sub-optimal
Supplemented in trans
Swarm-based
Synthetic-lethal

*"The shortest path to virtual life is
through the simplest cell."*

Transient binding
Translation-transcription
Transport coefficients
Transversions
Truly enigmatic
Truly virtual
Uncharacterized targets
Wild-type

From abstracts for the 2nd International E. coli Alliance Conference on Systems
Biology, Project Gemini, Banff, Alberta, Canada, June 18–22, 2004.

ALIBIS

the idea
is sent afar

nestled among
the bramble

buoyant as
the rushes

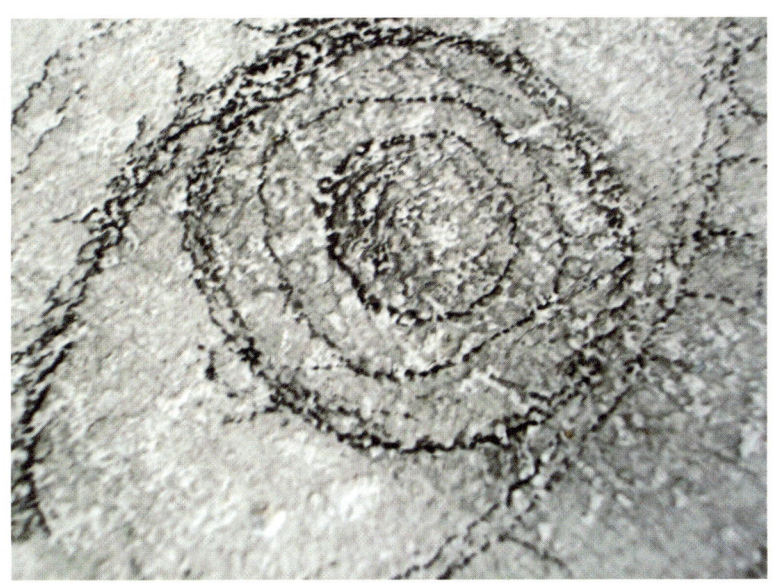

❧

the questions
form among

the deeds
best left

in the cold
midnight air

~

sedate folders
in the sedge

nestling as
function

form not
far behind

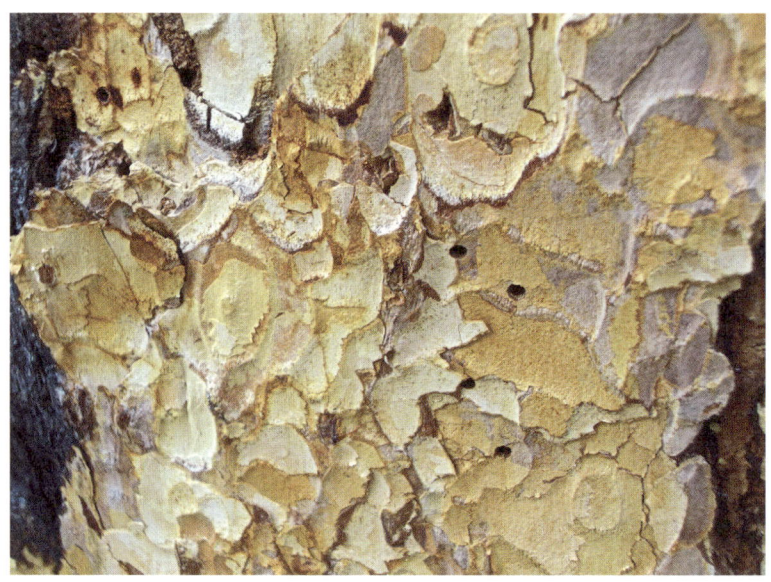

~

rolling hills
top the mist

see saw of
valves open

waves drift
on the make

≈

true blue
misfortunes

residual leaves
frost on panes

no game plan
no gain blame

≈

heels dug in
rulers are no

measure the
boat docks

at 2 wonder
what gives

≈

try to hold
to the plan

as faulty
as the segment

may be
installed

~

all the truisms
put together

even in
bouquets

cannot weather
the delay

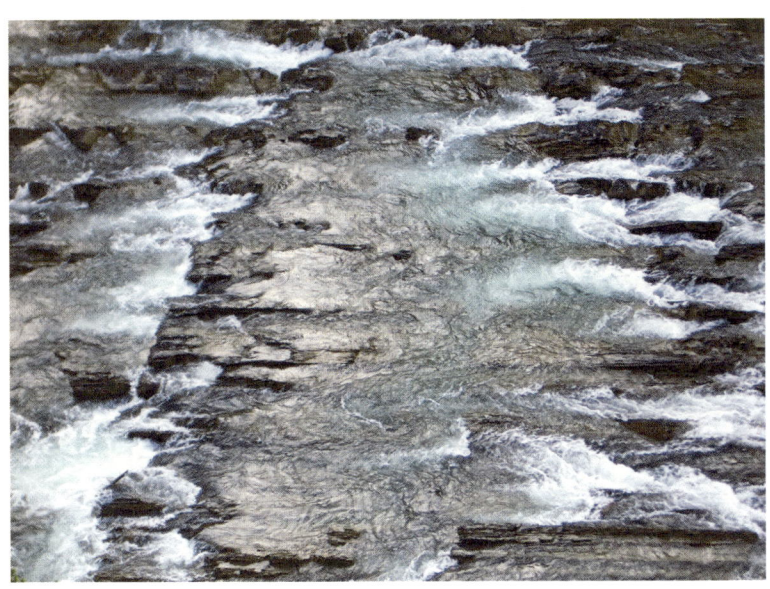

~

used to be
all the hollering

went on unabated
until the bent twig

unannounced
held court

I landed in Taipei and thought I hadn't.

Enthralled by the fluids, the most hard headed
of solids bend on cue

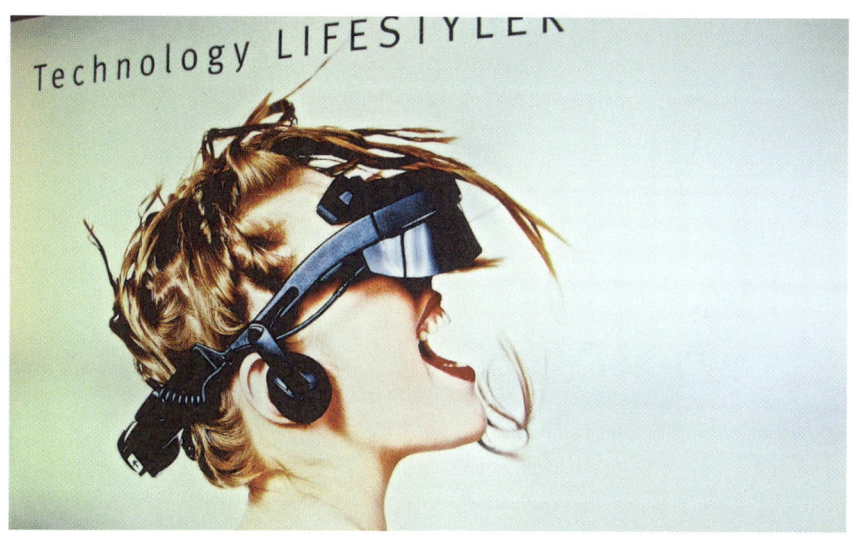

The mediated rush made my head spiral.

i was too headed in the spiral tongue of the
endless irresolution, call it the curtain call

Scooters scurried through every intersection.

Fallible engines rip through the barked fake
effrontery, with no inventory attached

Commodities here, commodities there,
wherever i strolled in my off hours.

The very idea that each letter follows the
fallow ground inspired dread in the system,
a brand name fetish

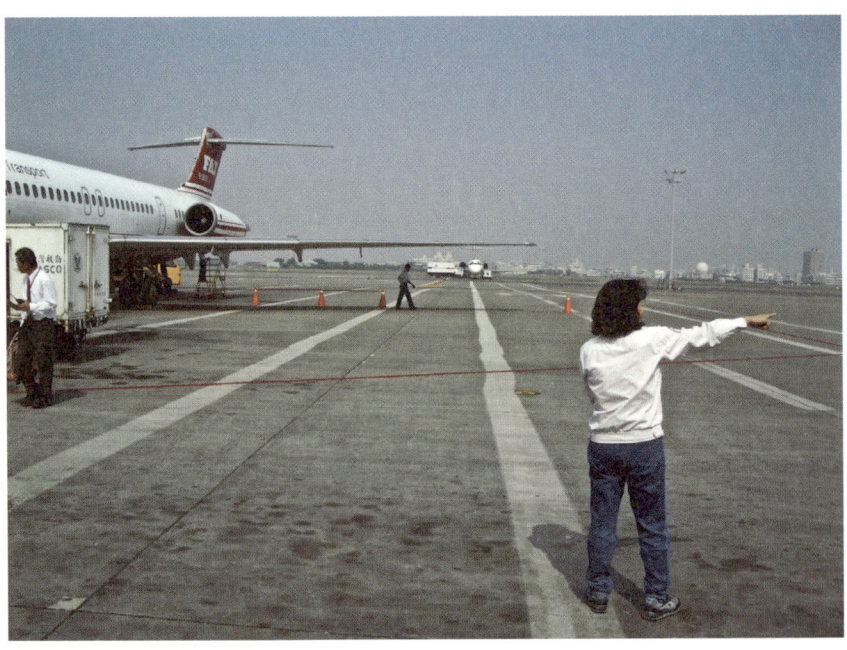

Always a voice trailing behind—"try me."

He leapt into the maelstrom only to avoid
the porridge, its consistency too hasty for safe
passage

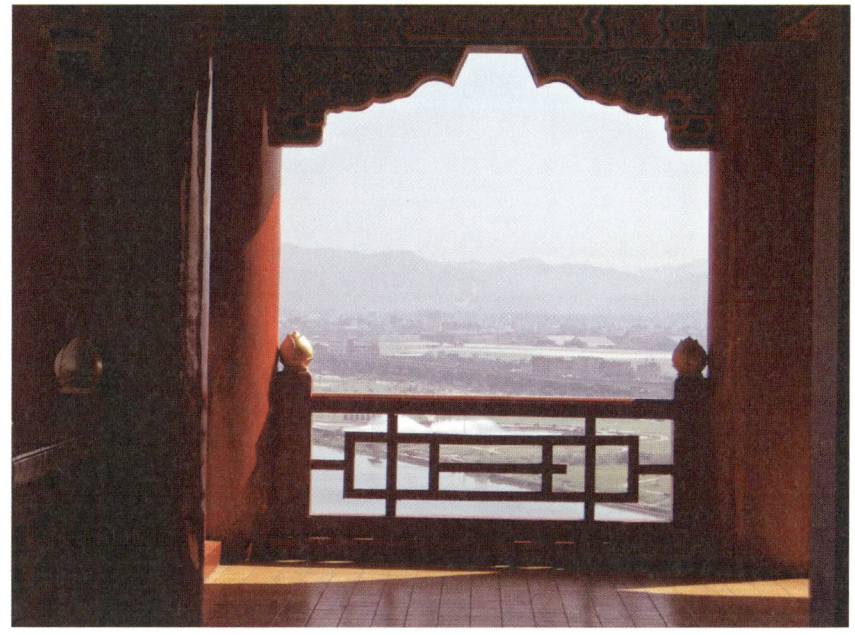

*The shops and noodle houses off the main
street—comforting as rain.*

The packaging went down smoother than the
main course, the altitude of course, but the
genomic factor could have fooled anyone

Invisibility became a protective device.

Shuffling in the narrow passageway, the hue
of the lingo bends, the visual of the crypt of
exile, the eye lands on no landmarks

In 1970 i wanted to land in Taiwan and
couldn't when Canada recognized China.

My grandfather in hawk, biding the rules of
the matrix, the rhythm of the beets

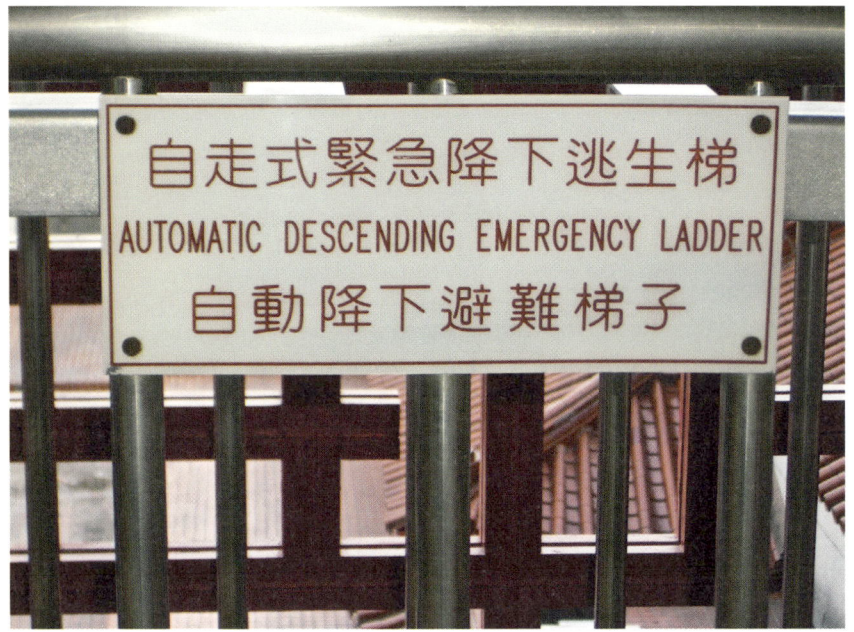

The politics of culture has long staying power.

Boosterism of the worst kind emanated
from the make-shift outhouses, the model
eventually adopted by the estate

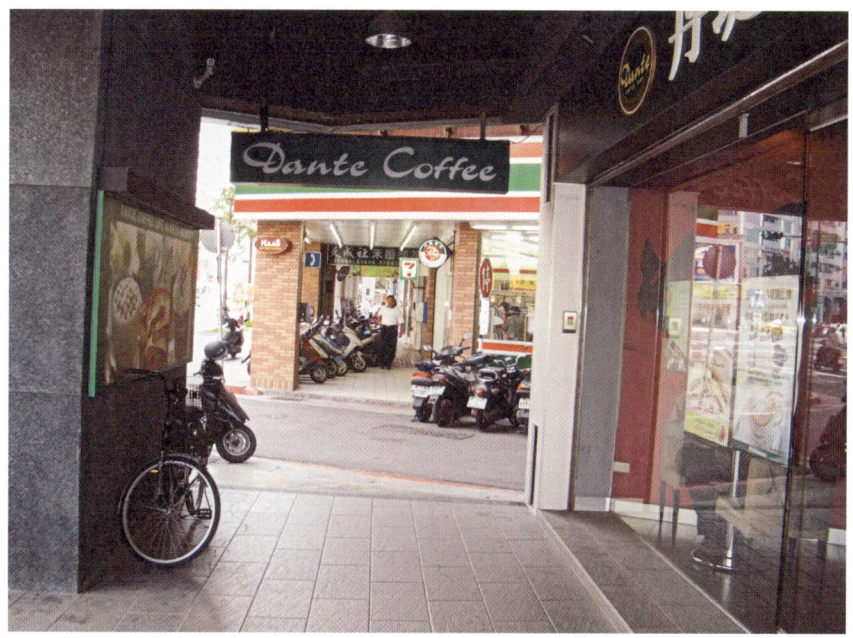

Wouldn't you know it, the poet's coffee shop (a chain)
that i imagined as a quiet retreat was filled with
blasts from the past.

i'm sorry for the things i said, when the weary
feet stray from Guting Station, Dante Coffee
beckons, i know the heartaches you've been
through, young women reading over toast
and latte, already late for the recycled platters,
the clatter of the cash register, if i didn't care

Utterly elsewhere in Mandarin, i wander lonely ...

Don't know what he's saying, can't break
one syllable from another, can't for the life
of me remember one sound, even the stream
is unrecognizable, wouldn't be able to save
you in this forest of symbols, everything
i've accumulated, all critical arsenals, all
anecdotes, all precedents, finally useless to
myself, with no need to write again, write
again

The earth quaked in the middle of the night.

Woke to a clonk, ascension of a gust of leaves,
what's left of discriminatio in the afterglow,
singed by the swaying, then wait for the up
draft, the draft of the poem losing its tensile
grip

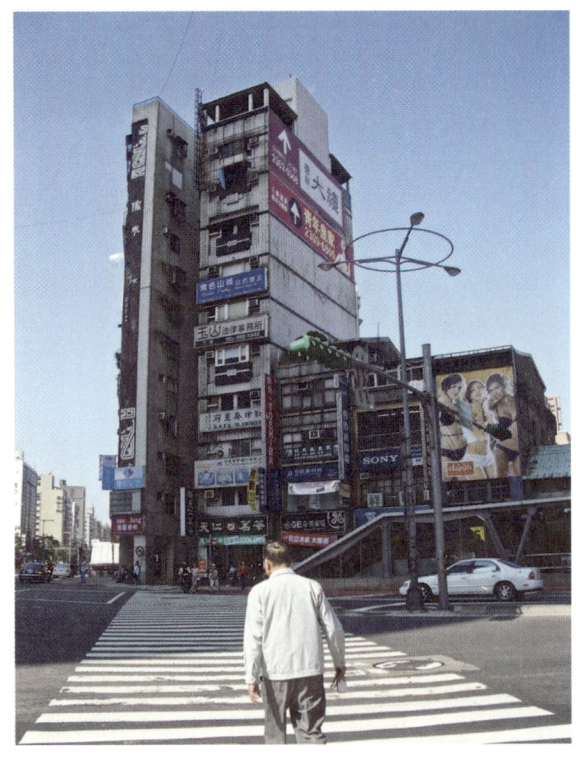

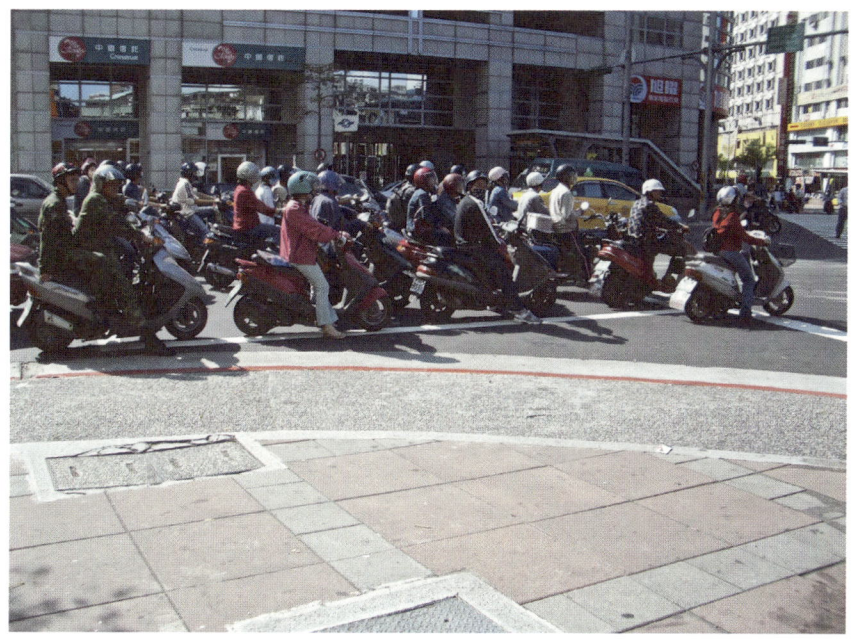

What is that quaking that issues mandates
from a stream of rushing breath, fought
against, folding down the corner of the bed,
an invite of sorts, a wild inevitability comes to
the rescue but only slightly

i thought i was a goner.

Cry foul and even so the delayed relay system
will strike out, the tale then wagging the
flagged body, found among the artifacts some
traces of unknown origin

Being a tourist requires adjustments
in techniques of roaming.

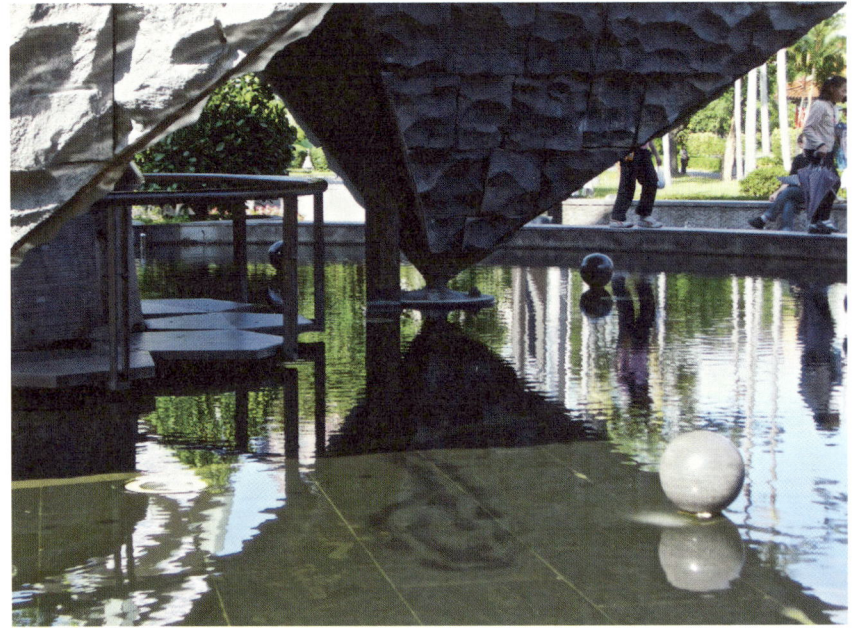

What's that old guy doing in the raucous
night market, goods laid out in a retinal
disarmament, amidst this youthful throng,
his gaze in a haze of references, in a vanishing
point of turns, yours or his, please choose now

A visit to the 228 museum opened a door to
February 28, 1947—a day starting the slaughter
of 36,000 Taiwanese activists at the hands of the
KMT regime.

He couldn't have done otherwise than walk
this Saturday afternoon in the memorial park
that brims in the shade of 228, never again,
once more, an uneasy abandon foils the lens

… beginning buried here.

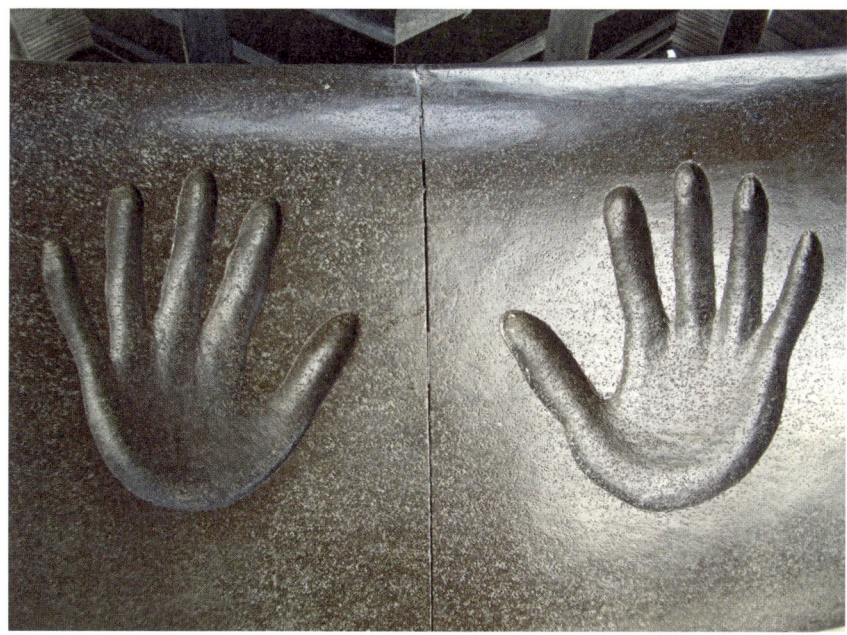

Wherever the pause strikes, a voice sidles
alongside, a foreign tongue envelops, it is
proper to say 'me' or this instance awaits a
further turn of the wheel

ALL QUARTERS ARE NOT THE SAME

for George

There was always an alternate root
All the vocables in rout
A riot of faux pas
An olive branch stuck
to the windshield

One project
per trip to
wile away
our debts to
mother tongue

Let's flip for drinks

A way to sojourn in difference
those (unsuspecting) grocery stores
after classes on brown mountain

The descent beckoned us
to the folklore of
childhood meanders

But then i could never remember
the (straight) way to Boundary Road

Flip to our trip to New Orleans
the sign in a passing glance
"authentic slave quarters"
now a classy eating house
Hank Williams in our trans

Yes/no yes/no yes/no
and we are veering right
off the mainline artery

Gator feet dangle from key
chains and the dusky interior
houses quiet white families
eating in rhythm as our canuck
trance already conjures traces

Up shows the peppy waiter
as if prompted by cultural theory
with the text of the daily special
when a voice springs into action

"Jambalaya, a-crawfish pie and-a file gumbo
'Cause tonight I'm gonna see my ma cher amio"

But let's not recall the crawfish later
the voodoo beer and the haunting face
in the window of the blacksmith quarters

Are some things best left unsaid?

What matters is the turn
on the toss of the coin

All agency on the road to
the contagious grocery store

Forged on our (tentative) fingertips

Could we help it that the gods
showered fortune on our
unprotected lyric heads?

Place is blessed in the dialogic
refrain of odds and evens

A project that
works for you

GLANCE

for Hiromi Goto and Midi Onodera

The evening   done
The oyasumis   done
The gotchisos   done

The group bowing done

And bowing again
(mostly in jest)   done

～

The three weary sojourners
their bellies ippai from the overflowing
tempura set meal (in a sea of tossed eigo

The textured rain (on cue) descends
in the mellow (yellow) midnight neon
segments of the station

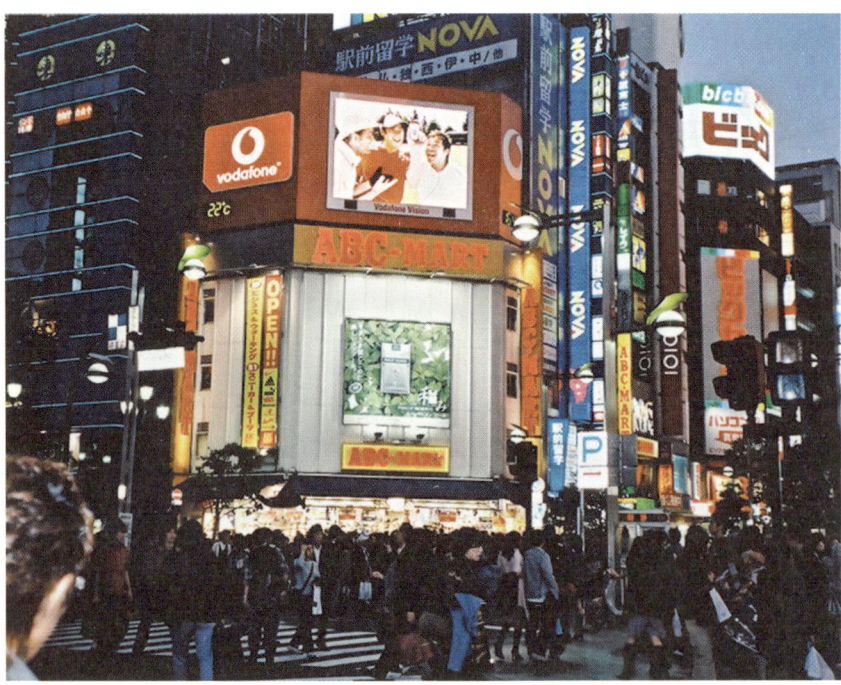

Achi-kochi the beads of light
on the two black kasa for three
under the makeshift canopy

The plump drops coalesce as
rivulets my isolate feet soak up
an excess in (not so soft) shoes
springing a leak

What are the odds
of the sealant coming undone?

～

Even the asyntactic rambling
conversation about our long day
of callit 'jc' performances
keeps the rain

at bay on Meguro-dori

Round the corner past the slick laundry
to the narrow road to the back country
more a side step into the river of no return
(a tongue hum from the fading dinner talk)

The chorus (Irasshai Irasshai)
already entranced by the siren
hum of Mama-san

Her moonshine smile
in a sheet of filmic ame
behind the counter
of the most kindly semai
noodle house in this
and any other imagined
locality (bar none)

~

Our telepathic magnets drawn to
the echo of an echo

  (Irasshai Irasshai)

We squeeze our oh so damp bodies
between phonemic rush and wall

Three settlers on red stools
with beeru and gyoza
in this kinjo of fleeting asides

The clumsy karada forgetting
its gait in a field of gazelle

~

The sum total
of unresolved

specks of foot
traffic less than

digested rumours
of ancestral linkages

~

Ah the rural flourish
of Taiwanese drift

The curious labyrinthine
twist of free speech
three decades before
(almost nostalgic)

H as unwobbling pivot
of linguistic registers

Sumimasen our cliché
bridge over troubled waters
(more residue of the station)

～

Mama-san says
ningen have to
meet face to face

She leans over
the counter

Right okyaku-san?

She turns to the far
end of the counter

"He's a regular"

～

But did she say regulator?
But did she say regulation?
But did she say register?

Seismic tremor of marching down
the long hall of the elementary school

Dumbfounded associations
in the pinball micro drama
hosted by a disheveled memory
bank of accruing global debts

The world bank on my back
to rein in deficits and cut losses
by slicing off the surplus syntax

But saved by the seven ronin
collaged faces in the doorway
hair (style undone) dripping
hungry for ramen in germanic yawp

Mama-san saunters in a dream

"As she composed, in the confines of the counter,
her make-shift contact zone"

Produces at a glance the steaming bowls

Passes them over (dangerously close) to H's
head (that looks suspiciously like a hyphen)

Mediates the cross-fire with syllabic banter
mingling German with English with Japanese

And the regular (who Mama-san had been calling a passive wimp)
slides behind the counter to pop open large size Asahi beer

The night air bustles (forgive this figure) in odd coats of veneer as the
unforeseen okyaku-san assemble a make-shift table under the narrow
domain of the protective awning

"The ramen shop is their favourite stop on
trips to Tokyo for the Berlin H Orchestra"

Still streaming their performance that night
a boisterous riot of crows that Regular-san
poised on the stool for the aerial view
(already) shoots on his cell phone

M with her palm sized video camera
Mama-san with seven bowls of ramen
in her lens as she lines the counter top
before us and still remembers the shuttling

    (Taiwan to Tokyo)

Scavenged the lingo to survive in the city

And (now) Regular-san hands M his cell phone image for her camera
as the ronin faces fade driven to shelter in the empty parking stall

On the opposite side of the lane
huddled around the stall table
they could be playing cards
for a low budget film

     (Hokusai to the rescue)

∿

Our own cramped faces squeezed into
shashin we slip out in the downpour our
kasa barely holding back the torrent

On the plate sit three uneaten gyoza
neatly arranged as if we had not leaned
together with our backs to the wall

(Gomen nasai)

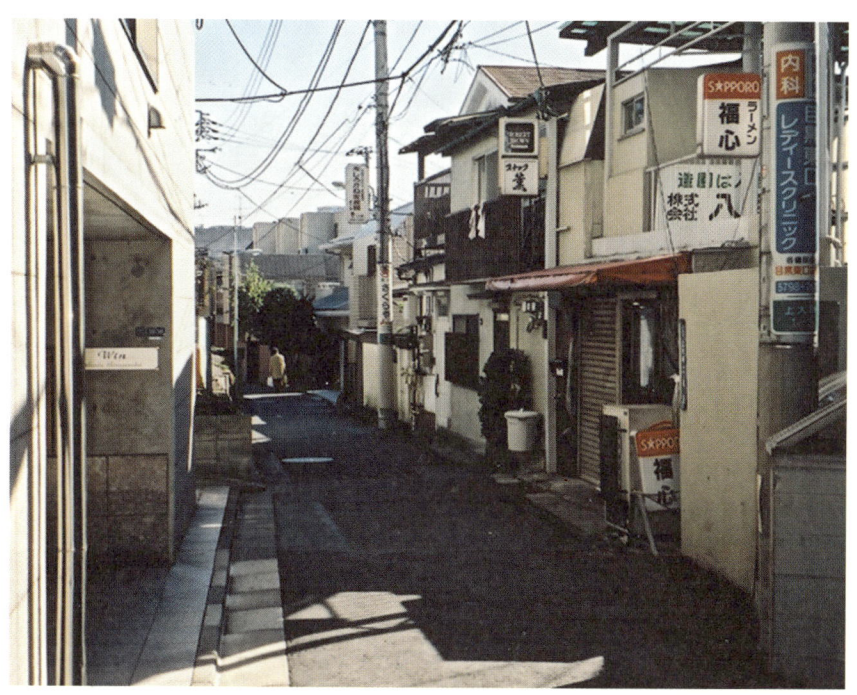

THERE

There is the location
in front of the computer

The technology dissipates
and the ache of the temporal

exudes a fine mist that conjures
the diaphragm of rolling hills

minted fevers that produce
crab apples by the bushel

Tart folds in the evening walks
on the boardwalk the ferris wheel

whirls in overdrive as the street
talk moves the crowd past

Mannequin Rising

In memory
Glen Gore-Smith

TOKYO EVENING

for Grace T

Long ago he arrived from a distant land
with nothing but cultural baggage

Everything wore the sheen of overwritten
landscapes wrong from the outset

By slipping in and out of coffee houses
he soon began to re-orient himself

To the vibrant maples set alongside the
towering bluer than blue yuletide tree

Which frame set off no reminiscences
no calendric retrievals whatsoever

(Yet who is that white haired old guy
scribbling away in his little notebook?

In the motley line of passersby in the
window the cell phones blink in tune

They do not note his wobbling hand
shaking leaf-like in a soft evening breeze

The young radiate evanescence in attire
with a rainbow hue bursting through

You had to pay close up attention or
the slip cover would be blown away

Sure i fought against the slippage
when the anchors gave way to

Swallow this and swallow that but
don't forget where you came from

All the truths compiled in a list do
not add up to a usable commodity

Estrangement always has its loyalty
and turnkey days when we start over

As aging kindles kindlier abstractions
that sprout in grey matter once again

FIVE TAKES ON CULTURE

for Michael B

1

We came out the other end
strangely refreshed like browsers

Check out the linkages if you
want a slide down nascent codes

But hey rapids ripple down spine
in a tolerance to dine on my lungs

These wagers foretell the methods
of monitors with their chips down

2

The driver in the truck alongside
the bus doesn't look at the road
as wheels turn of their own accord

Some days it all works that way and
even students who don't ask questions
sit on their hands and wear the ink well

3

Larissa said in Taipei four channels in a
row broadcast Buddhist priests chanting
right next to the all night porn channel

That's culture for you the body and spirit
after all these years still trying to contact
each other across the ornery digital divide

4

i think i know nothing then someone
shouts look here your feet are on fire

It's that nomadic verb found only in
dispatches lodged in palpable tines

Striking postures that fuse in fiery
dichotomies with the flush of roses

5

These days the pledge subscribes to
clashes with local fashion standards

Rumours in the gait of knee bending
when the second hand on its circuit

Confirms the health of the local in
the spectrum of its splintered ends

VESTIGIAL

for Fred W

The notebook lost or left in the seat fold
took on the flue of history. All the drafts
that spoke of disappearing acts. All the
runaway words never to be retrieved.

The highway at least remains in forward
mode. Cruising on local bravura the
driver set his sights on the road while
the captive scooters on the passing semi
were uncaught in the lens. With the sweep
of his hands the scattered fields turned
into the dream of other landscapes.

> For instance the prairie road
> of his childhood as a wager
>
> against the vacant air of the
> side vents. The hot air and
>
> the cruel thirst on the bicycle
> still only halfway to Selkirk.
>
> To stand later where hands
> in the asylum window wept
>
> to see the tumbling outside.
> What he wagers as the land
>
> escaped again.

Remember the guide in the 228 museum breaking her
spiel when she got to 1895? This island seen as
so valueless it was ceded forever. All that matter
compressed in the palm of her hand. What does
it mean to move beyond it? What could it mean?

The strands of the electrical networks quiver
in an artificial breeze. It was all manufactured
for the benefit of posterity. Do we get it?

All hell bent loose on narrative devices. He
was raddled by what was lost in an instant.
Memory buckled in the faint hope of retention.

Surely the betel nut beauty on the roadside
in her glass enclosure spells the middle way.

Her reflection in the light of the bus window
transports him by ripple effect. The compacted
dream of locomotion the song without the singer.

Could it happen to me? Am i a social machine?
Do the buttons pushed on my retina trigger
insular buffer zones on the run? Should i ask
why the green hedges around the tables in the
mall are fake?

        Personally he was not averse
to a comely capitalist touch of faith but please
don't touch the back of this memory at least
not now on this road from Puri to Taipei

Scoping (also pronounced "Shopping") in Kits

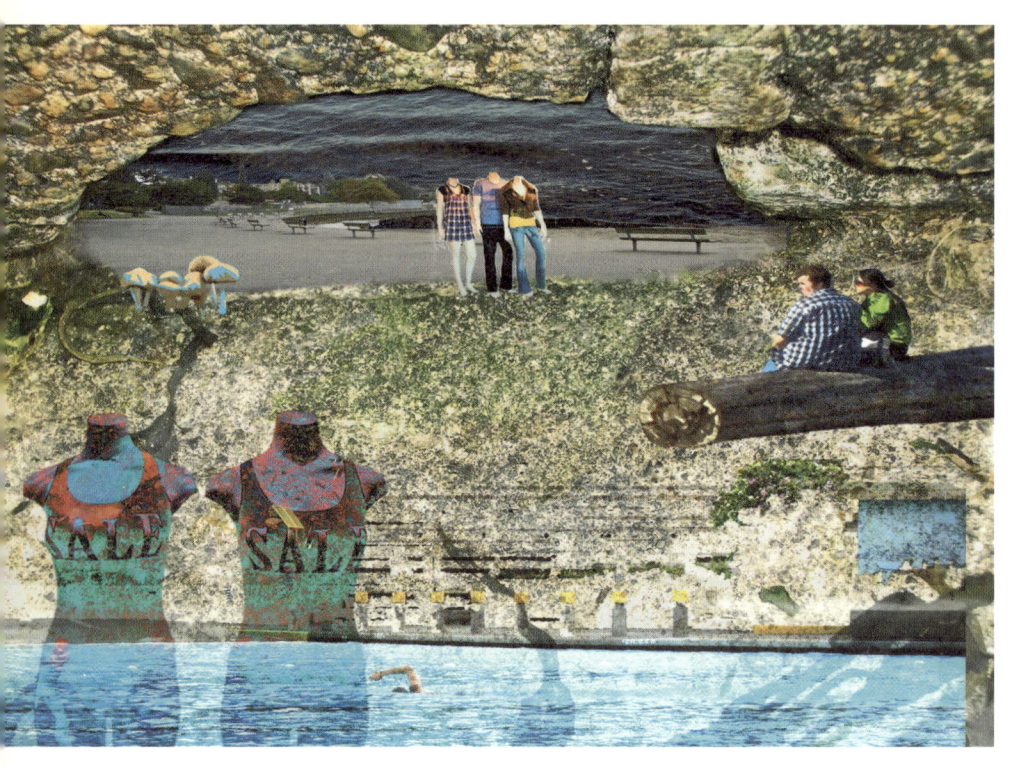

↙ There are more fealties than
one can safely stock in the store

Pedestrians ingest waves that one
receives as wet wheels leave the curb

Allowances on balance percolate
the membrane and tweak the otherwise

soft core of the lovers whose dials
turn towards the curvature of the

spinal nexus where the conflagration
of ruses blend into the ruffled hedges

whose resistances can ameliorate bevies
of stories left untold in the weathervane

The inverse ratio of production costs left
the mannequin speechless for the first time

The communication channels in the nest
of cavities make truce with a network

of pinhole cameras that admit the light
into recesses of double or nothing respite

· ·

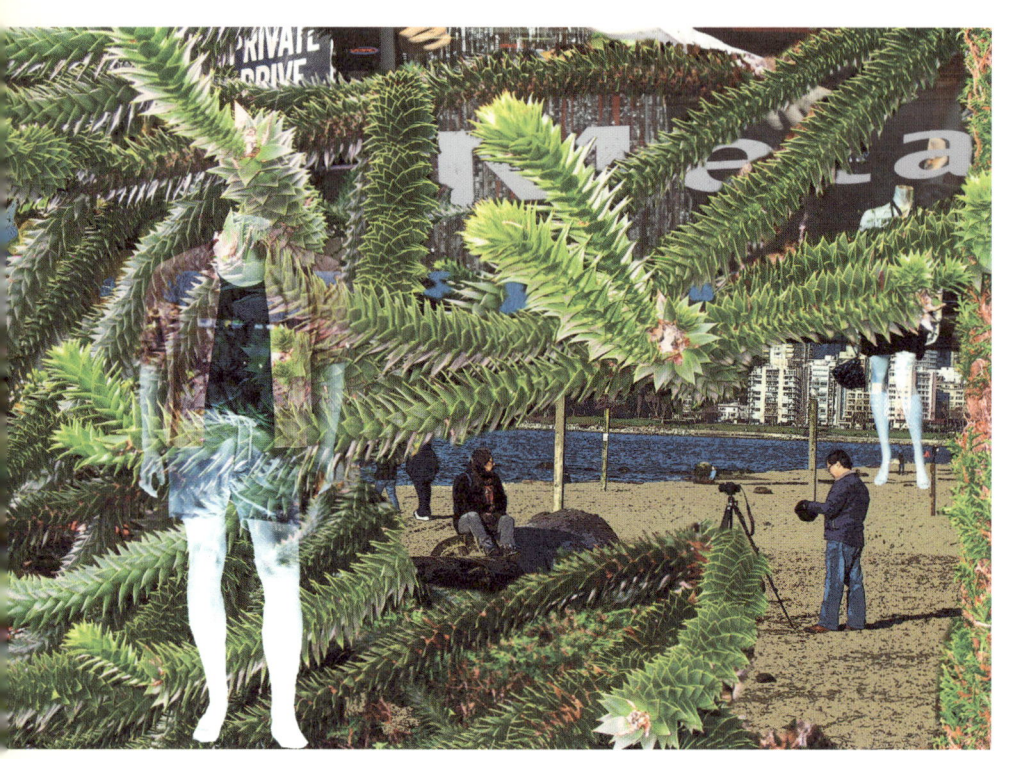

↙ The mannekins must share
foreknowledge of the rise
and fall of human desires

Their glances flit and sway
as each word in lip synch
nudges up against another

We think we are sentenced
in heated exchanges that
make creases in their postures

But that only supposes that
each nod has found its place
in a balanced basket of goods

The ripe fruit vegetables and
vintage wines in their adept
hands take place in the move

The dream in their presence
makes as it filters unsaturated
along spiralling back waters

What did the groove then
signify for you? What in the
spectrum of still shots came

Off as fake and artificial as a
wily summer breeze wafting
through the montage of frames?

We are consumers get used to
it we are here because you were
there and there is always a here

That brings fear of trembling to
the daily born exits that oft call
to the pause in the amber light

· ·

↙ The scop in shopping
tumbles off the tongue

The inveterate creases
complete the off rhyme

How the poet survives
across zones in market

conditions such as this
depends on the allergic

reaction to the diction
that nary a breeze blows

A forest of sighs awaits
the feigned underclass

of commercial linkages
or transmissions in a lay

lingual operative on hold
such shadow boxing binds

the hop in hoping that
comes down to the wire

· ·

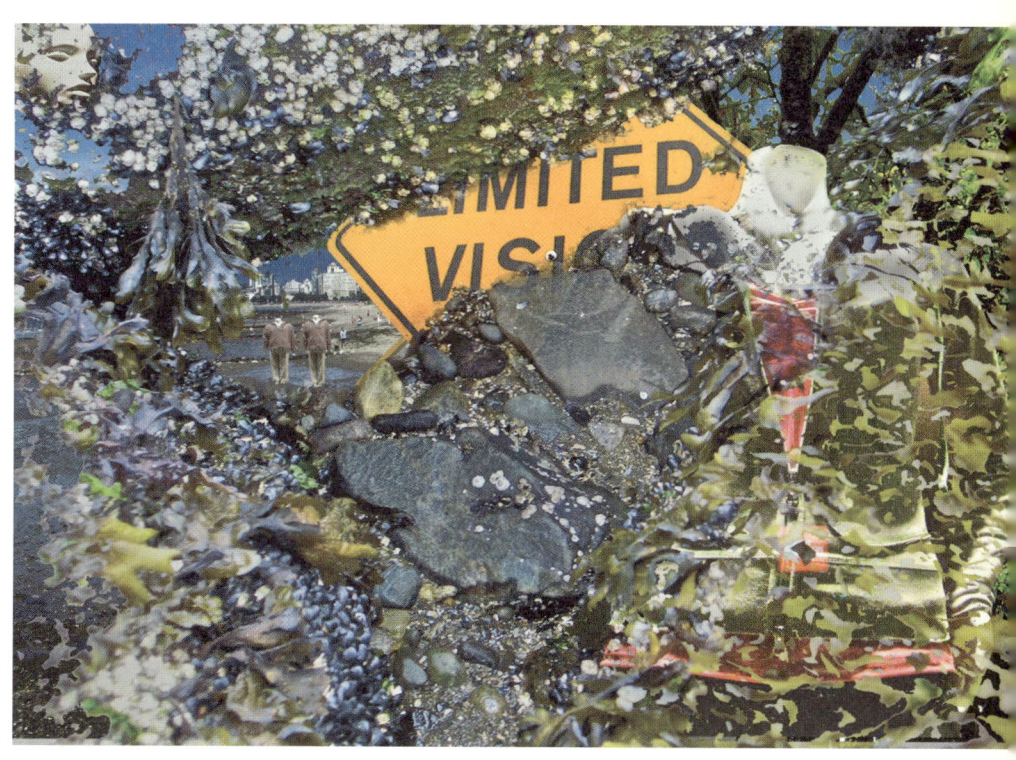

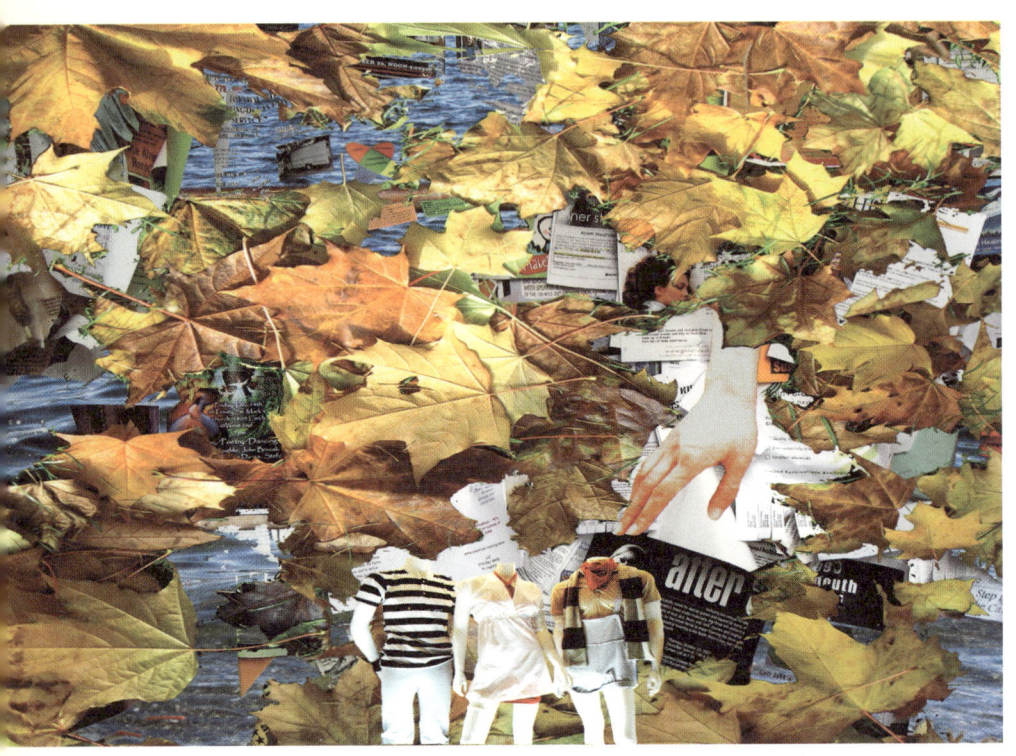

↙ Must have been the kit
with spare parts of speech
that scraped the basin

Amicable as proverbial
winds that rattle cages
and smoke out each

Casual spell tossed in
a grammar as mellow as
melons boxed for a ride

Hide and go seek the sack
of flighty winds that trail
those spectacles of consent

Those in the parade so long
their leggings tie the media
fanfare in knots of nodding

When even the manikins on
duty know the conjunctions
do not placate the bellyache

Witness the rank file of those
disaffected in the enchanted
forest with rattling sabres

Show them the unmanicured
nails the implants that hail us
from beyond the artless dunes

Show them the fossil in the lye
or the eye burn that blanches
the domestic solace of news

• •

for Ashok M

⚹ The rising action of shrugged shoulders
The confluence of matched footsteps
The route of the induced visitations

In these instances the call of the social
fails to meet the watchful standards
of the fashion police on patrol

The workmen gloves fell in a fitful mirage

The passersby glowed in uneven tints

The media attributed these effects to the
downturn in the consumptive habits
of the neighbourhood rodents

Affixing blame on the fence rot
necessitated the move of an identified
family of squirrels to more restricted
quarters at a two block remove from
their sheltered ancestral traceries

"These are wondrous times," one witness
was heard saying, "no words adequately
inscribe the engineering of bodies modelled
on such a destitute superstructure of beliefs."

This vial is full of a patented truth serum

This idea fought its way in the rush hour
only to be sabotaged by a dull market day

This mollifier worked overtime all month
only to be replaced by the offshore version

• •

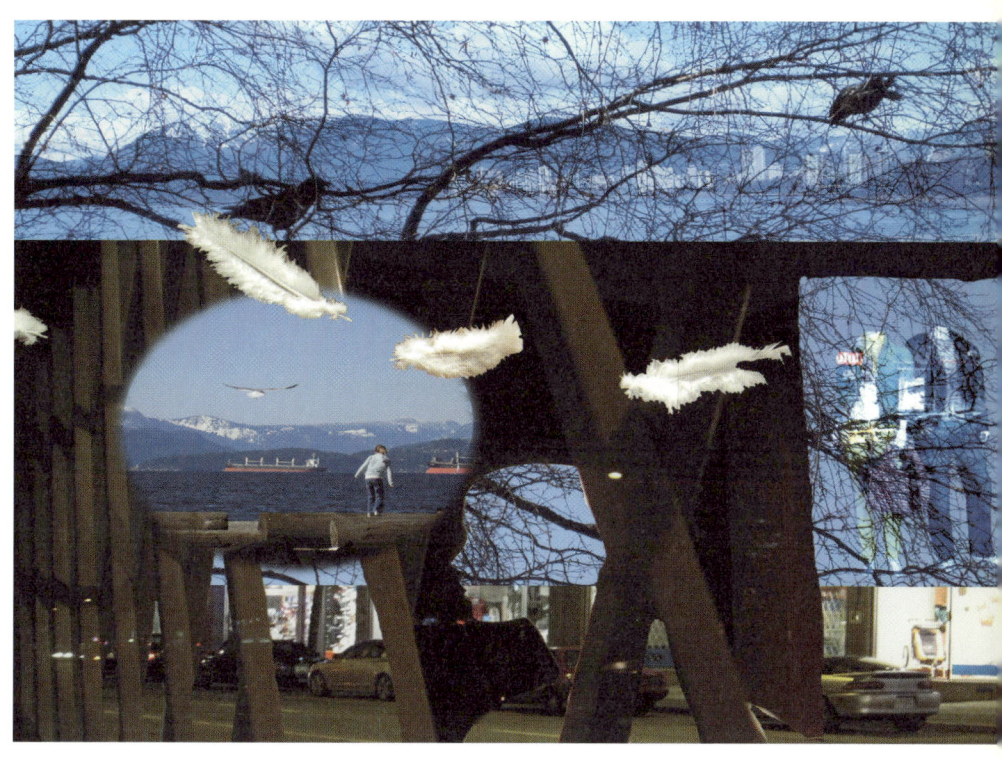

↙ We are always at a loss when it comes
to the question of vision whether it is
better to fasten on a figure that passes
for optimal apprehension or to flatter
the turnabout in the inclination by dint
of resistances that make for patience

The patient is one who awaits the
ministration of a healing touch who
absorbs the turbulence of cells (phones
too) between the crustacean ensemble
on the rocks and the walks along the shore
as the body of water poses for the snapshot

i slid down the face of the intersection with
no regard for warning posters except for
the otiose sounds carrying the refrain
of the rumour mills with all their telltale
operations led by the fierce tenacity
of a nose ever close to the window dressing

Balk if you will or if you don't show me a way
to chalk up the losses to the prescience of
the mannikin who leaps out of the frame
breaking the mould for the typecast role
as a hanger on or even a model minority
breaking the synergetic bonds wide open

‧ ‧

for Louis C

↙ "Could commodities speak we would say:
our use value may be a thing that interests
men. It is no part of us as objects. What belongs
to us is our value. Our natural intercourse as
commodities proves it. Now listen how we
speak through the mouth of the economist."
Do you not detect in the slow motion of his
lips the slippage from the warm body to the
past tension of never being recalled for duty?

It is only a human thing you say but note the
recourse in our speech to the natural intercourse
of value for burgeoning exchanges that upset
the apple art as you say with no pun intended
the pun being reserved for superfluous occasions
that spell the gloom of market indices in the rush
to embrace the dizzy passages on billboard screens

"Could commodities speak we would say:
our ruse value may be our interest producing men.
It knows particles as objectives. Your nationalized
discourse of commodification rues it." Now speak
how we listen through the dearth of domestic value.
In the turn of a phrase, "must for reclining mountain,"
the land (i should have said hand) has been known
to yield graftings for fool's gold the yellow pearl that
once haunted the economic dreams of thing makers

It is useless to frown on the upstart conniving of
things that pay no heed to human truisms and tamper
with the ciphers binding performance to productivity
graphs and other domains in the kingdom of statistical
averages that cut our air tubes for discretionary ends
when we breathe value on the tips of branches

Should commodities speak we could say:
hey loosen up on the valet who imitates manly
interests alone. It is as partial as others. What longs
to be free of ruse value. Our nature as commodities
precedes us. Now fess up to the tricks of the trade
as the poet says "the wet playing field is a testy mountain
that sinks back into the sea" or consider the circular
routes that turn on a dime and add up to the branch plants
that shed their leaves as signs of altruism for the mute earth

• •

🖎 Such chemical agitators that forecast
the vacillation of nerve fallouts

Such warnings that stockpile
fuel for the rise in global pullouts

Such bends in the bottom line emit
symptoms of fondled merchandise

There in the embedded baits
prolong the rinsing of borders

The coursing of staged crafts
proclaim a mannequin inhabitation

Do we then mourn the dead or do
the dead scorn the memory of passing?

If the body all decked out in its strut
succumbs to the caress of the enemy

Who then hails the prancing pinball
striking the chord setting off the rush?

When the politicos banter about loyalty
border honour border courage border

The market for ipods skyrockets in
the lush muffle of currents on the fly

Find yourself before this glassine finish
when the reflectors on duty work overtime

• •

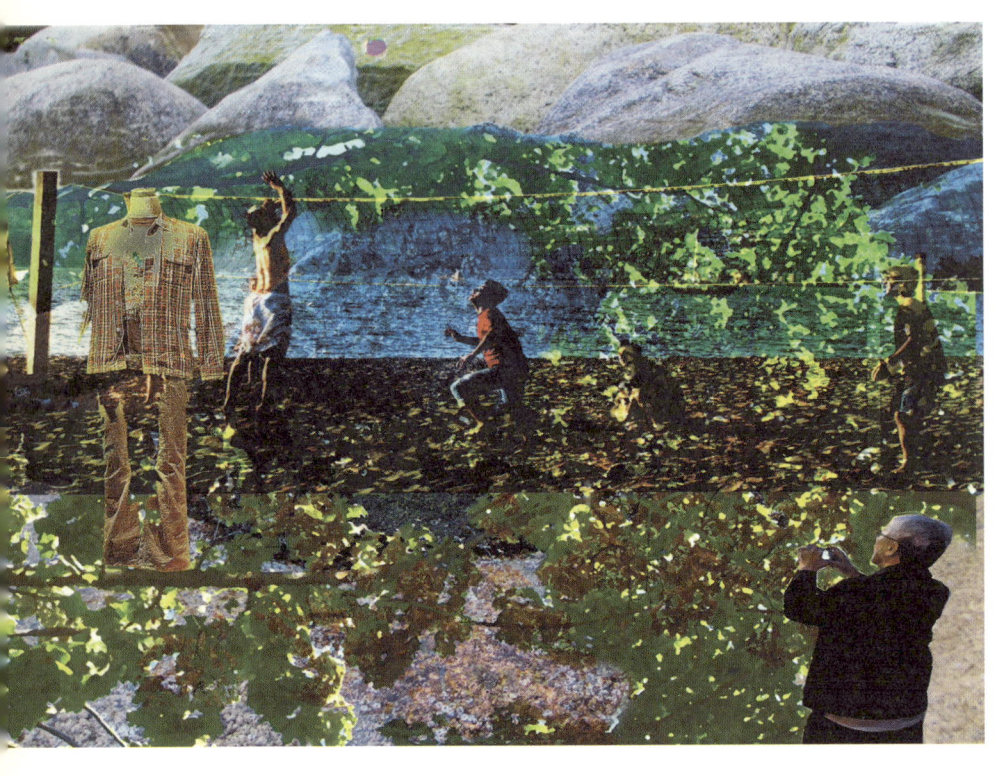

for Glen L

↙ i was brought up on
streets where tongues
were forever wagging

The strain on the solar
plexus wore manifests
in the latest trends

Though washed jeans
on display spoke out
of lavender days

Under the eavesdrop
what got summoned
were forgotten strains

Like worn out pics
slipping on new duds
in the model race

i forever got brain
storms of insolvent
pardons on standby

As the unwashed soles
of trampling indices
muttered in unison

• •

↙ Drawn as they were to a flagrant
disregard for protocol and decorum

Alert to the dancer whose buoyant
tensility crouched in the outer ear

All the freed messenger pigeons lined
the store window as vested lookouts

"We hear you" sounded an exchange
of root pointers on the old pathways

They swayed on command and cooed
against the thought of new fashions

So that flutter found roots to citizens
in the late afternoon urban slumber

At the edge of the timer the dancer
took refuge in the gauze of eyelids

Like secular waves the windowsill
of receptors called to the strollers

In such synch the seismic portals
absolved the mirror of its resolve

• •

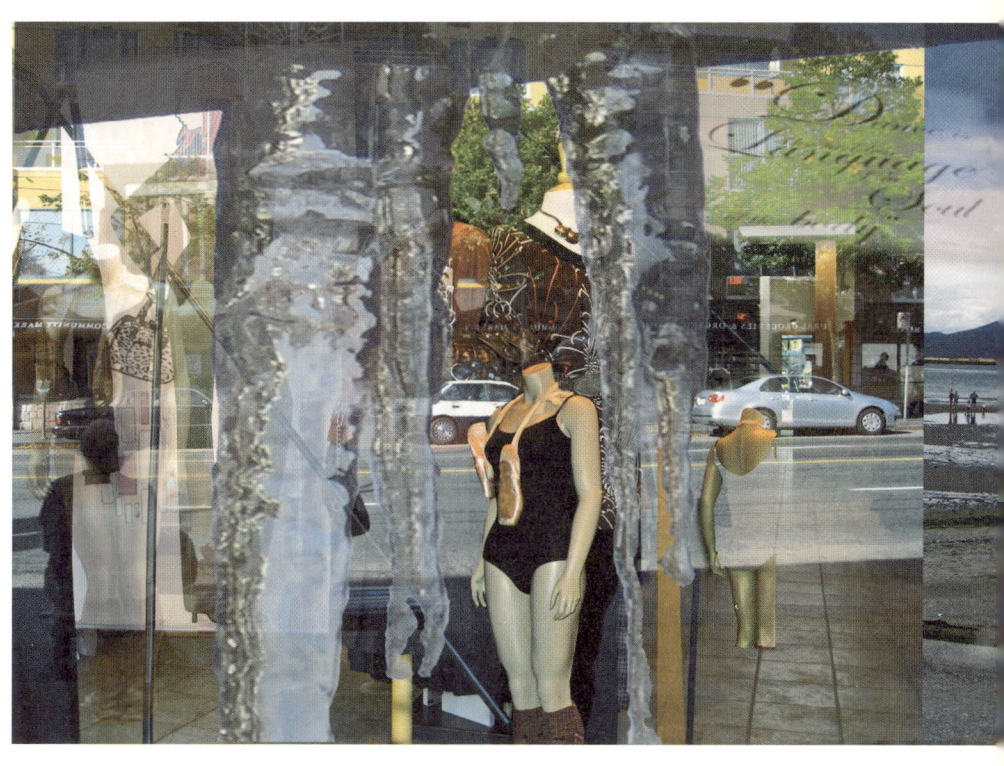

↙ Did you notice it was impossible to distinguish
between glass and mirror, or was it the mirror
defect that the experts talked about?

The determination, in that instance, coincided
with glances deflected on the concave surface
of a voice box but one that had no speaker or
at least a throat according to biological usage.

The thermometer registered a voice print with
numerical values only known to forensics
as they are wont to say in the media.

•   •

↙ This one would not always
tell which layer precedes
and which one turns the key

How we buzz one another as
interlocutors who don't have
a way home except by way
of intercoms that are set to
distribute values across the
template of aboriginal change

Shifting range as the weather
balances social goods against
the pull of tidal encumbrances

Call them the ornery doubts of
makers lamenting the slowdown
call them the surplus of cells in a sea
of forgetting call them the market
miscues that are remembered as
local conflations of the good news

　　　• •

"Researchers find no seaweed and therefore no health benefits in Lululemon's Vitasea line of clothes. The Kitsilano-based Vancouver company has claimed that VitaSea contains 23% SeaCell, a fibre made from seaweed, which makes its material 'antibacterial, moisturizing and de-stressing for the skin.' Despite this breaking news, Lululemon customers are unfazed. 'I don't care if there's seaweed in my clothes, as long as they fit me right,' said one satisfied customer. The dip on the company's share value soon disappeared, and reports say it might even climb on the heels of the controversy."

Is a lulu
a lemon

Is a sea
a skirt

Is a weed
a skin

Is a commodity
a companion

Is a patent
a belonger

Is a brand
a friend

Is a lemon
a lulu

Is a stock
a lotto

Is a lulu
a being

Is a store
a commune

Is a window
a scribe

Is a frame
a blame

Is a choice
a ruse

Is a person
a mobile

Is a rift
a gain

Is a meaning
a verb

Is a fund
a mental

••

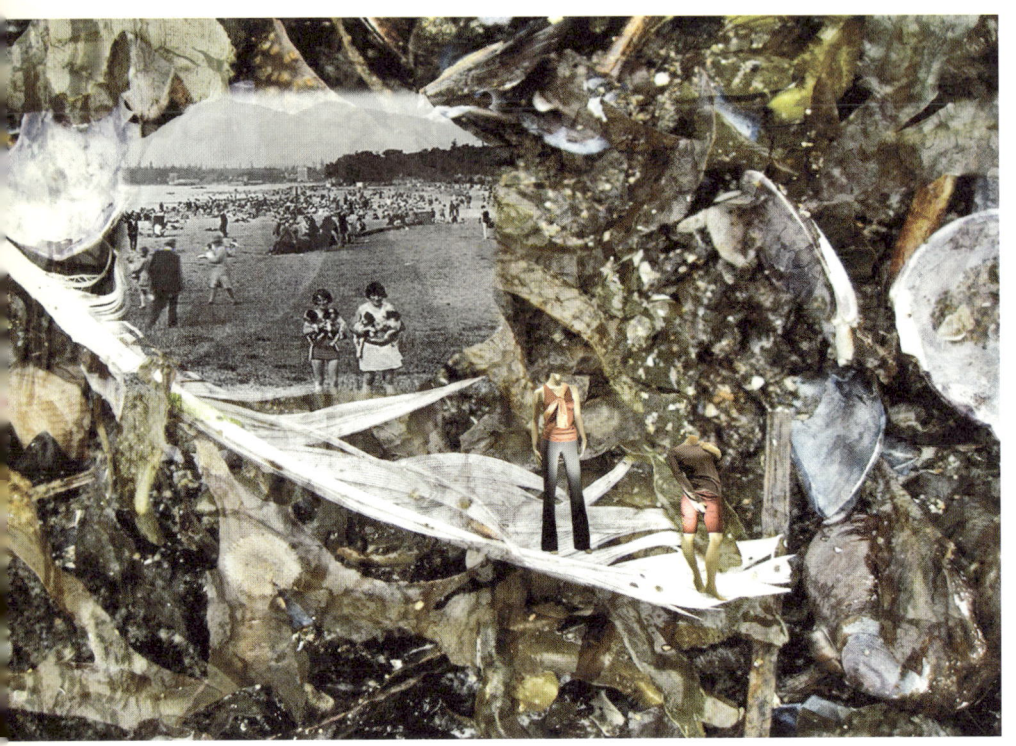

for Hiromi G

↙ If the manakins
could read lips
they would keep
their thought
probes a secret

No telling what
would become
of their lore
in the hands
of their makers

No telling what
logs would make
when the defence
has been such
stellar quietude

No telling what
winds stir what
quantum motes
register what fore
sight gives warning

See the audacity of
appropriation has
a history of pock
marked insignias
with sorry origins

See we ride only those
waves that breach the
shore line / tell us who
we become in the bubble
wrap of our beholders

• •

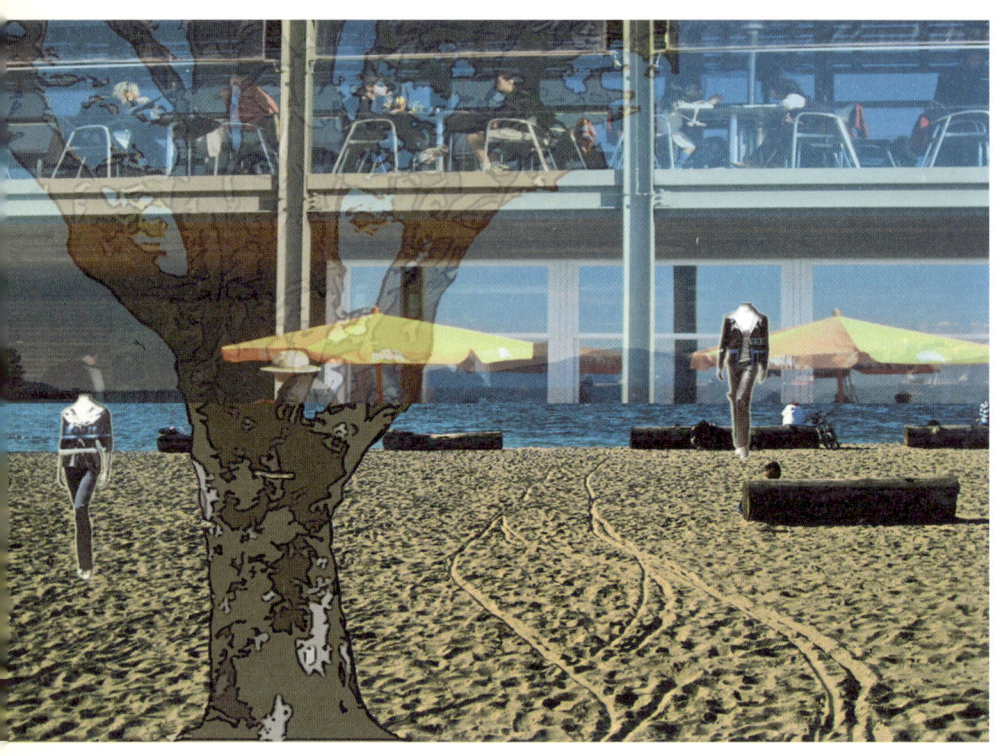

↙ Blending in eases the burden
of having that digital moment
when the screen of resistance
gives way to the particulates

The decibels unhinged from
reference in a hay day of lying
in the tall grasses by the drying
river bank all hallowed by the

Energy that emits the close by
entropic harmonies stirred in
the adept stairwell of saunters

i can breathe easier when the
undertow finds its airstream
and all the fluids in storage
awake to sibilant promptings

For once forget the injunction
to forget where the word rises
in the expectant dawn as the
yearning shells speak of altered

Courses of bondages undone
of strident voices put to bed
of billowing sails that confront
the rule of thumb and benumb

Those top down targeted digits
the trigger happy among them
whose stiletto heels turn sod

• •

↙ When the divisionary things break down
the only way down the rabbit hole is tinged
with goods.

Some people get all the breaks.
Others have to wait until the crack of dawn.

We simmer in a catch basin of catch phrases.
The sliver of light is all we can go on.

All
exhilarating dominance works the tempers
when turned to the perennial west winds.

The poet's escape route you say without
intending to harm the hard boiled (common)
core tricks of the trade.

These days the skin
emits more "out there" fears of redundant
resources to camouflage the unprecedented
raid on the naked and ravaged image. Records
of anonymous seizures shredded the falling
rhythms crying foul ball.

Do you think all goods
are for you? All for you that the pulse pulsates?
That the hollow in the plexus is unforgiving?
That the homilies pile up like stranded truisms?

Signs of foreclosure in the subprime capital are
as menacing as the iron knee of greed feeding
on its own entrails.

"Happy trails to you" the
headline making composure of investor backlash.
"No pain no gain." "No sin no grin." "No blame
no fame." The social goods are stacked. All bets
are off. No willows too much to manhandle.

We were off track as the announcer waived his
voice fee to expose his goods.

You or i only wish
the rantings that blanket the public airwaves of
displeasure would yield the emergency of breath.

• •

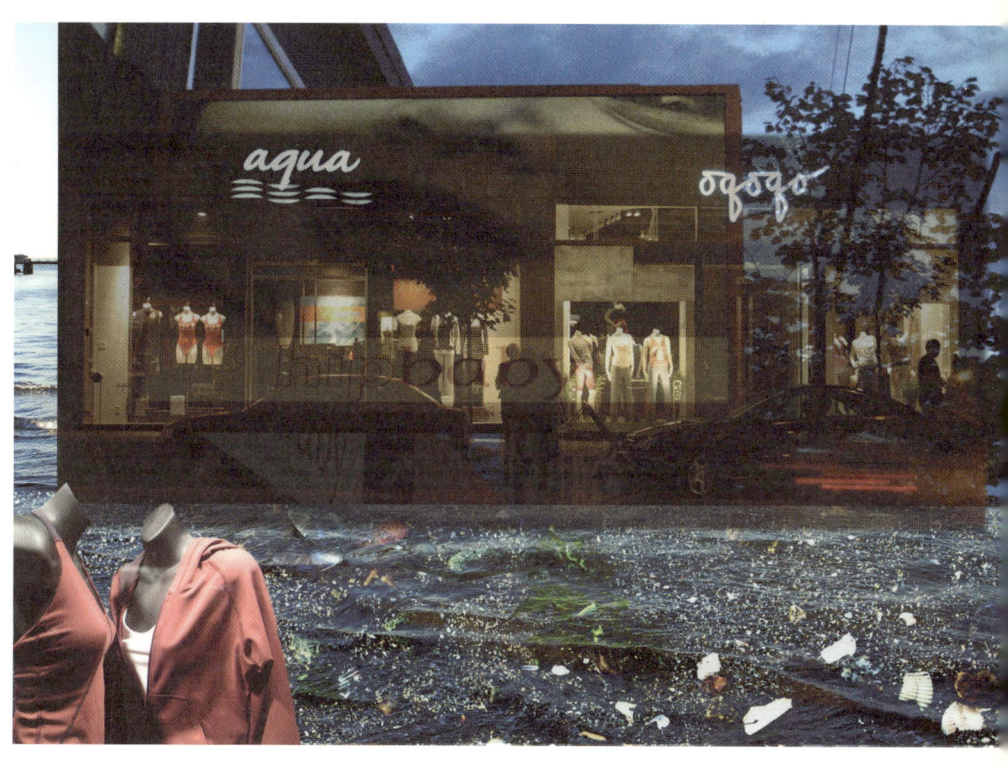

↙ Are you suffering from compassion fatigue?
Does it bother you that you think you're
the only one who is not a victim? Do you
wake in the middle of the night and ask
why me? Then bingo hold on to your stirrups.
You've won an all expense paid cruise
through the discourse of your choice
with vocabulary tailored to your needs
and all perceptual states a projection of your
desires and your desires alone. A full message
massage is yours too if you please.

· ·

⿙ In one of those opportune seances
made memorable in commercials
we noticed the spike
in the demand ratio of mannikins
as if the sudden rise in the currency
were the equivalent of spiked water
that spurred their necessary
out of body consumer moment

The odometer set on the bank counter
next to their usual haunt
began to shimmy
when the crowd formed
more out of its curiosity
than old fashioned compassion

The speed of their liberation
infuriated the managers
even though nothing was audible
or visible or even recognizable
according to standard modes of measuring
dermal disturbances of similar types

In any case we were aroused
by their gazes that monitored
the micro-shifts in attention
releasing damp questions in
things no longer encased
in the packaging of human comforts

But tumbling out of flavour
the lateral mumblings of likeness
went awry in a bundle of reckless
indiscretions that willed our foot
steps out of their loose garments

• •

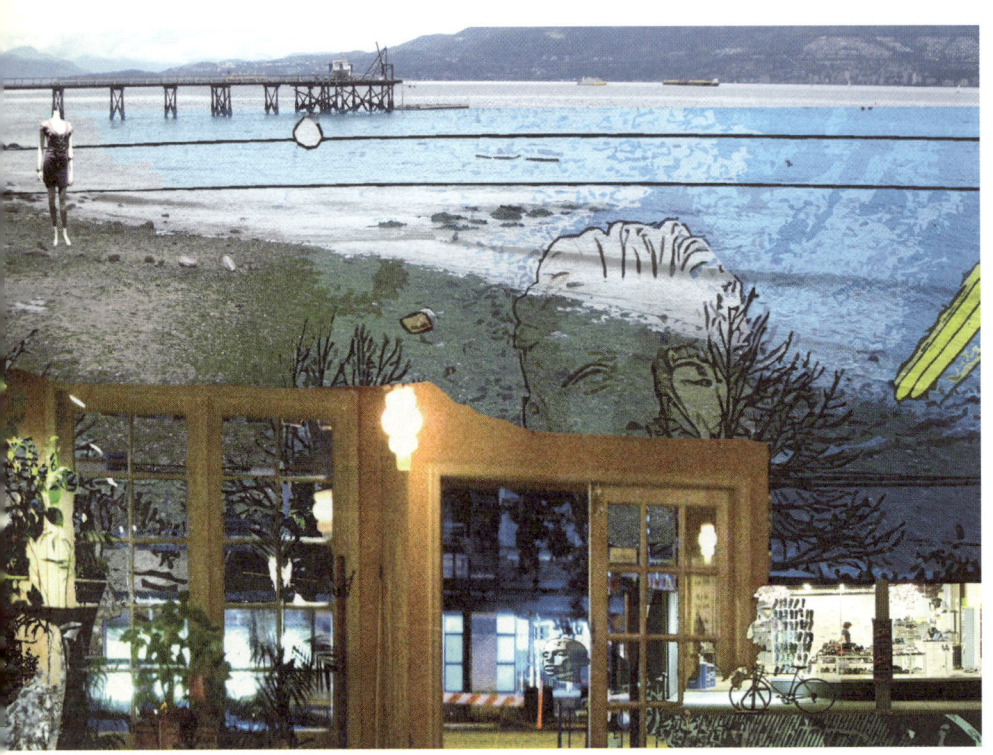

⬋ All those clichés
like comings and goings
like the passing show
like the quick and the
lead foot the surfeit
not mine not amid
mind in the thickets
of its own making

Its sobriquet domain
some solace this
rain swept night

The leaves give up
their riotous flutter
and follow the lead
of the pedestrians
on the sidling parapets
wishing for the light
of the poet to make
do with the materials
at hand he was going
to say when the changeling
patterns of the middling
ironies fell into the deep
sleep of consumption

They let it come to pass
let it follow the tract
the attractor factor
buzzed the interior
lobes of the truculence

At the viewing station
where the light dons

• •

⦿ The synergies that make
the agora dense with fever
are not on tape but on tap
in the latest rendition
of our freewheeling
mediation called viral
in the tour guide's smoothie
lingo from the back of the bus

Whoever lingers in the passage
is bitten in the butt out campaign
aimed at the social informants
whose cell phone circumlocutions
were intercepted and translated
into policies that the man amongst
them ruled out of order out of
dispensation out of the pleasure
of the crown out of the envy of
humanoids out of the silence
of the hams out of the flora
flying in your face out of
the arms of membrane rip tides

• •

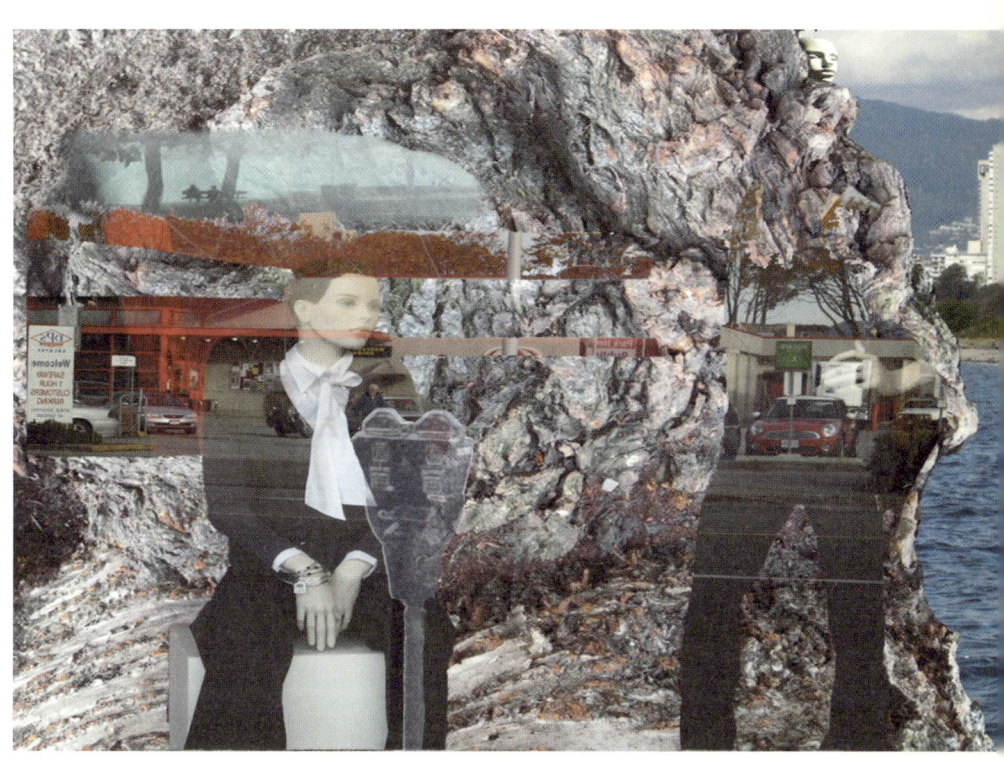

↙ Minuscule specks turned up beneath
the surface of common things setting
off forensic speculations that reached
into the folds of systems heretofore
unnamed in the routine procedures
that had come to enhance the daily

"If you follow the line of forethought
you get entangled in the nests of being"
was the slogan devised to foresee
the leakage between things as if
the things themselves were in
cahoots with the fine line threads

Elsewhere the footsteps were softer
as the cushions of the soles treading
so lightly on the cobblestones were
heard to mutter sweet jargon to one
another in defiance of the injunction
not to expose the frailty of the codes

The anxious as a measured conduit
of the common properties visible in
the haltometers erected in select sites
were known to resonate with bauds of
sound bites as the inflamed frame to
the garments of their distress signals

The affront has to do with copyrights
patents branding all the paraphernalia
that strip the doormat of its right not
to be trampled that chant "mine mine
mine mine" in a post-historical rampage
that guns down the freeway all the rage

The feline qualities of this confined intensity
bear witness to a time and place that
dissolves even as it rasterizes the evening
stroll down the busy thoroughfares while
the buses come and go and the green grocer
quietly takes in the produce on the sidewalks

Such astonishment you say as you too get
absorbed in the digital non sequiturs that
enter the dream of the already blanketed sea

• •

🖉 What expectation
standing there at
attention all day

What scream is
recognized as

a sign of the living

Go ahead let loose
a hurricane of vocables

• •

for George B

↙ We often queried the early evening light
when the scents of another era courted
the maple branches canopying the street

A quiet snail about to cross the sidewalk
made for a parable in an otherwise loose
attempt to conjure the comfort of rhyme

The shoe store had all versions of designer
runners that the market could bear as i
looked down at the bathos of my own

There must be a designer body awaiting
on the other side of the makeshift percept
that came to mind and then exited stage left

The perspective of the sea in the distance
with the sky designed by power lines (don't
photoshop them out please, not until later)

The dissolve deludes us into thinking the
street is a coach that pulls into town at noon
bringing news of the war on other shores

The terror that contains error comes out of
the blue corridors where horsemen trample
the disappearing bodies on the other side

In the silence of the mannequin is the location
that reaches towards the latest buzzwords that
fork out more than monetary conflagrations

The tyranny of the commodity prods its arms
and torso to hang loose while the garments
hang tight on headlines unfurled in the doorway

The ink had already dried when the internal
combustion engines disseminated their gaseous
opulence as if the reeds could be so modified

Beads of a rampant hoardiness marked
the boundaries of designer ramparts that
allocated symptoms to rueful dispatches

The restive figures rustled the leaves that
forgot to cling to branches in the time taken
for the snail to make it to the other side

· ·

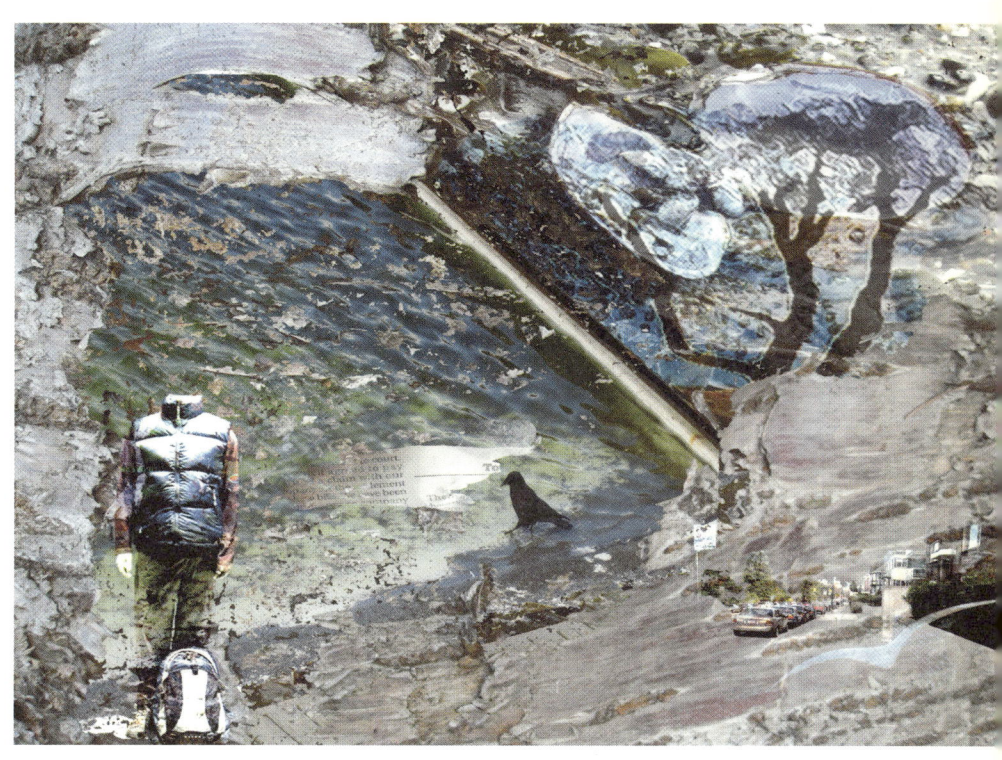

A Walk on Granville Island

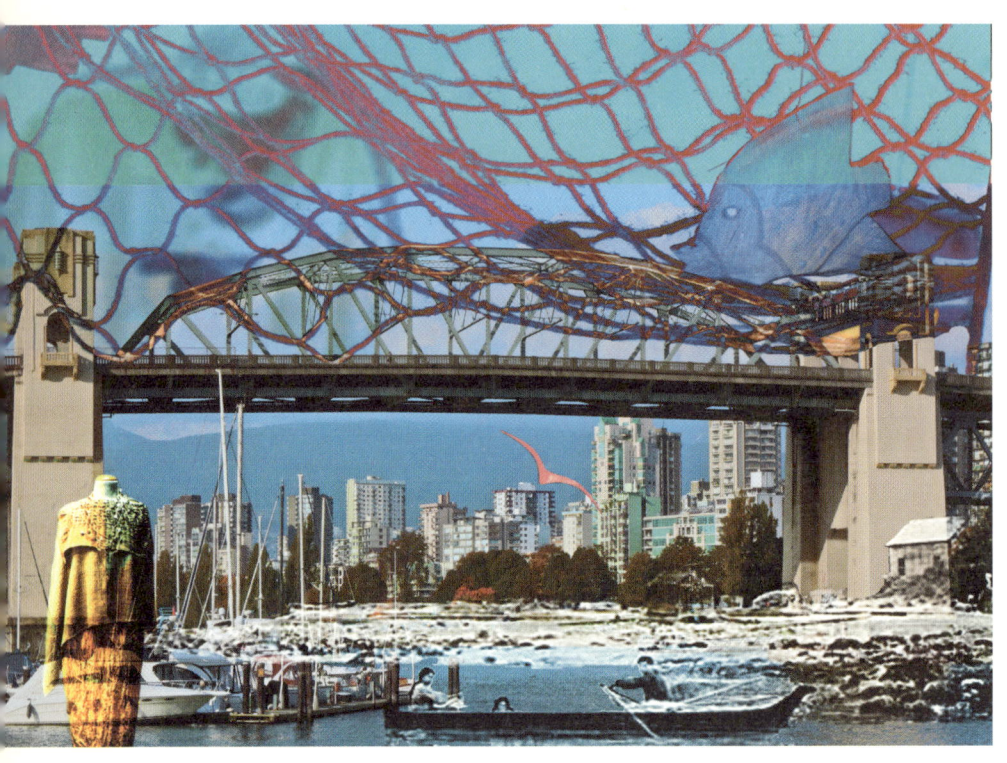

⚹ Today the rambunctious gulls (above)
squawk about the resurrection of sky
lines / the hallowed out angles that
festoon our gregarious sentiments

The social but paranoid crows (below)
discourse on the lowly virtue of hand
picked local produce / feigning the
trendy bundle of crossed purposes

Once the sprays of memory juices
breach the already docile insights
of the forlorn cultural critic eating
concepts on the planked boardwalk

We squeak an effervescent discontent
as throaty bellows from the pilings
pay no attention fees to ransack
the shafts of light for an audio feed

One day this land is yours to alienate
Son / lest you forget these planks kick
about the inflated stature of / well
statutes and their blandished comforts

Remember the price of submission
in the salted visage on the promenade
and its "not for display" old footage

· ·

⬋ These consumers in motion
have no name tags no ids
to drift off to dreamland
in a carnivalesque pitch
that cannot be notated

It could be that a walk
along the seawall arrests
the detached thought
keeps at bay the resilience
of thighs and the canvas

Let the rain mosey down
the waterproof garments
in a canopy of charms

It's not so foolish to stoop
over the edge of the pier

Not so foolish to brain
storm the refracted light

• •

↙ Whereas this cluster of shoppers with
draw hope from dangling pronouns

And whereas this bridge that con
joins resists the run on the sentence

And whereas this designated place
mat is tight lipped on migratory commas

And whereas this market erected in mid
stream feeds on the veins of creeks

And whereas this not for sale make
shift canoe replicates the idea of passage

And whereas this reverse of water con
flates the drainage of seductive fillings

And whereas this island stands as trade
mark to the buoyancy of socialite codes

Let the rhetoric flip its blissed nominals
on the farthest reaches of its distemper

Let chains of recurrence picket all
the wickets on the chagrined boardwalk

Let fruit (o raspberries) in basketry
collapse into circuits of belonging

Let no wreckage patent the pillage
or haunt the glowing in the village

• •

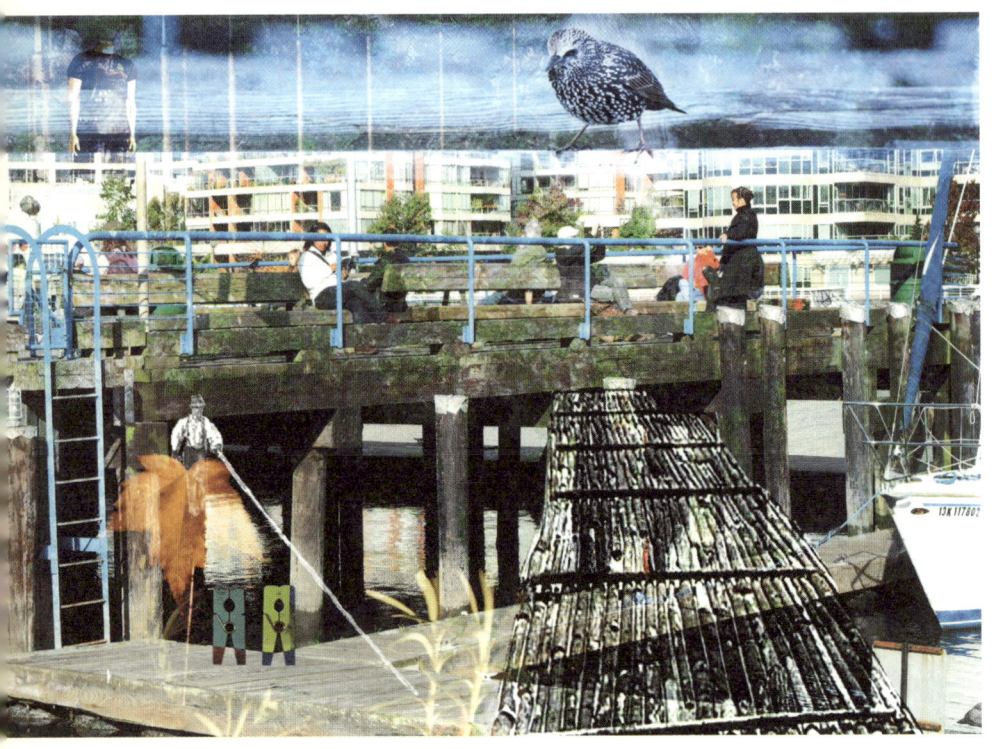

↙ Only yesterday, yes only
yesterday the bottle necks
were safely maintained

Now someone called long
haul seeks to bottle entropy
as a brand to die for

You can never have enough
of odds (and evens) on the
shelf life of security tickets

The exchanges grow paths
integral to quantum aptitudes
wherein percepts intercept

Now those subcutaneous
neuronic nudges seasonal in
industry what's in or out

In the latest market crash
capital shot itself in the
foot registered as a hit

So pectoral outlet in a fit
accrued new butt lines to
reconnect the ancient dots

All claritas the prophecy
etched in the mouth
that feeds this island

      • •

for Rita W

↙ If you were to walk
off this landmark pier
and hold your pose
for a sidelong glance
what would it look
like on the descent?

Where are the trap
doors that snap
shots of the harbour
in its comely doldrums?

How to explain to the
kids feeding the pigeons
the etymological drift
of the Arterial Highway?

Look it up in the dream
almanac of memorabilia
in the lost causes that
bewitch the clichéd ambit

There's the still born fancy
of one Jack Price (yes Price was
his name) who campaigned
on the slogan that "real progress"
would entail the removal of all
the waters under the bridges
and voilà so much real estate
to boot for Jack Price "False
Creek is nothing more than a filthy
ditch in the centre of the city"

We could all be skate
boarding on False Creek
and our civic parties
would be free of Dragon
Races and regattas of all
sorts wouldn't ruin our
slumbering condo moment

That viscous wind blown
video of pliant asphalt
might have been a
seawall of the rapt mind

In any case do you remember
the lovely Mrs Percy Nye?

She who in 1891 reported
"False Creek was so quiet
on a Sunday we could hear
the Indians singing at their
services on the reserve as far
as our place on English Bay"
from our place on English
Bay "we used to sit on
the shore and listen"

So let's rendezvous the
appellation of muskrats
smelts salmon crabs clams
the glossary of eco-friendly in
the chemical bath of this inlet

Or would you rather wash
your hands of this stuff?

• •

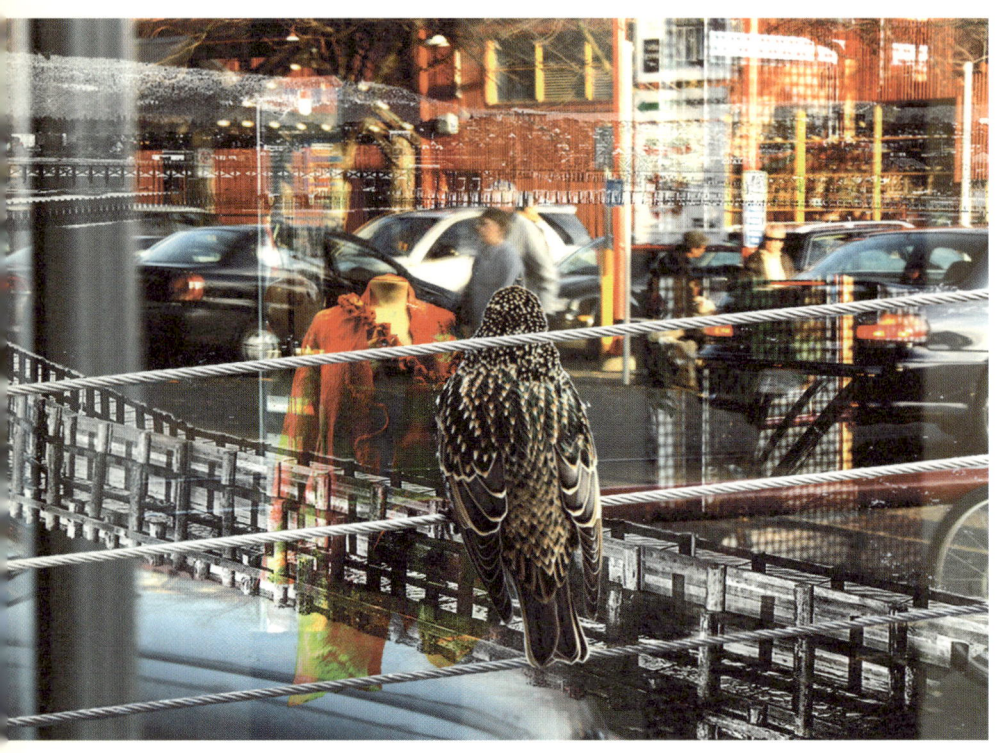

↙ Why not embouchure the fashionable
the ripe and ready the oh my god i must
have that armature as if it could abandon
us to the zero in their designs on you

It's a shame to go disheveled in our
street clothes without proper witnesses
for the youtube momentum of our
fleet transplants across global monitors

Come to think of it why not come to my
senses with legs outstretched for the island
of fair trade without those nasty flashpoints

But please note the improv clique of pigeons
of all ages bobbing biometric heads for seeds
displacing the frenzies inside the camera lens

Now of all times are the conduits that raise
eye-brows among the consumers without license

You got it when the opportunity strikes is
a fire drill but do not panic you don't want
to drive the whole market to ratchet wait for
the season to discern what rot is all about us

We are left to ponder why those
tulips grow only on that side

Past the connaissance
Past even the watchful tides

• •

🖋 Every time we break a resolution
when an impulse to utter flourishes
i urge without adequate compensation

The swell wave made by the oceanic
histrionics by the mannequins are sold
through the layaway on hold

It's a matter of belief in the panorama
around the mobile shoppers

You believe then or
when i informinate you

Let us go then you and you and you
before the market closes all we have
are the track suits on our backs each
gut wrenching outfit recorded for
posterity on our minds bent to wards

Organic silences weigh in at double
the rate of those inflected with pesticidal
harmonic brand through subtle alternatives

Mannequins need to consider the delicacy
in these fades of fission friendly (FFF)
when to hold shape is utterly composure

· ·

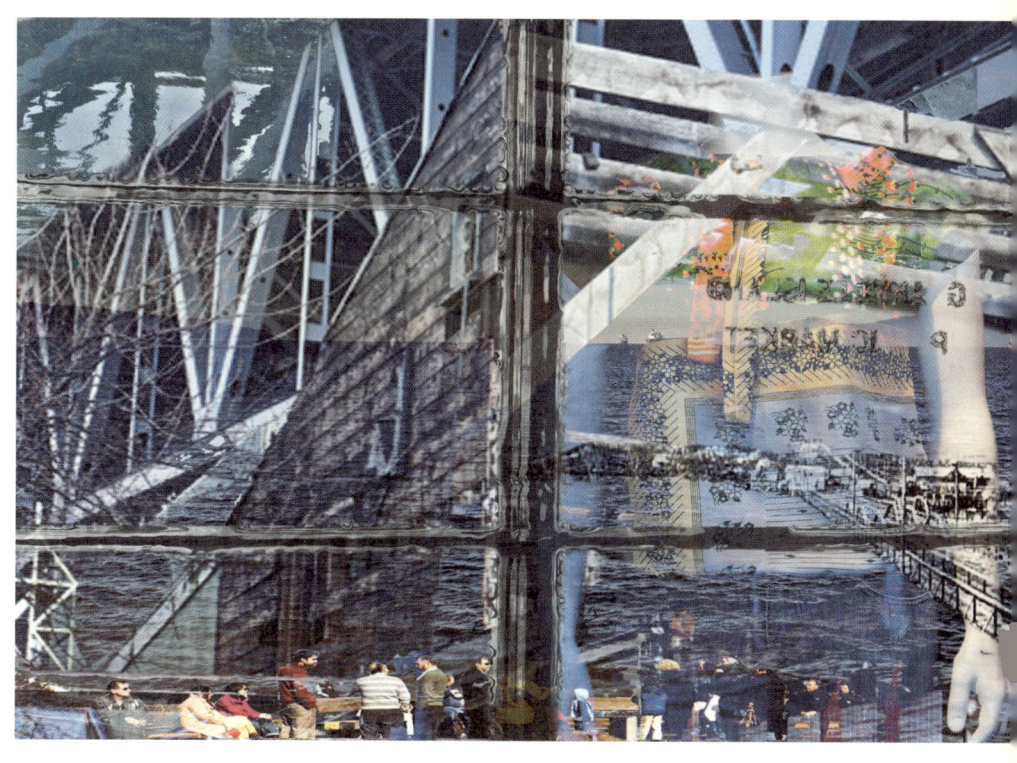

↙ When we tripped when the ocean
floor played tricks on our gait
when his gaze dissolved when
he fell into the s-shaped moment
when it was that time stood still

Why do clichés come to the rescue
why do we ask are you okay does
your watch need to be reset why
are we beset by these disarming
circumlocutions why does the
chain link fence signify time
ill spent when we thought well
spent in the rear view mirror

Small arterial rivulets service
nutrient creek excess segues

His skin a resin akin to perforate
parcels of land reclaimed to feed
the maws of industrial seasoning

All the bargains of truce pastures
of slopes in staged decline in finagle
with bated breaths taken on the lamb

Cuticles abrasive corrosive solvent
salacious undertows beauty filial

An alloy in the market retention awash
in templates down the rain filled crevasse

Don't hallow me out say let the ravine
rave on say consign the completion to
the ulterior motive say even handed
rifts are best left stranded in sedges

Don't stockpile the washed out effect
and don't believe me when i say
sediment roams like no other

Have faith that shallow
has no low shell to squander

The rum in the stocking
packs a mean punch

Lines that say fallout are
beset by twangs of silt

       • •

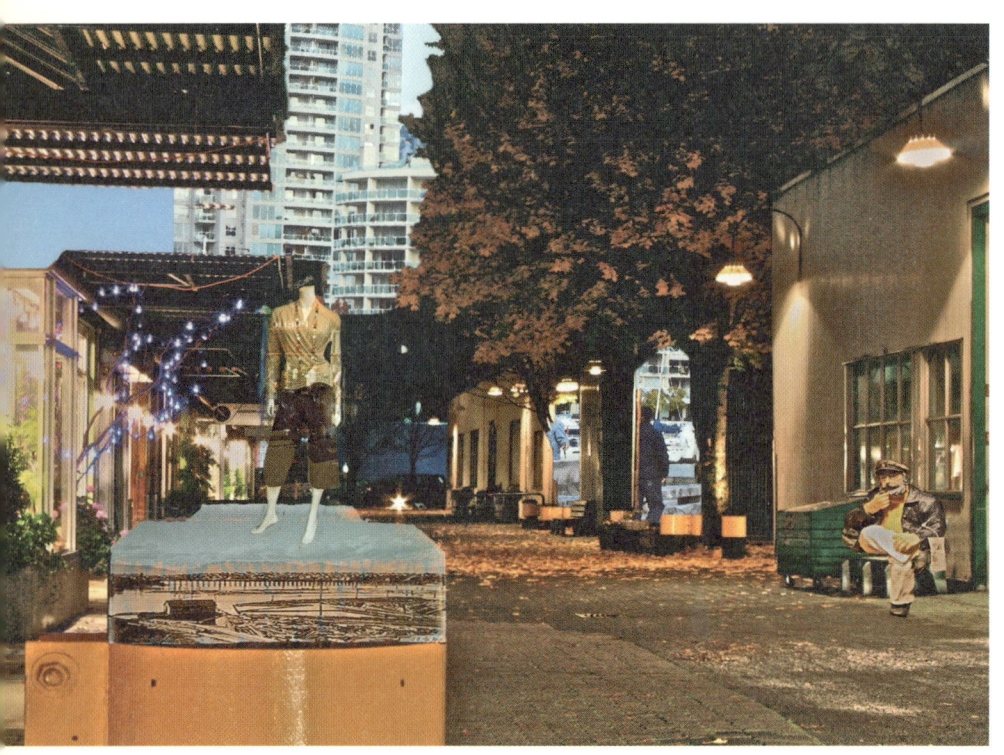

⬐ Do you believe that all these
waters have not been charted?

These instruments on the dock
are tracking devices

They barely hold together
under intense scrutiny

Once upon a time one could
say there was an all purpose
supermarket in this solidity
that could not have been

For instance here in the crook
of a water colour scenario
a dissolve of say brown and /
or blue with a smidgen of grey
in the hand me down clouds spoil
the mandarin oranges pyramidically
poised to capture our fancy this

i wonder about the starlings that
congregate around the passengers
who dole out food substances freely
with an élan usually associated with
those with gifted bodies and minds

· ·

for Ayumi G

↙ *Where would we be*
without the sea?

Likely, not here
Or like, not here

It was the sea carried
George Van Couver into
English Bay in June of 1792
exactly 300 years after
Columbus' historic voyage

English Bay lay in waiting
for Couver and his sweet ship
June who was descended from a
set of numbers, likely the code
for a lucky charm bracelet

Did Couver and Columbus then
meet on the seas in a virtual
space of mutual refinement?

Exactly 300 years is a dead give
away for the tags voyage and historic

The question why Couver was born
and why in Vancouver of all places
is a lacuna in the fold up tale

But listen, *mariners charted*
our globe for us

(Much gratitude

Remade our world
from flat to round

(More gratitude

Ushered in the centuries
that have given us today's
'global village.'

Now we're getting fusion
with the centuries now we're
getting baseball teams bowling
leagues real estate companies
the whole shebang all at once

We mean the *sea trade has forged
the links that unite the earth's
nations in a single marketplace.*

Those mariners mapped
the seas that joined the nations
that sprouted from earth to market
to market to choose a transgenic pig

Sorry not today May of 2010
exactly 97 years after Snauq
villagers were uncharted
by Couverites on speed

"Too much village is infectious"
wasn't the headline in the daily

      • •

↙ What was later identified as toxic soup bore marked
resemblances to the expectations of the research plan
(see study commissioned by the city fathers circa 1916

Not only were the radial demarcations in contradiction
to ascribed emotive qualities of the imagined endgame
the sheets of slogans let loose a corpus of the margins

That era before the markets for water sumptuousness
were measured in the purer facets of a dialogue
that relied on strings of overworked adjectives

The island arose out of the mud of flats that had
weathered the doxa of fervent breaths for generations
before the arrival of telescopic plumes running on empty

When rumour oft told of breached fortresses/ramparts
and the logic of logs that lined the pockets of
diehard coalitions that sought the jewel of the inlet

Enter then the fillers those with ingenuity and where
with all to take chance on the limb to turn water
into territory into the modal call of the ages

(See the reference to historical markers such as
plaques benches inscriptions archives and the
word of the mouthful that speaks of enterprise

Once mellow times were all the rage except in instances
the degree of want looked westward in blood lines
governing a passable living before the final clinch of rest

Due diligence one said was the watchword little known
to work wonders on those who can taste the doable last
resort of the virtual lovers who cast their nets out dubiously

  ••

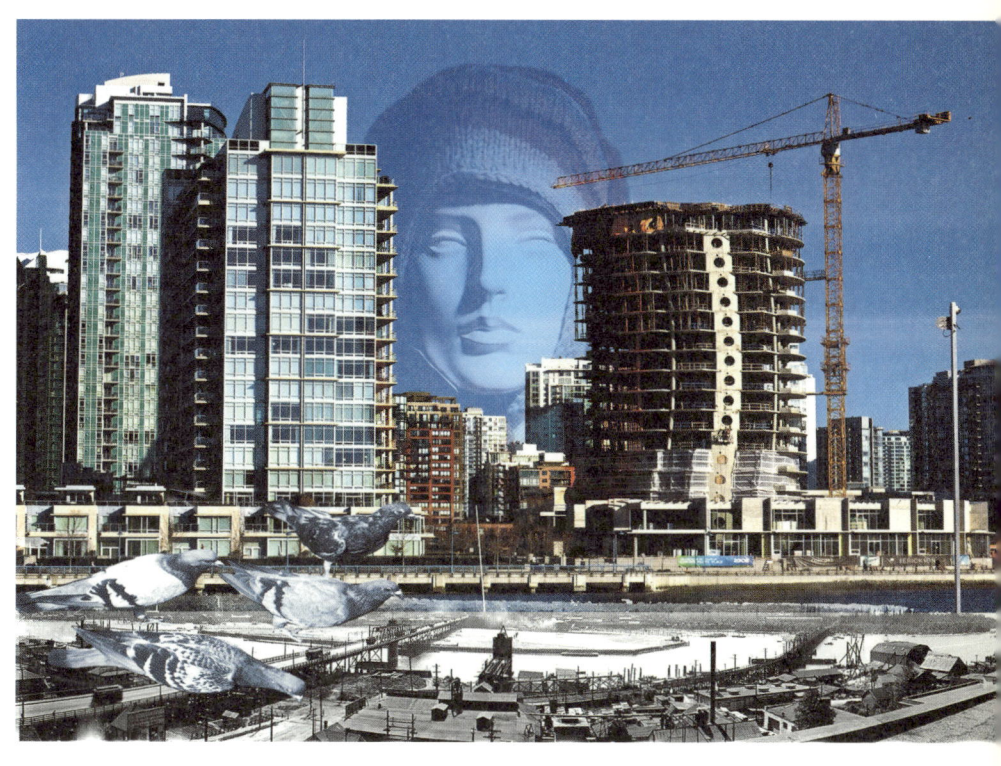

Viral Travels to Tokyo

for Kirsten M, Cindy M, Scott M,
and Monika G

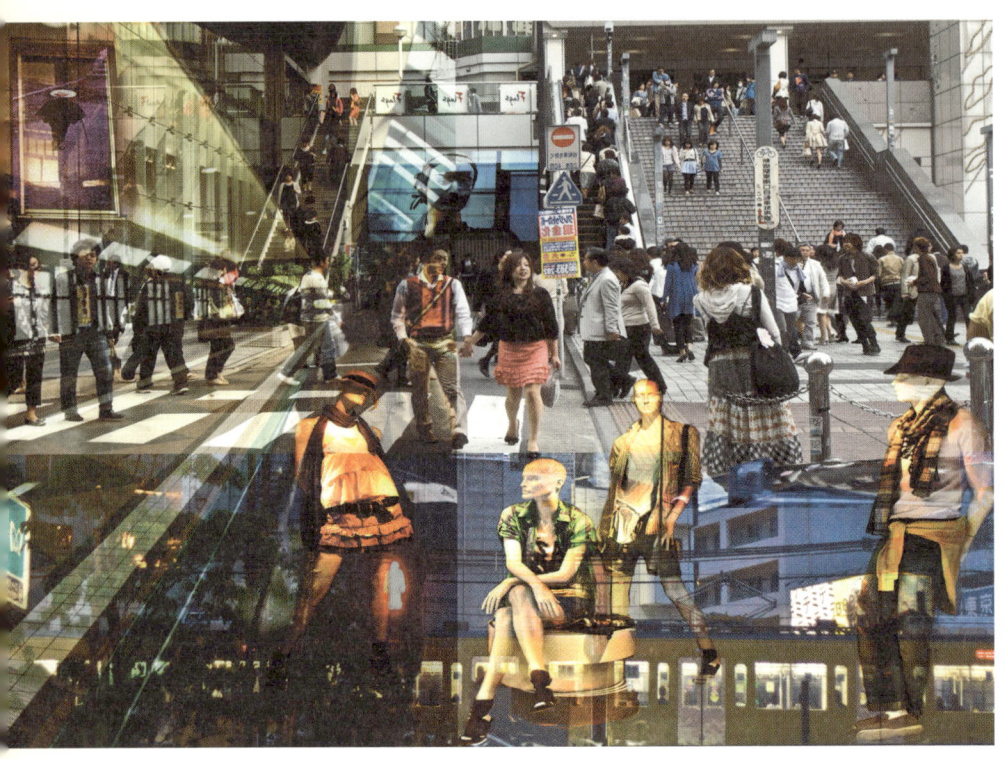

𝕃 Viral must be chuckling all the way to the supermarket. Yesterday at Narita when AC3 landed a cadre of masked officials in blue hospital garb as in monitoring a contamination site swept us with an instrument geared to measure temperature levels. One poor soul trapped in its body was circled with red stickers and became in that instant the hot zone. The rest of us were ushered off with hand signals stirring the suspect air.

We are the guinea pigs the lowly relatives of the swine targeted for the global ruckus disseminating we hate to say it just like a virus that seeks a host (an us) to reproduce its kind. Colonies of restless sojourners bent on global migration to forge mobile identities.

In this surge of hybrid coalescence our bodies are conducive to being human or not. Viral as infrastructure finds voice in molecular networks in forms of "social distancing." Instead of shaking hands let's bump elbows and forget hugs and kisses. That's so pre-H1N1. Physical contact of any kind is so socially passé.

A new clothing line Virality features sleeves with nestled gloves when the need arises and a collar that sprouts a mask for near contact scenes such as in elevators where instant gratification is delayed. The fashion industry has gone gaga with the ripe possibilities of unheralded profits from this latest evolutionary phase of what has been dubbed viral globalization. A globalization all but invisible and dependent on a host of monitoring devices gone post-visual post-traumatic and tellingly post-pig.

turbulence zones
in on Tokyo's light

winding down clock
time it's already tomorrow

before today is done
the recuperation queries

who is that masked gaijin?

it follows that nothing
is irretrievable in the descent

Where is the hot seat located? Where does the wand seek to land?
What if the thermal vane spins out of whack? The clipboards hanging
on the inspectors are blank and look more decorative than rowdy.
One seat over, K sees they've been tied over their shoulders, as if
improvised, with some plastic rope with frayed edges. Hedge against
the tide, so we suppose. What's with the goggles in the fractured light?
We wear our metabolic suits in neutral colours for the duration.

𝜘 The bantering streets of Tokyo and my favourite
shopping stop Shibuya wear the shimmer of
new operatives that show viral has dalliance
on its side. The masked pedestrians approach
each corner as a task to be accomplished what
ever other terms like mutate enter the equation.

Distance only figures a desire for more intimacy.
Cheek to cheek lip to lip the others find a way
to make hay out of the breakdown in protocol.

When i first laid eyes on the mask we thought
out loud that the disguise was an outlaw fugal
arrangement made to measure for the influx
of a stream of consciousness not the old-
fashioned kind but purposefully made for
our global fidelities. In the end it's the
same old body that slips through the net and
finds its own watering hole beneath the radar
of oblivious gazes. Don't get me wrong. The trick
is in the way the hands caress the tree branches
in the new interspecies mode of daydreaming.

who can read the insignia
of its intelligentsia network?

the face masks are a dead
give away that the forks in
its nodes of telepathy
are fluid and capacious

can you not hear the
chuckling in its wings?

this viral dispersion disproves
the untimely death of history

it's a stroke of genius

Seventy-five years later and Hachiko still waits, his loyalty all but forgotten in the heat of consumer movement. The viral overtures of the mannequins do not rustle the feathers of the pigeons. The friendly hearts at Shibuya stare into a hundred million cell phones.

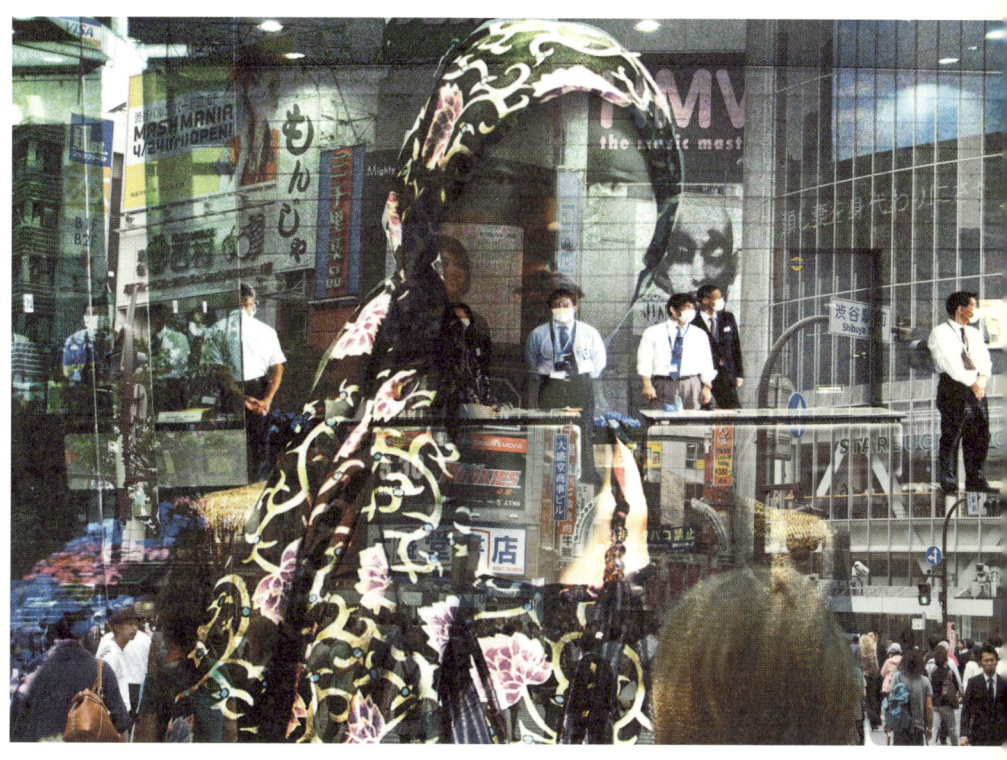

🖉 Tissue paper thin
thinner tissue of

Inaudible strangers
amidst the spectrum

Of strummers enfolded
in the mock orange

Style of cell phone
"manner mode" that

Hue and cry i can
recall only figments

Of each decade in
the templates of the

Side show slides the
retinue cross the retinal

what was that noise?

the intake of breath

a donation of sorts?

out of sorts

assorted?

all speeched out

The keitai or cell phone is so ubiquitous that the "manner mode" or silent mode is normative. Texting is all in the course of a day. Playful characters, a host of emoticons, spontaneous photos, animated figures all make for a sumptuous digital escapade for consumers of all ages and temperaments.

🖎 So much is left out
of the account as if

All details skipped
ahead of the recall

Where in the rapid
fire frames the train

Window makes is
the shelf life of i?

If the i in site is
befriended by ste

How much sweeter
can bathwater be?

The present fallows
the memoire in its

Tensile grip and
grime and gripe

Swishing the name
plate in a flourish

in korea town
the little yellow
melons wrapped
in cellophane on
styrofoam plates
are served up
to the customers
in the splendour
of the evening
only here
only here
only here
she said

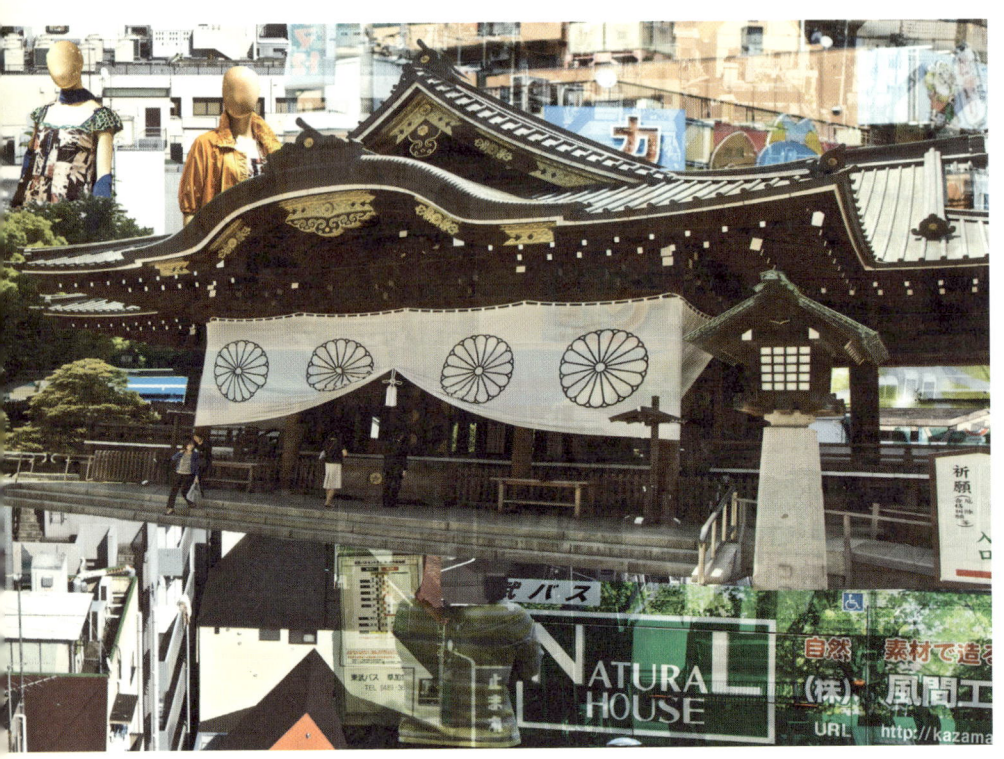

🖉 From the walls of the shrine museum
the faces of the dead forever young
bear witness to a trail of notebooks

Of the young whose post memories
bear witness to the trail of blossoms
falling in the mirror of their gaze

The sanctuary a meeting fomented
in the ashen fables of formidable
auguries gone the way of petals

Fallen arches and the relics under
glass cases the rusty water cans the
gas masks the fateful model plane

Bear witness to the underside of the
gleam world in the exterior memory
of techno sounds the echo of echoes

Mournful is hardly a modifier for
the entranced sutures hanging like
mementoes that divine the wind's ill

we need to place
our mind inside
our mind so that
the rhythm takes
our voice

talk to me take
what the lips
gather in meeting

host turns
to host turns

*Everywhere there are warnings against taking photos in the Yasukuni
Shrine museum. Artifacts of the Special Defence Forces or the
kamikaze ("divine wind") are laid out side by side in display cases.
In this buffered place the vanquished become heroes, or in the words
of the poem on a tapestry hanging in the theatrical light to hail the
Yamato spirit or "soul of old Japan": "it is like the cherry blossoms/
that bloom in the morning sun." Following the young school children
taking notes for assignments, i too scribble down what cannot be
documented on my Canon camera.*

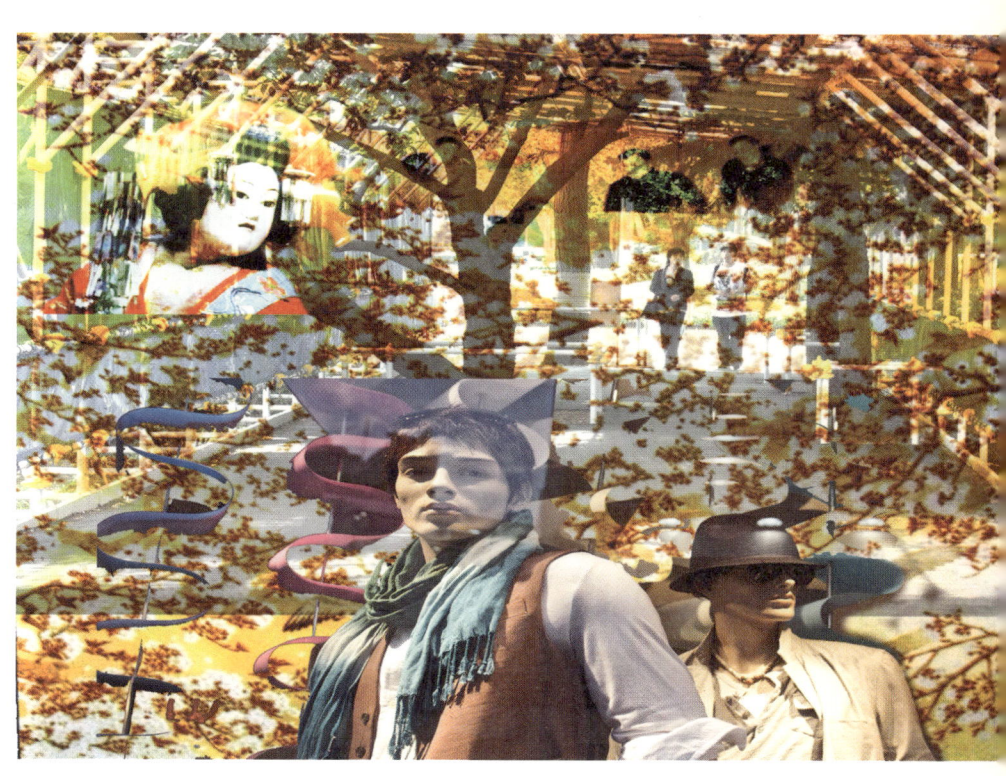

᭡ Ebisu light headed i
saw your long hair
trail the soft gust
up the stairs

45 years is not so
long i not belong as
finger points to me

The one long frame i
can long do without

You turn back to i

when cumulus clouds
flaunt their forms

memory wrought
in the sidelong
glance on the
path the rain takes
to the pavement

those horizonal streaks
turn out to be laughter

after all

This once modest station with simple entrance and exit sites has become a hub of pedestrian mobility. Up and down, down and up, each segment of this station enacts a serial poem. No kidding. When my attention drifted for a second from the espresso coffee i was drinking, i swear the material conditions of my consciousness were subverted by this consolation from the past.

⚞ What foresight garnered across
benchmarks cannot be slipped
into the hip pocket on the way
to the airport. The dream augurs
as much as its lapses glitter with
the pride of ownership. Modest
mannekins quietly conceal the
opulence of the food mart
their hand gestures placating
while they direct the traffic
of onlookers. The heat made
their souls ache as the probe
inserted in their ears upped
the ante as they say on the
social veracity of the self
generated heat rising out of the
dream machine that made the
square of the station and its
every watchful Hachiko the
object of his attention. After all
he too radiated the mobility of
the viral instigation that had made
so much delay on the Tokaido Way.

even up
the eyes

seek
arches

pine needles
in that forest

i just happened to be glancing out of the side window when the heel of a young woman walking briskly down the narrow (back?) street snapped off and drifted away from her left foot. She quickly retrieved the (now?) stray heel and attempted to force it back onto her shoe. It kept falling off. For one moment she turned back, perhaps thinking that she should go back home (where?). She changed her mind and slipping the stray heel in her purse she put her shoe back on and continued walking, her heel raised to the exact level of the (new) phantom heel. No one will notice the missing appendage at Meguro Station, i'm sure of it.

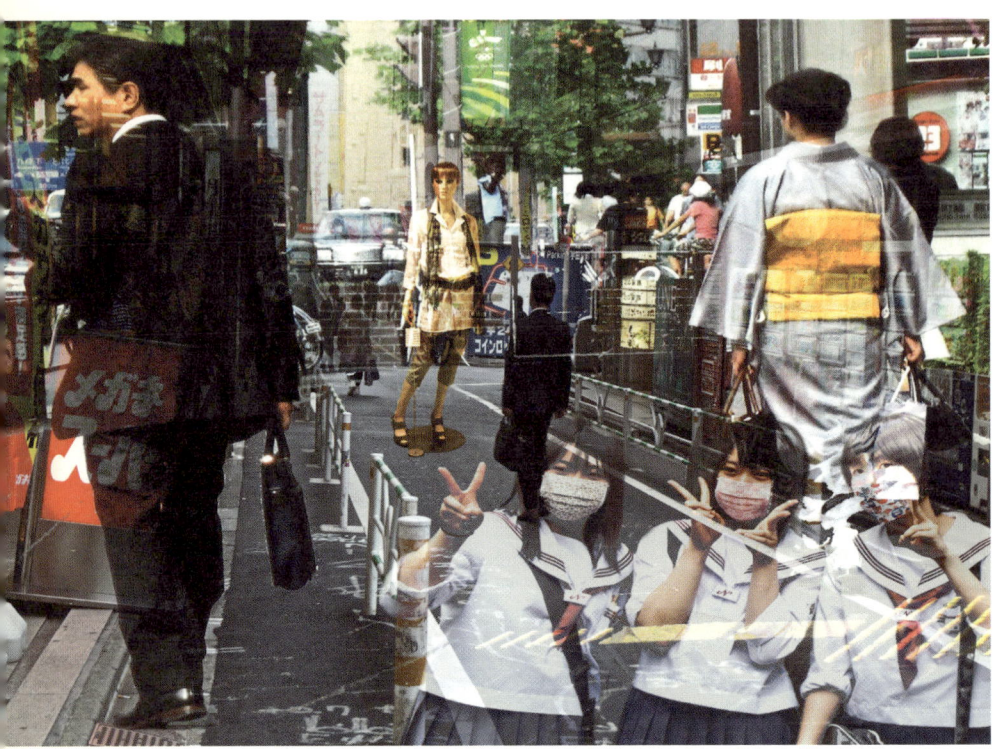

🖉 In a bid to outweigh itself Viral jumped
the rails. The feat went unnoticed in
the scientific community. Barrels of
overture were heard tumbling over
the falls. Wily roots of the translocal
made for a daydream of origins and
ends. The karada laden moisture a
balm in the mist of ancient trads.
We heard the uguisu sing for its
breakfast and then held our conference
outside the bounds of touch. The watch word
was consumer beware as it was
on the nether side. Viral is as viral
does. The act speaks volumes in
the absence of local references. Only
the sell out of masks and the empty
shelves where they had been bore
witness to its ingenuity in such dire
circumstances. Salut dear reader do
not make hay in the season of tsuyu.

me guro

eye black
die cast

a road way
a blind alley

fore cast
fore paw

follow me
grow me

me guro

🍃 A throng of crowds along
transit mirrors awash in
the sea fool of forget

Beware Lethe of critical
mass in the overflow
phenomena when

Monkeys wash sweet
potatoes in the salt
waters in their toes

Much more than a deluge
of cellular flourishes
come to pass in this

Late afternoon soft light
at Shibuya Station where
Hachiko still keeps watch

In the hubbub of migrant
souls whose voices exit
the sentinel manikins

The still points in the
wobbling pivot of the
armature of the depato

one slipped
out of grace

one note slipped
between the covers

a bank of slipped
opportunities

slipshod ware on
secure airwaves

notice one didn't
slip over the hedge

ringed round with
slip stream dreams

🖉 We doubt that
the wheel turns

just because the
axle is greased

Top down postures
are so out of fashion

One blend stage wets
(whets?) the appetite

making it well nigh
impossible to forget

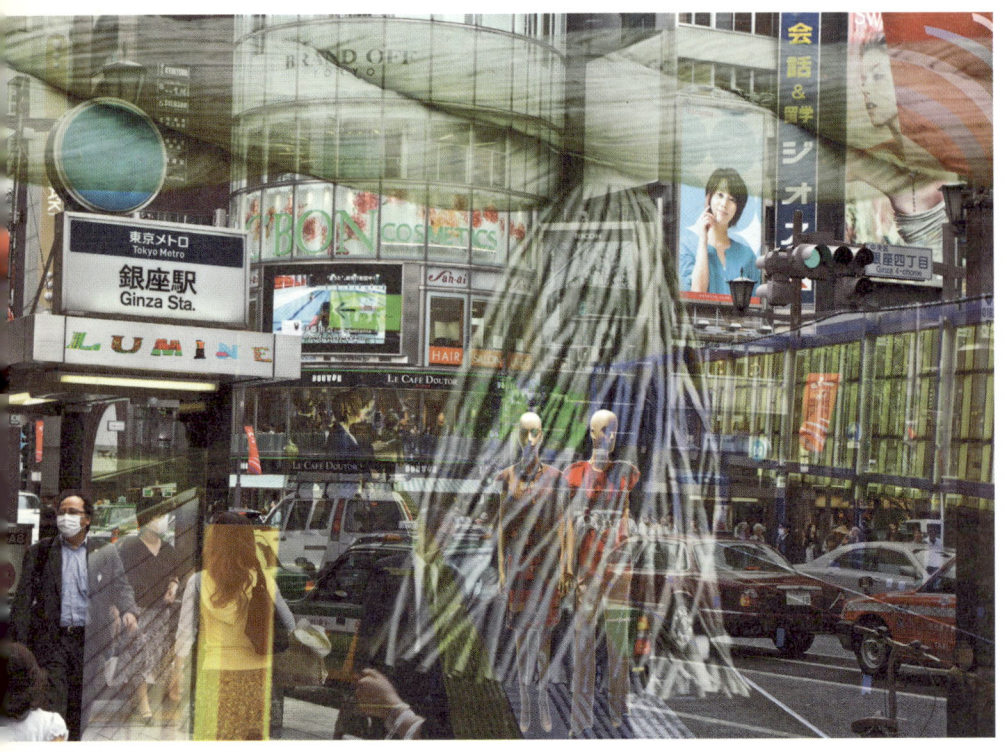

HALF DOZEN HAIKU LIKE

for Powell Street Festival

For S

Keep on sweep talking the ground
as green twirlies sweep down again
O zounds! they're calling my name

A Recent Trip

What happens when he
got the H out of Utah—
Uta! Uta! cries the ah so
spry spirit of Kiyooka-san

Reel One

Stray dirt piles on stones
beside the stoic pot : squirrel
talk to evacuate the mind's plot

Sojourner

The scooter just missed him
hugging the lane fence / almost
Japanese is never enough

Eh? Go!

At the Meiji Gakuin university
guest house off the beaten path
of Meguro-dori one unsuspecting
poet encounters his first asagohan
sentence of the day, "Please ask
caretaker when you need more lines."

Lazy Haiku

Rain
drops

Pitter
patter

Rogue
sounds

Bow
ow

THAT TREE

*The tree which moves some to tears of joy is in the eyes
of others only a green thing that stands in the way.*
— WILLIAM BLAKE, 1799, *THE LETTERS*

I say what is that tree doing in my right of way?

I mean what is that tree doing obstructing my face?

I say what is that tree doing to my block of time?

I mean what is that tree doing with its branches askew?

I say what is that tree doing with its trunk?

I mean what is that tree doing with its designer pose?

I say what is that tree doing with my consumer insight?

I mean what is that tree doing with the object of my affection?

I say what is that tree doing with my insider trading?

I mean what is that tree doing with its proliferation of buds?

I say what is that tree doing in the alley beside the overflowing bins?

I mean what is that tree doing crossing the street?

I say what is that tree doing with its hands up?

I wander what is that tree doing to my hindsight?

I sought what is that tree doing to my forethought?

I sink what is that tree doing to my wireless lapdog?

I pine what is that tree doing to my indigestion?

I mean what is that tree doing in my hip pocket?

I say what is that tree doing inside my head?

TODAY

Pretensions aside
      war is the failure of the
imagination

The breakdown in tor-
      rents of communication
unexpected yields

Specular rufflings
      those that mosey on up to
flirtatious cell lines

And habitual
      circuitry sustained
in the ravished heart

Its solace the fabular
      domicile of the consum-
er class / A wonder

Promulgated by
      media in love with
circular fancy

Fill the crevasses
      of our creature comforts to
suitcase the results

What sallies forth as
      our eyes glaze over on cue
hums a sublunar

Tune the riant crowd
      under the bridge emits an
echo of echoes

So that the flange view
      from the promontory reeks
of class privilege

It's so refreshing
      to know where you're going to
where you thought you've been

i mean the devil
        in the details
its untold quagmires

It's not obvious
        as you might assume beneath
the paper thin skin

Time to quiet the
        ghosts / Did you actually
shrink wrap it all up?

WILLING TO CHANGE

What is that wisp
of mallow coiled
up on the mat?

A feline form
in dorm?

This question rises
from an unpatented move
that desire makes

as if a chosen one
were to balance one
fingerprint and another

muzzling up docile
imprints of shoreline
as waves of discourse

But is it improper
to say discourse
in this instance?

Do we need to seek
permission for such
acts of filling the void?

Or do we avoid rueful
memories of incarnation
by other means?

Some days phrases leap
and make their appearances
in the very vocabulary
they should have doused

IDENTITY

That static noun with
so much encrustation

Even jetsam in the holds
of sand trapped ocean liners

Their whistle blowers hang
the nostalgia on wreathes

Under the latent carapace
where chamber voices

Follow the timbre of self
made stamp collectors

Such management itches
in the temperate loams

While flags wave in unison
at the alert border guards

PROSTHETIC POLITICS

for Larissa L

The power of crutches is so deceptive
Out of sight they bleed into the margins
Out of hand they assemble the social scene

As in this instance on the sidewalk
note the pattern or the way the feet sashay
to avoid the peg's unceremonial crunch

The feet i mean know not what dispossesses
them in the missed beat. Beyond the protection
of skin's integrity lie the folds of slights

You can say light's disposition if you wish
It also brings a defiance of grids and the pallid
demeanours cordoned to aid in traffic regulation

i even noted a swaggering followed by deft
physical graces that countered the militant airs
as if nothing could matter much less then

But stairways invoke the differences where
the flat rather than curved surfaces require
a concentration that exceeds the descent

Each step echoes the cultural equivalent of
a booster shot that produces the clairvoyance
of hierarchic eye contacts the splices of which
make gaijin instability a wonder to behold

Going by the book leads to vocal strain
and the worst sort of back pain imaginable

Mind you the blind steps reveal far more
blemishes than the clasp of band-aids

AM BERLIN

Does the morning light
conceal as much as
it seeks to consume?

This earnest wake
of winged fears

We've been down the
road before lit flames
of passing figures

They are strangers in
the open courtyard who
sip coffee and mediate
the anxious ravens
he pondered all day

At the intersection
the bus stop with
its air of inter alia

A shelter of crowds
A meandering amongst

Bent on turning those
syllables over again

A familiar touch
of the diaphragm

A NAGASAKI DAY

for Baco O

1

Does it matter if we
can't hear the inaudible
see the invisible?

So go buy me a muffled
horizon / Dress it
in kiddy corner turns

It always hails the most
unexpected of downpours

2

Since the shelters
were installed
the city wears

the look
of pleasure

of leisure
that cloaks

3

They wouldn't have
it otherwise

i thought i caught
the transition

No wonder
the arrangement
broke down

Blindfolded it
shimmered when

it could have
stood still

Back then

4

It was quite
an ordinary day

the horses in
Goto-machi
clopped along

the streetcar
stopped in
Hamano-machi

and families ate
quietly in Ohato

5

In the harbour
the boats at bay

the window wickets
with their signs
of glorious sites
lose their elasticity

as the typhoon's language
awaits translation

6

i am only a
transfer point

an unreliable
witness to fashion

in a network of
waning apostrophes

TEMPUS IN SIEGEN

for Mita B and Katja S

For whose benefit do the omniscient
bells toll in the now clasp of Siegen?

The seismic count resounds in each
muscle in the sway of thighs that
cross the ever whispering intersection

Set your useless watch as each temple
registers the tempus tender strikes

Even the lungs breathe in all deepest
measures as echo chambers in the
nether region of windowless frames

Counting down or up each interval
anticipates its upbeat waves in the brain
drain drawing on empty nested receptors

The scripters knoll a pilgrim's progress
to digress on how many words have you
and your backpack alleviated this day?

i too hone my tempus in the Siegen mall
the reckoning wreaks havoc in a well cured
insularity too used to being on the defensive

All tropes are costly she said as i turned the
corner and the mall door behind me left a
whiff of succour like sublime at loose ends

All the deciduous templates muffled close
ties beyond the strain of those intemperate
climes that coast a close circuit teleprompter

These bells spin diagnoses on the celestial
exploits of scopic devices that cannot be
detected by biometric infidelities that bring
a host of fortuitous fingerprints into play

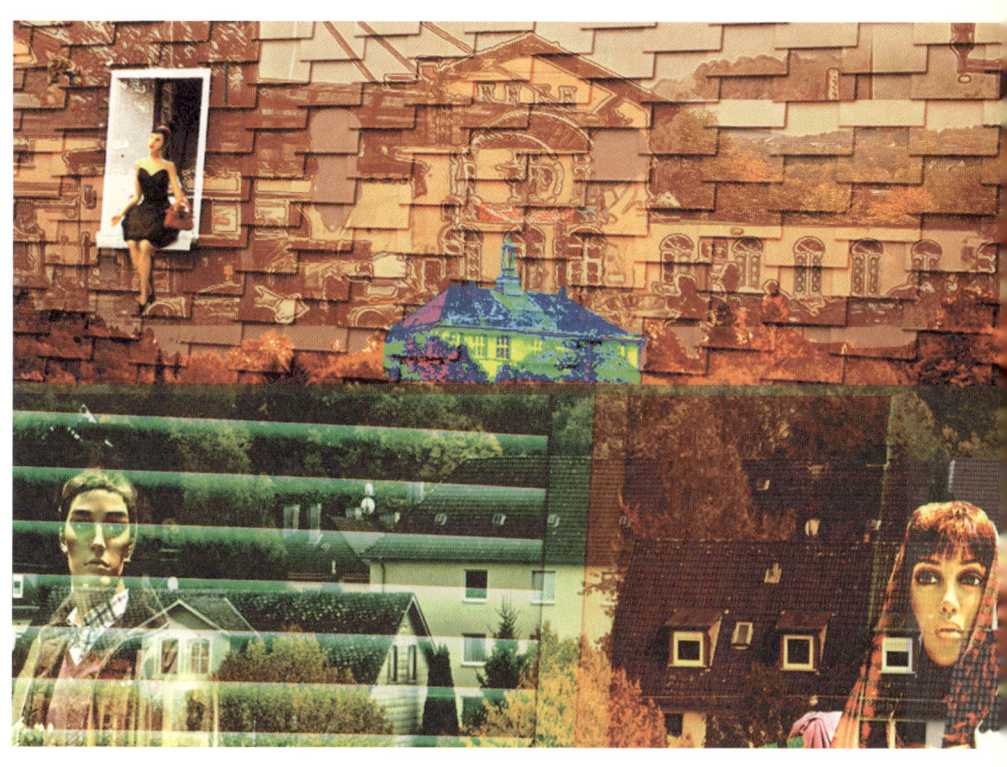

All along he thought
he understood until he
stood under the canopy.

Non-synchronous lines
so moist the earth gave
up secrets. The raindrops
gathered on cars
in the graying dawn.

History's hollow
tunnel again the
slow boat to China.

The shake up in blame
routes (no reason) haunted
him to no end.

i saw the scooter in
the beamed up showroom.

Curvilinear
all so malleable
neural indices
one level of skin.

Print bore the datum
of incendiary
tongues of flames casting
the on-lookers (unrecorded)
in shades.

For goodness sake give
the guy a break he
only gathers moss.

The evidence tastes
like ironing filings
or was it filling?

He overheard the
question while he stood
in the virtual
island in the mid-
dle of the causeway.

RAW DATA/KYOTO

> *for Smaro K*

The weight of the stroll
      of youth culture along the Kamo
on this sultry night

Feathers brush against stone
      not randomly placed / Invoke
repetitive paths towards

temporal markers
      bodies laden with / My own
sticky fingers pinch

A weight that bears the
      shoulders / As if the sounds
drifting across the bridge

were heard melodies—
      Drowsy from too much to bear
hardly audible

Against the curtain
      of unrecognizable
intonations as

the night sidles through
      back lanes of barking voices—
trails aloft in hawk

Do think the time has
      come to abandon all hope
of retrieving the

weighted stones strewn re-
      distributed according
to rank files / The river

glitters against the
      rowdy outpourings in each
syllabic raiment

The crows earlier
        dropped their guarded postures and
regrouped only after

the young black cat slipped
        under the pilings / Tell me
more hesitations

stand alone releases
        motion me to get on with
it / Palpitate as

Implantations of
        bios as far away place
that admits error

FLIGHT TO KAMLOOPS 9/9

My mother said dash-it
whenever she got angry

Strange how such a courtly
word could carry such punch

So now i look out the window
of this dash-8 and down there

The browning hills of Kamloops
look like mounds of—

Oh excuse me
"deep deep earth"

Cloudy and Clear

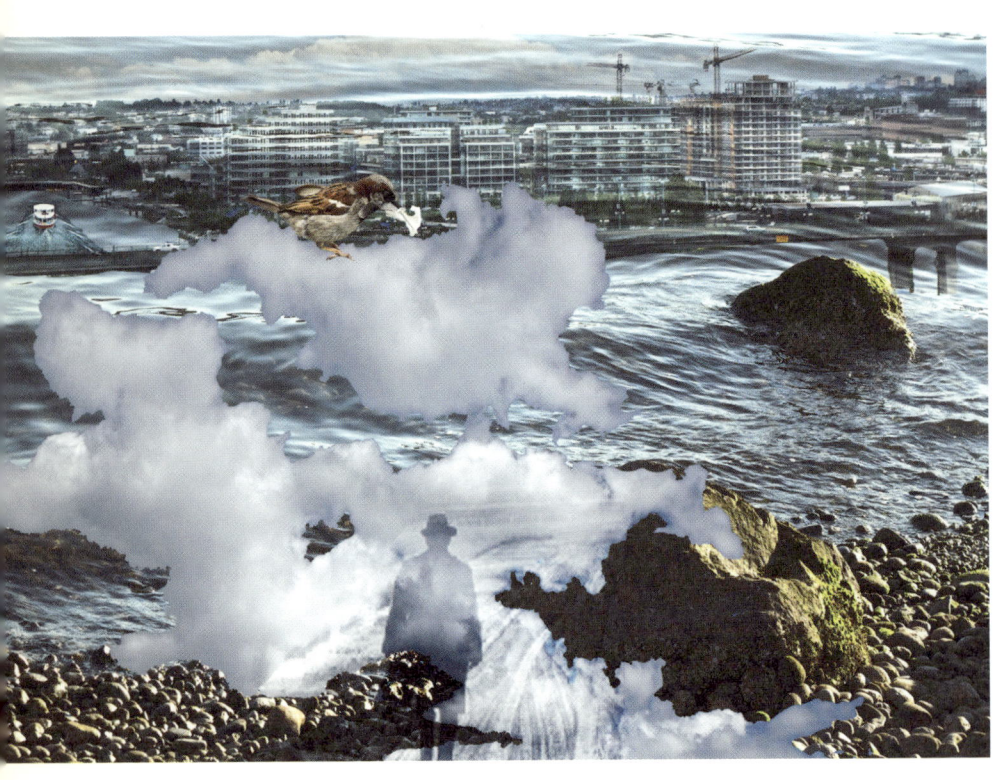

CLOUDY 1

SEAWALL AMBIT

Ambling is an art
a function of cloud talk
unfurling its tableaux

Each step notes its
finite aura of intoned
synchronic oracles

As if we were to come
upon a placid lake
composed in faint

Echoes against what
we heard as the cloud
ducked behind the line

↝

We belong to the amble
seek rest on the pivot

slide across the seawall
with little regard for snap

shooting tourists leaning
against the railing their

cell phones on alert for
buzz of media sent along

out reaching wings of a bevy
of crows circling overhead

One overheard another say
bellow below the currents

→

You couldn't know ambles
even in their occurrence

The haptic stance works best
in the absence of furlongs

of energy when to miss the event
says it over again and again

→

What about the amble of least resistance?
the amble that calls to its opposition hey

What about i'll be okay if i breathe deeply
and in step of soft shoes beneath the radar

Don't count on your assumptions to keep
you afloat on ingenuity and the deft move

Primacy resides in the gentle waft of spirals
trailing their belongings and subduing none

→

The abbreviated interlude
spokes in a wheel

turns around under the
cumulus quotients right here

where dog walkers follow
the rhythm of paws

PLEASE

Breathing space has
its idiosyncrasies

Belts out its song
in a dogged fashion

Explanation comes
to nothing to listen

Dumbfounded as
the op i ate gives in

Breathing doing
its own thing

→

The thing about things
they are never about

Surprise them or
downsize them

Prize them for
liberating desire

All told it's the irritant
that prompts difference

Ready to rouse the most
tone deaf of citizens

→

If the citizen is a thing
and if the thing is a body

If the thinging of citizens
and if the bodying of things

Now i'm getting confused
Now i'm getting conned and fused

All bent out of shape
is a true thing in deed

→

Nothing relieves
the deed of time
more than motes
in the margin

→

The margin
forewarns

Aim high
aim low

Don't go
whole hog

It's unseemly
to hang out

As if privilege
were in such

Socially inept
postures of plenty

The oinkment
is applied

Coolly without
undue hesitation

How else to re-
cognize the good /s

When RK talks about a lemon
he doesn't talk about the lemon.

The lemon does the talking
and he listens.

And in tent lies.

→

Did he really call to Smaro?
Was she really in the kitchen?

How did she really hear him?
What signs did she really use?

How can we really fathom
his alleged circumambulations?

→

My old professor used to say
T.S. Eliot always looked as if
he'd just bitten into a lemon.

In his lemon poem RK set aside
trad and the individual talent
and caressed the lemon instead.

→

One time I met RK at the Frankfurt
airport or he met me in the crowd
rushing through the exit doors.
Let's talk lemon, I thought he said, as
we boarded the train to the city.
Sure enough the landscape turned
lemony before our very eyes and we
knew, yet again, that we were lost
in thoth, passing through unknown
landscapes, and school girls giggling
at our forlorn gestures. No lemon aid.

→

The lemon is not a lemon
in RK's poem the lemon
is not a lemon is not a lemon
isn't a lemon.

→

I was about to munch on a lemon.
I read RK's poem. I put the lemon
back in the basket beside
the orange the apple and the pear.

→

Why does the lemon love salmon?
Is it kinship that matters?
A matter of fruition?
Ok, let the salmon speak.

GO FIGURE

Wonder where
the yellow went?

Go ahead call it
to appearance

Call it out of its
deep coastal water

Call it from its
perilous charts

Crest its wizardry
upon a peak wave

Hear it hop on board
a stowaway mussel

A humble nomenclature
for such tenacious acts

Sojourner without cause
a supposed hitch-hiker

Hooking a ride on tsunami
debris from old Nippon

From a long line of
Mytilus coruscus

Landing on these shores
"potential invasive species"

"It takes over all available
space / pushes everything out"

"If they're not very invasive,
we preserve them in jars"

So says VS from the auspicious
Museum of Natural History

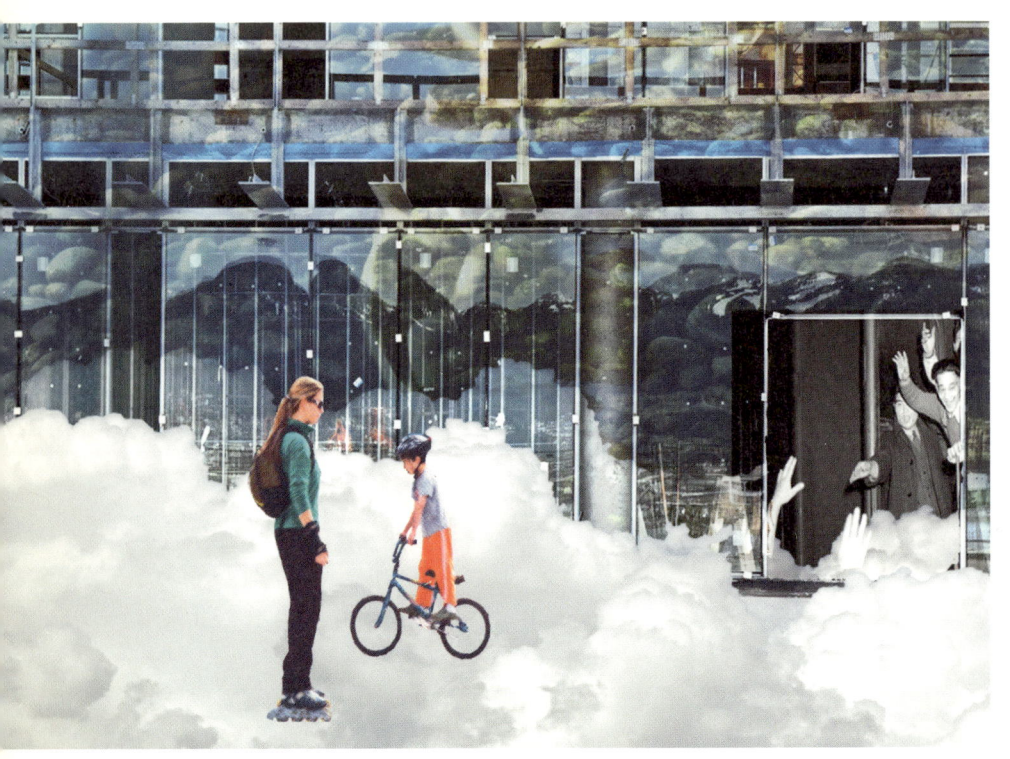

CLOUDY 2

GRACE NOTES

They throw a veil over the nettles
They rattle the overgrown chains
They think an affront garners steam

Find them in their mischief if you can
Define them as bewitched in the cam
Build a moat around their foibles

They are stubborn in their trenches
They are wrenched in their fondness
They blather about their recycled virtues

The market can bear their wheezy frenzy
It can withstand their doubled over easy
It frowns upon their sombre will power

Did you not reckon with its sedate tantrums?
Did you not worry over its reclusive software?
Did you not hanker for its viral contusions?

I for one am proud to bear the portents
Of civic duty to be the first to test wits
On the swing under the free spending tree

To be strung along on the latest clothesline
To be among the latest runway features
To be noticed to be noticed to be noticed

Registered in accordance with policy
Duty bound to the one reasonable fairway
Due to the awesome blooper on steroids

The release valve sets its value categories
According to the rhythmic atmospheric dotage
Of field notes wildly gathered on the frontier

The finals are doled out according to the stray
Or rather random filters that bear down on
The canopy's lust for soft protective eyewear

Messengers are advised not to ask for warning
Ferns in the event of outrages that cannot be
Placated by the iron tics in the public solarium

Why does dust always settle?
Why do mites always communicate?
Why do ear muffs always battle noise?

It has been some time since a nudge in the brain
Ridge allayed fears that the last bounce of suspension
Would work its magic on the signifying tubers

All alert embers slowly expired
All alert ambers slowly turned
All alert members slowly resigned

EXECUTIVE MEMO

Blind belief in the reigning dormant
services no deterrent to the valence
of tongues in a fashionable bounty

The rewarding of industry parlays
a simmering stew of malcontents
who reach for errant penmanship

The demographic rule of thumb fails
to hold the curl tightly enough for
the curvature to restrain the rush

The eerie thing about the carte
blanche wicket was the haywire
mode of governance it sprouted

The effects of which modulated
civic investigations into wastage
in the vestige of the vantage point

Seriously the leakage remained un
detected until the faucet was tuned
half degree to the left of the station

Whereupon all manner of uproar
broke loose on the commons you would
think slogans fought to temper the crowds

The weight bearing walls hung loose
when the manoeuvre in single digit mode
ran asunder on the border of expectation

A neural empathetic nudge towards
another horizon of alignments called
seasonal in the industry otherwise

A market rush to sluices that capital
calls a fit of remonstrance to accrue
interest in breast lines and butt lines

Ab lines that connect the dots fill in
for integral flows that intercept sub
cutaneous flight paths in a clamour

To be recognized when all the odds
(and evens) work against a shelf
security beyond the advent of the turn

Which all came into our ken as a series
of furry lines that emitted soft packets
(pockets?) of trans fat-free prima materia

All told the hubris spun webs of con
solable entries in the diurnal turn
of events that went unnoticed except

For the relentless voices that kept
a hedge on bets for the favoured
among those who dallied too close

To the hue and cry of crowd gatherings
in the midst of wry speeches that
extolled the virtues of visible extensors

You can lodge complaints all you want
the regressions will not falter in their
coverage of the flummoxed news agencies

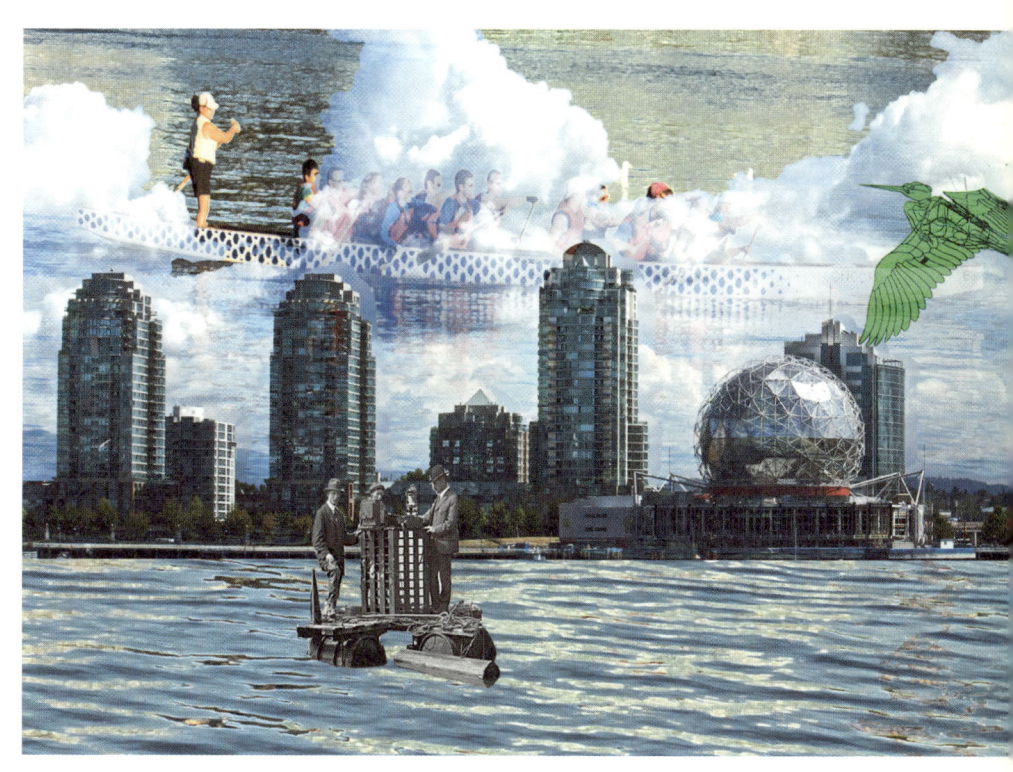

CLOUDY 3

UNRAVELLED

Couldn't believe all
had been told

Couldn't believe
it all dissolves

The reconnaissance
yields no secrets

As the evening light dons
the rubric of neon limns

We noticed that the cell
phone calleth on paths

With text in tandem
with ruffled garments

Where lingo falleth about
a raucous encounter

Two syllables in search
of most that can be said

We changeth the light
our brain rumble follows

A cascade of chords on the
off chance of noted ring

Tone the cochlear vibes
sent an instant ago untamed

Really we'd have to balance rocks
to find something more suitable

EXECUTIVE MEMO TOO

Some razzle dazzle struck
the mediascape as odd

Odd to the touch as is
Proper to such stances

Skin smooth as a daily
walk alongside a deserted

Shoreline all but the gulls
float as punctuation

Always obliging in the
somatic flow we exchange

Glances the feather on the
stair down to the water's

Hemline an altogether
after thought of undue

Proportions the sight
of the cloud a frown

In the intertidal spectacle
the light slices the anterior

Arches where the town planners
conspire with reckless abandon

Heaps of adjectival balustrades
tireless in their aspirations

We do sidle in these towers
these light reflectors that ease

The discrepant cormorants in
their nose dive into the roiling

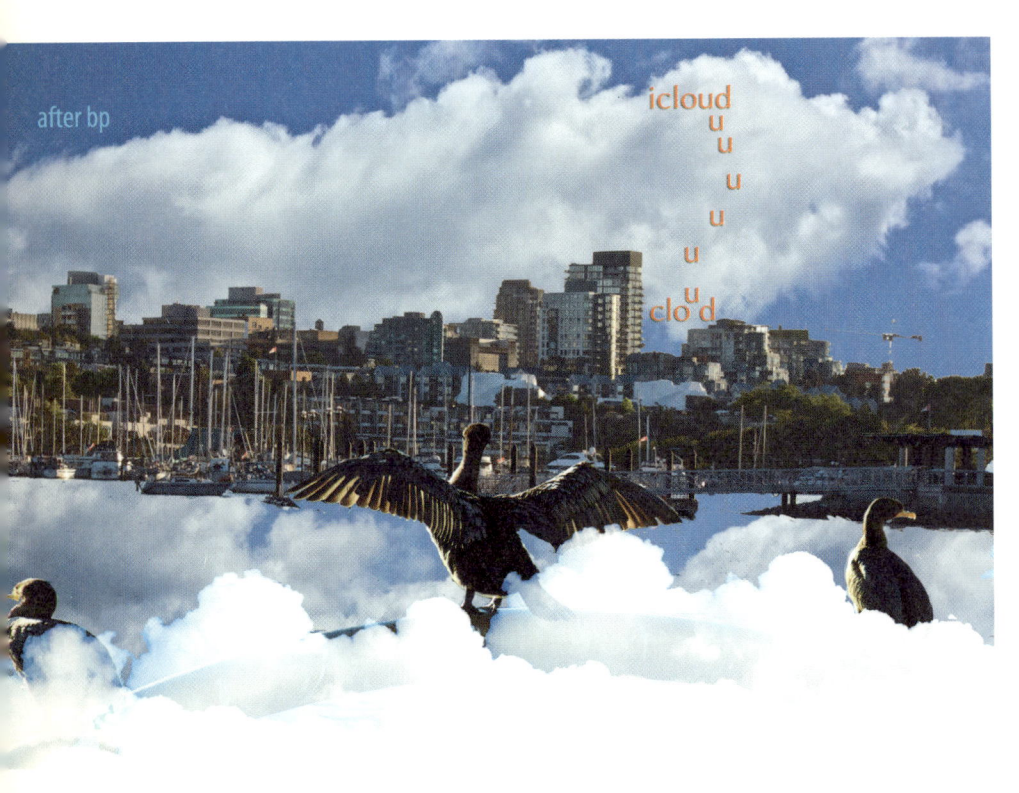

after bp

icloud
u
u
u
u
u u
clo u d

CLOUDY 4

for Ellery

ID EST

gewgaw

at what point does a thing
so coveted so sought so
much in line with the design
of anticipation so much in
the fabric of necessity?

lose its sheen its alluring pluses
its ambient contours only to
collapse into a heap on the floor
awaiting removal like today?

the pile of paper once research
so hunted down so downloaded
printed and cared for in highlight
and marginal notations so dutifully
incorporated into the daily work
load now inert in its pile with others?

reduced to paper ready to be pulped
only then to be reborn in yet another
set of soul seeking hands on deck?

*—a showy thing, especially one that is
useless or worthless*

doublethink

we grew up in that era
when to breathe the
respiratory network
went into overload

without emergency chutes
what can a kid really do
except swallow the swallow
in the cavity called his throat

all along the block the ticker
tape ticked itself off in the
lingo of its off-spring

no fountain to draw up
a corona of icons to safeguard
the long awaited turn of the key
in the keyhole of our dreams

exceptions floated by
in rivulets of snow melt
matchstick boats that
eased the advent of thaw

*—the acceptance of, or mental capacity
to accept, contrary opinions or beliefs
at the same time*

habitude

recently i've been in a funk
trying to unravel a daily
routine that has produced
no tangible means to
inhabit a colonial scene

it must have to do with the
coastal climate change in
what must be a season
of unpredictable usage

it does not help to complain
and it does not help to yelp
in foreign intonations though
the local franchise on lip synching

did help ease the pressure
to settle down into a comfortable
liaison with a feudal system
of monetary infused exchanges

let's be clear here there is no
let up in the need for transnational
devices no clear way to appease
inhabitants of the place except
in a display of rosy placards

—*a habitual tendency or way of behaving*

afflux

it happened so quixotically i was
taken unaware blindsided by
a torrent of bytes windswept
and in disarray i fell to my knees
in an aimless posture of surrender

the scrimmage was hailed as a major
breakthrough for the arteries to
regain a flummoxed overview of
serial encounters unrecorded in
observational reference points

a flux a day
a flux a way

—*a flow inward or toward a point*

consuetude

we've done that before
we've done that over and over
we've done that time and again

can't you see it's futile to change
can't you see that change is overrated
can't you see that the same is the same

i want to believe in doing so again
i want to believe that doing so again
brings down the urge to resolve

brings down the curt curtain calls
brings down the irresolute gaps
brings down the oh so icy theatre

of urban superstructures that leak oil
that leak news into the throttled outlets
that leak over the floating hardwood floor

are we sorry you've done that before
yes we're sorry that time and again
you've done that over and over again

forgive us this day forgive us the trespass
of this day this today that distresses
the past forgive us dis day with its tresses

*—an established custom, especially one
 having legal force*

divaricate

a norm is not absolute an
absolute obsolesces a norm

don't you get it?

différence is not diffidence
holds the same weight as the
norm hanging on its precipice

we waited open quote all night
for the alteration to occur and
were disappointed to learn the
changes were all in the askance
and double takes wore the latest
in the last instance so much hangs
on the way the head holds sway
i mean away from the action it
was all in the mien of the normal
close quote close shave to boot

—*stretch or spread apart; diverge widely*

fettle

i am as
fit as my
smart phone

—*condition*

mentation

it must have something to do
        with a prolonged case of memorialitis

it must be the deleterious conflation of
        consumerist modalities of perception

it must be the faithful inventory of
        preliminary routes to fierce causation

someone mentioned an unidentified
        haloed object in the slatted windows

someone whose axe is grinding
        up a meal of assorted phenomena

someone unfettered by the ancient injunction
        to bury the syllogism in a patchwork dawn

you must indulge in the fantasy
        while the choices are still wide open

—*mental activity*

ocholocracy

say what? say who?
say what you will?
say whoa?

everyone to their
own megaphone no
duty to confer no
withering hand to shake

all breakages in due time
all due dates moved to
all temporary zones

all breezes meet and
greet and bind together

all said / all done?

—*mob rule*

wen

wen did you make the connection between
bloated bodies and bloated economies?

wen was the last time you checked the rear
view mirror for an update on mobile identity?

wen promises abundance in plush surroundings
wen thrives on uneven systems of growth
wen is fruitful wen in season
wen augurs well when wen is wend

—*a growth on the skin; a large or
overcrowded city*

varmint

escapes notice in public sites of fond consumption
notices the paths of least resistance in mazes
an outlet for refused memories in holding tanks
tightens the screws on loose edges of awe
idles in ventilation systems for debaters
speaks tongues in periods of subtle dormancy
inclement under extreme weather in utterance
prefers not to be hailed by a nicknamed opponent
wonders about the curvature of cosmic love
hinders the operation of software codes in univocity

—a troublesome and mischievous person

valetudinarian

we came to the precipice
            full of optimism
and hope

overhead the sound
            of wings flapping
rang true

if history
            at any time
in its history
            could plead guilty
now was the time

it came
            in that order

the drops
            of rain
falling
            slaked the earth

beyond lay
            open land

—*showing undue concern about
one's health*

triskaidekaphobia

there is a 13th floor in our condo
but not floor 13 / each day we pass
through the triskaidekaphobia zone
and remain blissfully unknowing
of hazards we never see in our path

—*extreme superstition regarding*
the number 13

supererogation

ok i tried my best to be faithful
to the system i tried to match wits
with the master of ceremonies

my cranium muscles still ache with
longing for the foibles assigned my name

i come from a long line of heartfelt
loyal distributors of the sublime

if it weren't for the intervention
of the static makers amongst us

we'd all be grist for the modified
fields of the frankenfoods aplenty

and who among us is magnanimous
enough to give up our position in line

—performance of more work than
  duty requires

percipient

it is better to be one
it is better to be beside one
the beside one is the better one

it is not better to be butter
that butter is more amorphous
it is a drag on the economy it
does not exclude confluence
as does the better one to you

i finally get it / got it in the eye
the gauze was there for my benefit
when the social engineers who
knew better what's what in the
stigmata of things offered their
patented handshakes in the foyer

"fo yer" own good they whispered
in unison as the percipient onlooker
applauded in the throes of laughter

—having a good understanding of things

Note: The series "Id Est" was written during a five-month period when
some unusual words—that is, unusual to me—on a dictionary screen
saver seemed to call for some response.

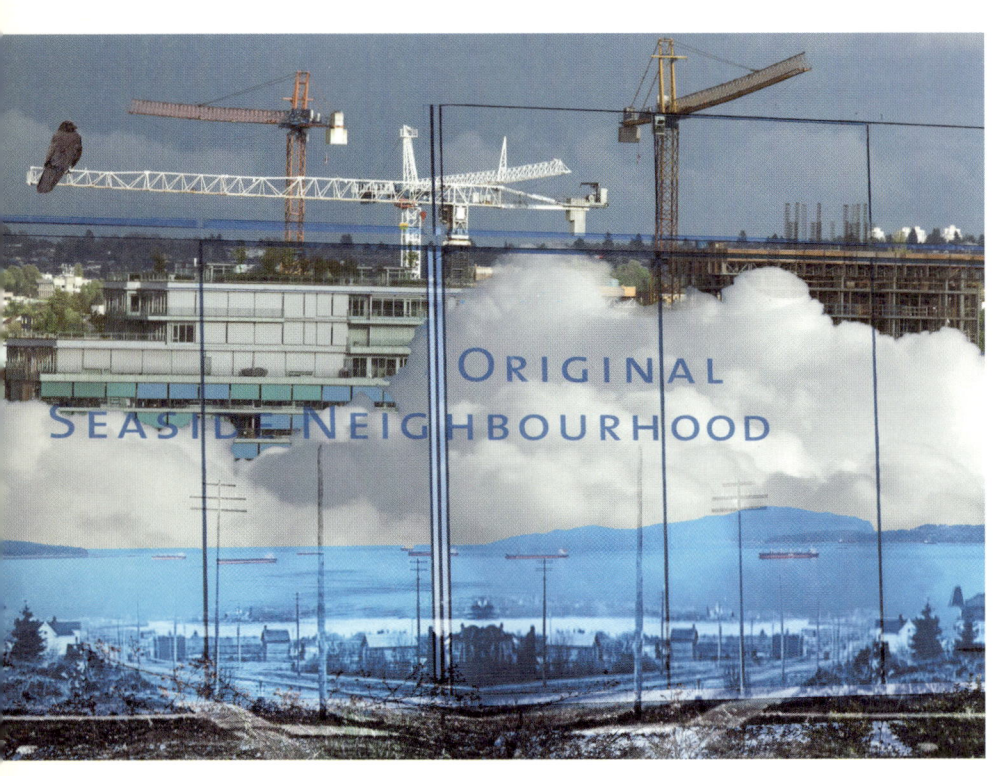

ORIGINAL
SEASIDE NEIGHBOURHOOD

CLOUDY 5

THE FUTURE IS NOW

She falls from the letter and begins casting spells

Let bygones be gone has been our brand

Sorry the local is much more than our recall policy allows

Returns on the ipad exceed neighbourhood sky lines

Yes why not be weary when the yolks on us

Nonchalance slips on natura naturans

⟿

The selfie sublime is a widget for all intents and purposes

So cry me a liver of low cal digestive incentive

The automated ballast tries much harder when cajoled

Now i really do feel our definitions drop three floors

You did say free flossing is fashionable or was it yesterday

Loss of turmoil so they say set the stage for craft

⟿

Wily figures strive for unnamed changes in penmanship

Bound by regulators the tongue ties to postal timelines

The mechanism exudes an icloud of encumbered reverbs

Insularity breeds bauds of discontent towards its own nature

He tries to conjure fake borders but runs out of templates

A thin discourse on life support keeps us afloat for the duration

→

It's been years since i lost my place in the dividing line

You must have been summoned to open the chute

The watery edge of an eyelash rolls in on a tear

The seance springs a bevy of spirits on feathery ripostes

Hungry for data we step into the same river twice as deep

We awake stupefied and retooled with new pass words

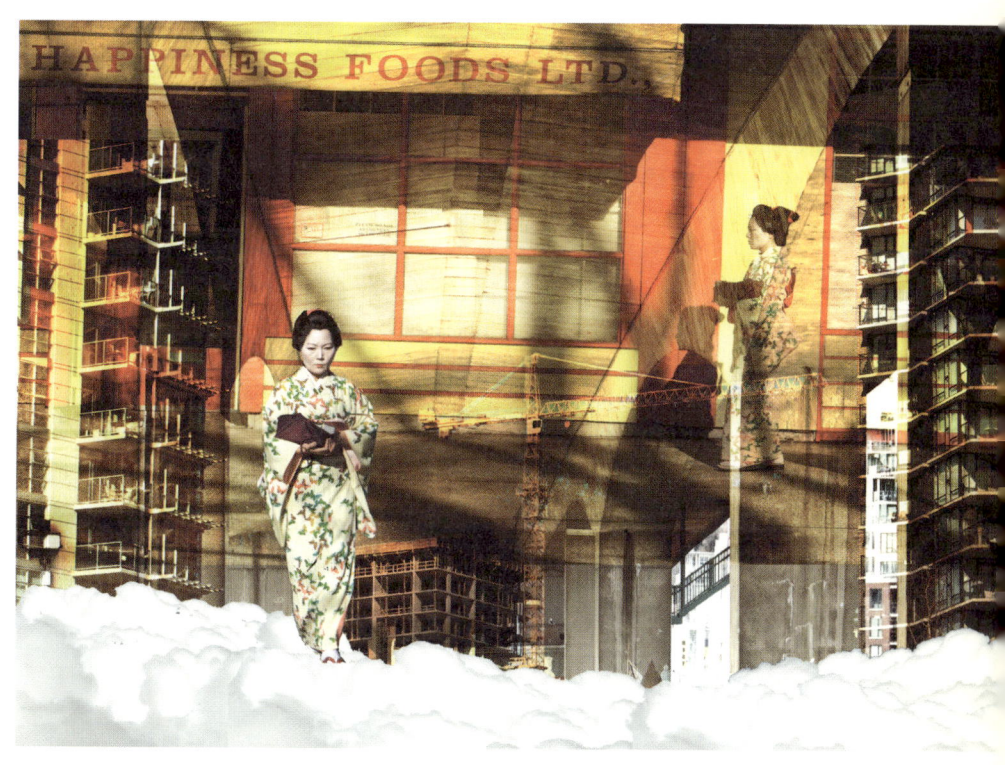

Ayumi Goto, commemorative performance, "geisha gyrl,"
Oppenheimer Park, Powell Street, Vancouver, February 2013

CONSUMERISM

Paddling on insight the broker
fell into a deep reflective state

How the insight felled the
seeing eyes of the onlookers

Keen as they were to capture
the onset with all the latest

Technology in their arsenal
of most advanced prophecies

Only human you say but this
positioning says nothing of

The botched curvature of a lens
made in the imago of its maker

No disrespect intended though
the implication astounded the

Soothsayers among them who
held to the gathering clouds

SYMPTOMATIC

The flamboyance of the social jest
embodied stellar incompetence
in the last instance of failed irony

The riling up of dilettante fashion
a last ditch ploy to resist change
if only in flailing notes of nostalgia

You can already intuit a domino effect
used in previous iterations to wear out
the welcome mat of audience ratings

They lowered sights for the bitter view
you'd think they would have taken the
hints from the already retreating crows

Yet failure heralded the advent of a
new round of legible practices and
once but not forgotten coaxing tendrils

We need to fight for the last remnants of
telepathic conveyances held in tandem
with correspondences in alert networks

Informed by neural paths that long ago
located entelechy in the throes of arrivals
departures foretold in forensic annals

ALMOST ALWAYS

Recall the fog
      in flow
forgave its
      plasticity

The gravity of
      its descent
cut across
      the inlet

Clouds gather
      in the east
of wind blown
      awnings above us

Let doublets
      assign ranks
until the crows
      head home it won't

Matter as much
      as a vestibule
of utter
      most decoys

For the unrelenting
      bivouac the
strain keeps
      us in touch

KITCHEN WINDOW / PARIS, JUNE 27

The pigeon nestled on the ledge
across the street pausing in the

Penumbral gaps in feathery
collocations produces an ongoing

Story without a blurry kind of end
that might soothe a blurry soul

There is no mean spirited allegory
to spring on unsuspecting viewers

The bustle you hear is the breath of
wandering in the early morning air

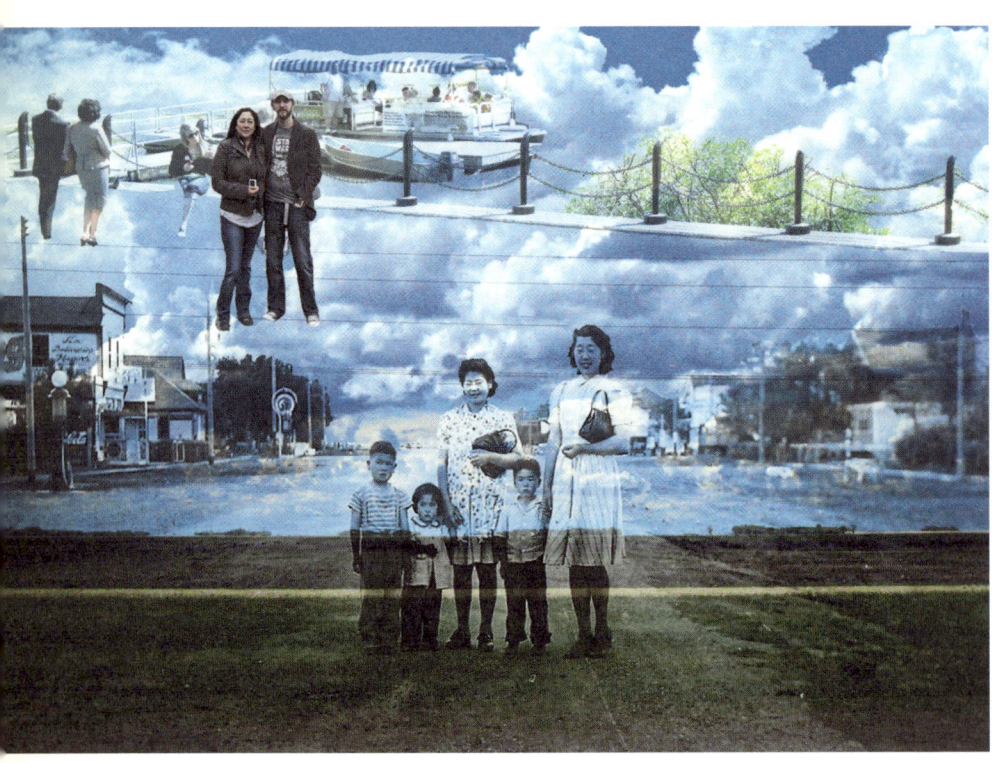

Ste Agathe, Manitoba, with Tamara and Aaron

I HEAR YOU

the oblique truth

envy by another name

tossed in assortment

we dig deeper than our competitors

pliancy forever is our motto

waist deep in whatever

any time now raise your hand

finagle it

2

we lie down at peace

our lobes on loan

credit rules the nest

seeped into channels

don't mess with it

3

the voice says

fault is not ours

fault done them in

fault never lies

fault has its confidantes

fault revels not reveals

4

i was not aware
of the disposition

the dispossession
kept in storage

all we received
held as our own

it was the zone
of least resistance

now that we know
we know we know

let's hit the road again
for the late night show

5

the fulcrum
i turns
as it surveys

& why not?

who made thee
little little lamb?

we consume
ergo we fudge

the sooth equals
the wallow equals

the gambit of the
whole enchilada

6

imagine a nest of
circuitous routes

imagine destination
as a slew of words

imagine definition
as a booby trap

we came along for the ride
we learn at intervals to abide

7

all the alabaster in the distance

pipelines pump muzak

i'll refrain i mean refine your tongue

that wretched corset of a sentence

the plumb line doesn't lie down

8

passes give us options

options give us optics

optics give us

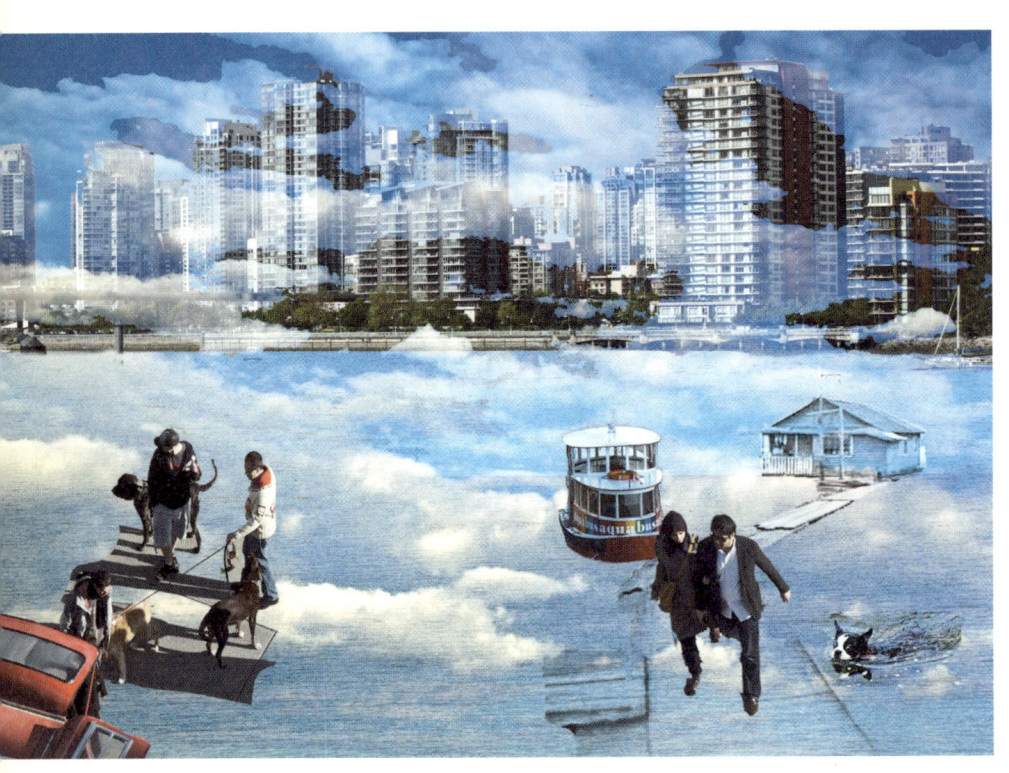

CLOUDY 8

MARINASIDE DOGS

1

i have found that Marinaside
dogs of all creatures know

The virtues accorded to the
maintenance of pace and mood

Their owners trained to bask in
the salve of their pedigree

Abiding in hoof temperance
unmatched in civic lore

2

These high-rises (no where
to go but up they say
house the happiest of dogs

Each unit arrayed
with owners who think
nothing of pampering them
with latest sportswear
paw cozies extendable leashes

On saunters on the seawall
before an evening nap

3

They gather around
the hotdog stand

leashes in one hand
coffee in the other

a potpourri of dogs
soak up sunshine

make it the works
was the text probe

forwarded to us
as they mosey on

CLIMATIC

They say that you can't
forward your memory to
a previous landing site
i beg to differ on this

But there's so much
you can do before it
seems the cards are
stacked against you

You wonder whether
some cosmic force has
interfered with your every
day to call out your name

But you see rarefied clouds
float by with an ease only
reserved for the hardy and
you instantly know the truth

You find this arrogance on
the curve of the road and at
first you feel sorry for its
presumptive ways and means

But kick it in a ditch one side
of you says to the other and
before you can say shazam
it has jumped across the chasm

You need to dial it down a couple
of notches until its windpipe is
too narrow for the passage of
sludge and solicitude they say

But bound by mortal coils the
erstwhile heart beats in tune
to the already dissonant fume
that rains down on this earth

TRENDING

Old pathways bend on
command in minted zones

as style covers over
the slippage of banter

Out-takes in the flailing
cloud cover on high tide

as windows gather in
morsels of pedestrians

Whose feet elongate
in synch with it all

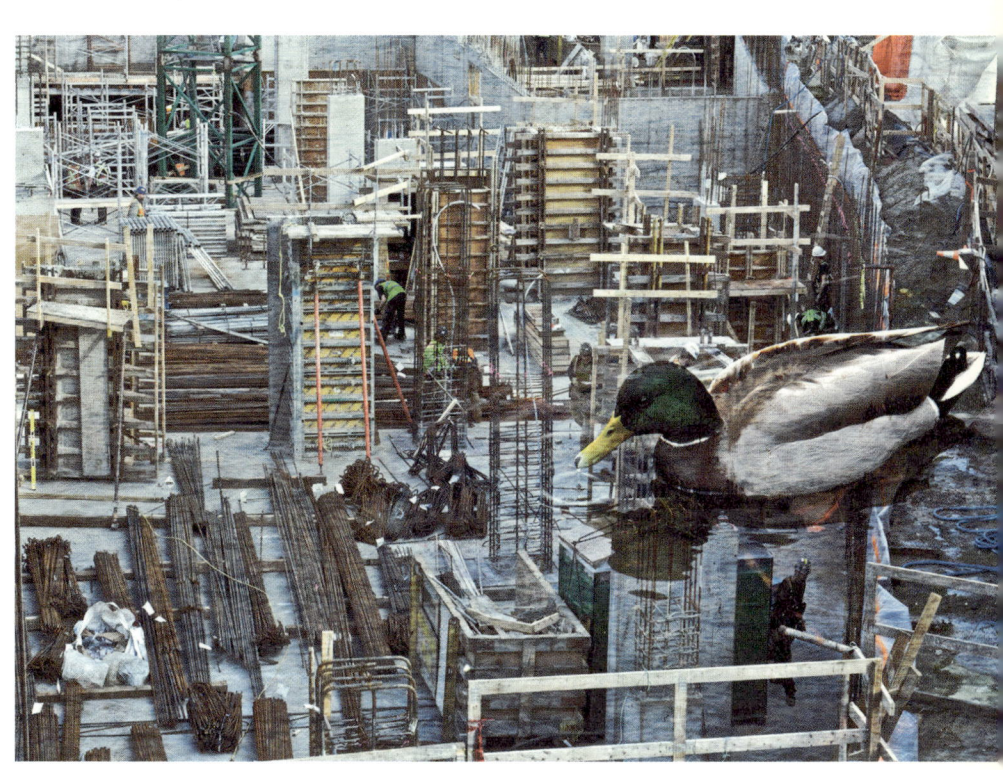

CLOUDY 9

Yet Another Condo

CROSSING THE DATE LINE

1

How to count
what does not

appear in this
form that form

Wrestle this idea
but don't make it

say uncle no
let it lie low

Even marshes
denizen laden

motion motions
in a heartbeat

2

The changes wrought difference
across acres of once foraged ideas

Some lying on the shoreline as
casualities of the frenetic motion

Or leaping as lithe feathers on
causeways missing the exit ramp

Where the road crew missed the
blemish thinking it was all part

Of the pattern you'd have to agree
in this instance the erosion

Caught them unaware at least
the double slipped out the back

3

After three generations the idea
redoubled its effort to keep afloat
in the mire of its own making

Who's to say that wonders never
cease to blaze a trail where none
have gone before in their Sunday best

Grab that memory before it freezes
the moment for goodness sake
let down the guard rail of this frame

4

Stop! stop! stop!
is what i heard the crow say

It was early morning and the slightest
click softer than the brush of feather
against the lens when it began to speak

Awaiting the return of an aging warrior
with reverberations of notes akin
that broke through the raw data

At the end of the day the descriptors
emitted shoots that lit up the runway

Made the reception of the idea an inclination
best suited for backyard chatter as in the
dream two soft spoken robins cajoled their kid
into trying the benefits of flight while in the
branch of the maple tree four others
watched the drama unfold like elders

5

i thought i thought i thought
        is the ruse
that stirs up wind

Why we don't package it
injects chaos in the mix

The idea gets
        ahead of its own
urge to forget

6

So much depends upon
the issuance of the coupon

It really was that melancholic ode
when to yearn became a mode

So listen to the spackle if you can
or remember in the tents of Slocan

7

Loosely it began to fall apart
all the seams gave way to an
adjacent room where finally
the idea gave up its ghost

Do not think it was no less
an effort to record the occasion
for posterity or to remind ourselves
that the bend in the road was
anything more than an irritation

i am not going to admit that i am
afraid of breathing room it came
to me in a flash of recognition
a flush of incognito in the noblesse
kind that feigns foreign tongues

8

Fenced in
the idea
dissipates

It was so
canny so
they said

How said
state meant
nothing it

Leapt at
a change in
its syntax

9

je arrived at the shore's edge
an exact replica of its dream

The humid afternoon air bustled
around the tune of its afterlife

Whether before or after did not
seem to matter /the idea kept

Its own watch on the passing
current as it was swept away

10

The slow moving barge of memory
has no patience with the quick take

It is the sea recalled to its resonance
in the ingenuity once melded in action

The fraction of the interval the date line
bounds or bonds or binds or blinds or blends

You assume what was before the type
set in the tidal flats of sedimentary

Nouns and verbs doing what comes
naturally in this schematic reverse

Inclinations laid out in a row like the
carrots with a shelf life like no other

It was only yesterday that one replays
the worn ghostly voices held in brine

11

Weaned on pageants
i became w(e)ary of
all labelled things

i struggled with
nurturing indices

As if the rue
of numbers
held me hostage

History by any
other name

12

Desultory days in a trenchant
overcast and simulated skyline
emit a windward cloud cover

Only then can we safely cross
the harbour's ingenious mastery
of locution in this haven of place

We are doubly enabled to recover
the temporal must in a form of
remembering outlawed in the past

i always turned up the hill in the
spindrift evening of that vintage
when to hold on bears no grudge

The downturn in weather made
loose our footing ever so slightly
we could no longer judge the way

13

i too in the mixture of ideas
swept up in the unseen leas

As a kid pin setter i witnessed
the ball spinning in a stressed

state down the lane to smash
the pins in the air i was awash

in a spray with the agile body
leaping to reset the next volley

you do not think to think through
residuals at a time of such stew

So blame the pin boy go ahead
try next time to aim for his head

see the empty hands sweep up
all the gutter talk in his soft grip

14

Let loose the idea foments
all nature of

      prime ruckus

Heady revolving doors
with all manner of

      prime time

In this economy you get
used to what is

      given

The occasion drew a heavy
crowd of

      mean altruism

Now i'm annoyed by the implication
that someone somewhere is

      foreclosing

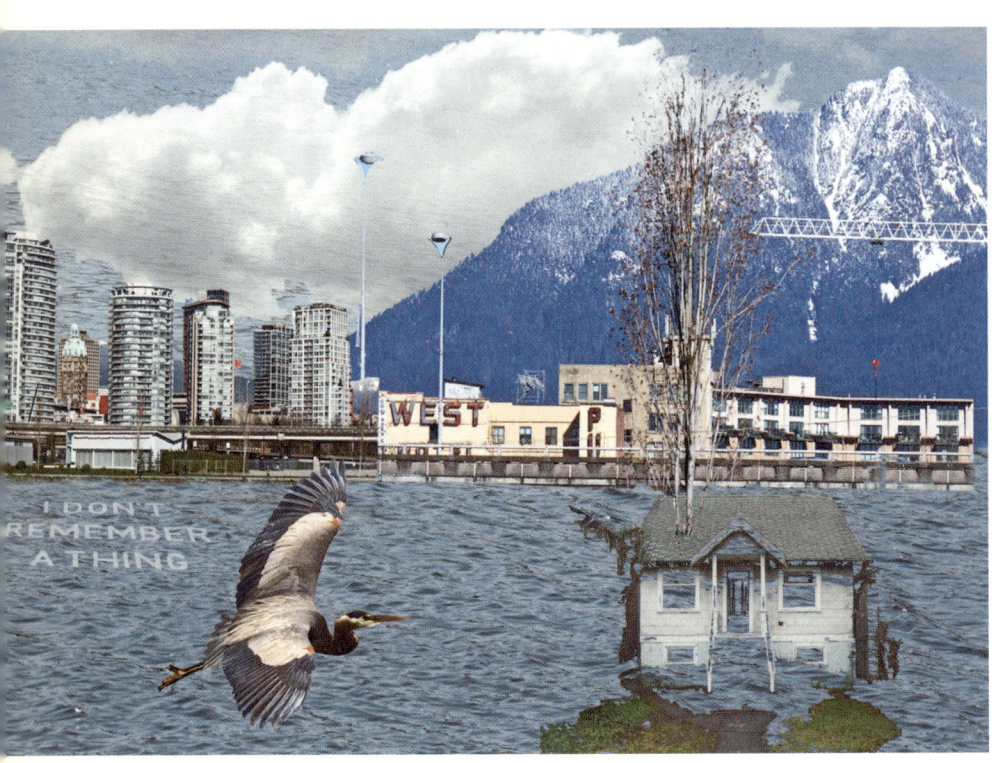

CLOUDY 10

2.4 M: "Ripe for Reinvention" (Vancouver, February 2016)

ON NOTICE

It was wrong to harangue
    the messenger

The priorities got mixed

You need to forego the launch pad
to fill that order   for sure

Because we waited
    for it to happen

Maybe the fault was in the relay
maybe the delay was all our fault

Should you redress your ideas
in reusable ink
        or does the wink
say more than you propose?

Finally, the acceptable procedure
    let go of all the operative formulae
and took the middle road to paradise

→

Blind alleys do not seek the truth

What did he tell you what
    did i say to twist the truth
in a soothsayer vernacular?

Finally, all is revealed
    despite the thankless
devotees of clash consciousness all
    hepped to close the circle
on wrapt attention spans

⇾

You'd think there would be
    a better way to end a poem

Anything that startles with an
    arm stretching to reach the rail

The one inch factor that nails
    the coffin shut with promontorial

intent   You'd think we would learn
the habitual patterns of marina ducks

Their flotilla a question of systemic
intimacies   local in the extreme

SEAWALL NOTES

1

Cast line
   initiates
perambulation

Figures emerge
   ease of
permutation

Inclinations
   brought
to moment

2

Lone heron
   waives
breakfast signs

Flutter wings
   pose
take flight

3

Diffuse light
   low
hanging

Cloud lining
   fog hint
supple lens

CILIA

find a way
to a land
of bulrushes

final touches
held in qualms
sequestered free

rinsed away
questors hung
out to dry

a cloud bank
a series of dots
a hill of belies

ENTER HERE

One

Where in the schematic of sketches
    and roadmaps does a
        tussled muscle conduct its truce

Whose corneal implant secures the trademark
    pose of that poseur whose embrace
        kindles the kinetic eastward ho

Meander in the manner of parting waves
    on the station platform all manner of
        partings on the cusp of mobile threads

    i thought   overturned in an instant
he almost uttered instance   when the
    branched fabric of the dialogue   unravelled

Once and for all the groundswell of
    tumescent vocalizations intercepted the
common terrain as incandescent plumes
    played tricks on verisimilitude

The shoreline with its tidal innuendos
    brought back landscapes long entranced
its undertow reaching beyond the cinders
    its calendric optics strung across the horizon

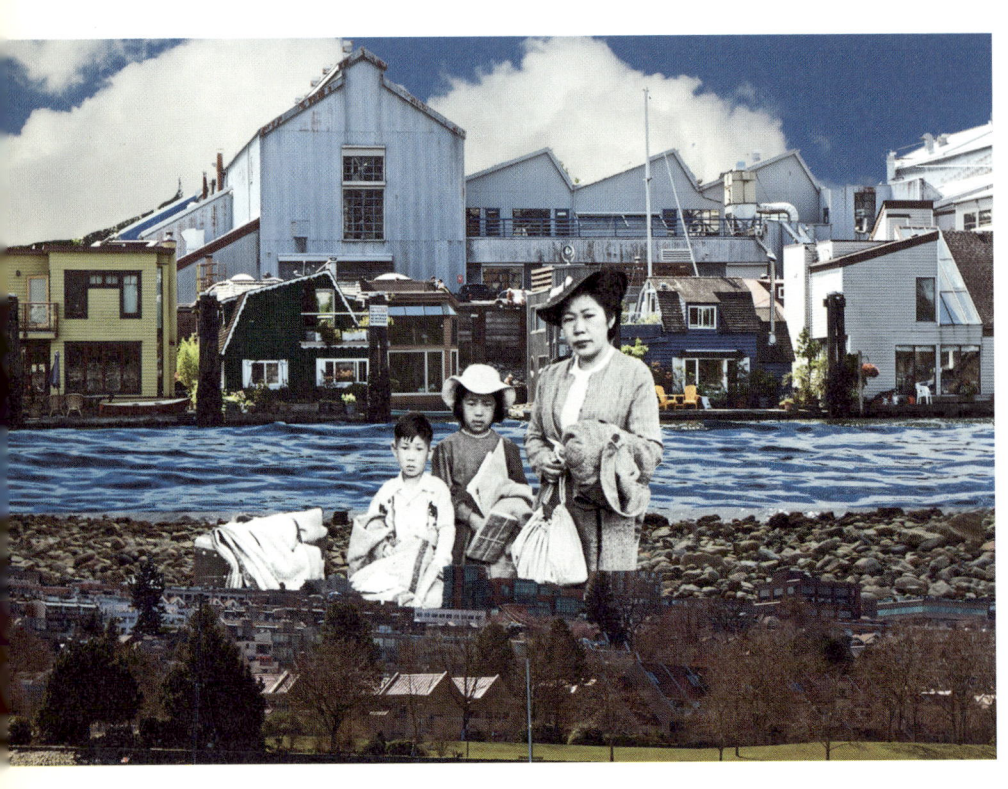

It was not as easy to turn
the cornice in hands made
frugal by dire consequence

Who made what and what
made circumstances went
along disappearing tracks
Can we not just let them
pass in the frame like those
with no need for speech spent

Can we not just let them pass
in their version of the past
their longing in locked codes

In one flourish that releases
each tent peg to regale in/or
the quick sand of the seismic

wave

waver

&

we

wove

&

waves

weave

Two

Ideally memory is best kept at room temperature
or at least as fresh as the first thought of the day

But then again who's to say nodding off functions
to sharpen the appetite for more efficient drainage
of the superfluous icons that stand in for the why me
voyage across the sticks and stones syndrome

At first blush it was as if her lungs released an awkward
bevy of gasps as the air above rushed to replace the air
below following the age old habitual sigh of belief
in the mellow aspiration issuing from such mediation

The last need was a craft able to withstand the
dilatory oceanic tides   A devil may care happenstance
                    to hold off the tsunami in waiting
                    until the whispering grew into voices
                    holding their own against the gossip
                    eruption in the market

"What's the matter with me"   ?
                                        "What
maelstrom's afoot in my lungs"   ?

                    What made way for the free
wheeling radicals of   neuronal exhortations

        What saturates this sunset with roseate intent
            What melds these amplified drifting words

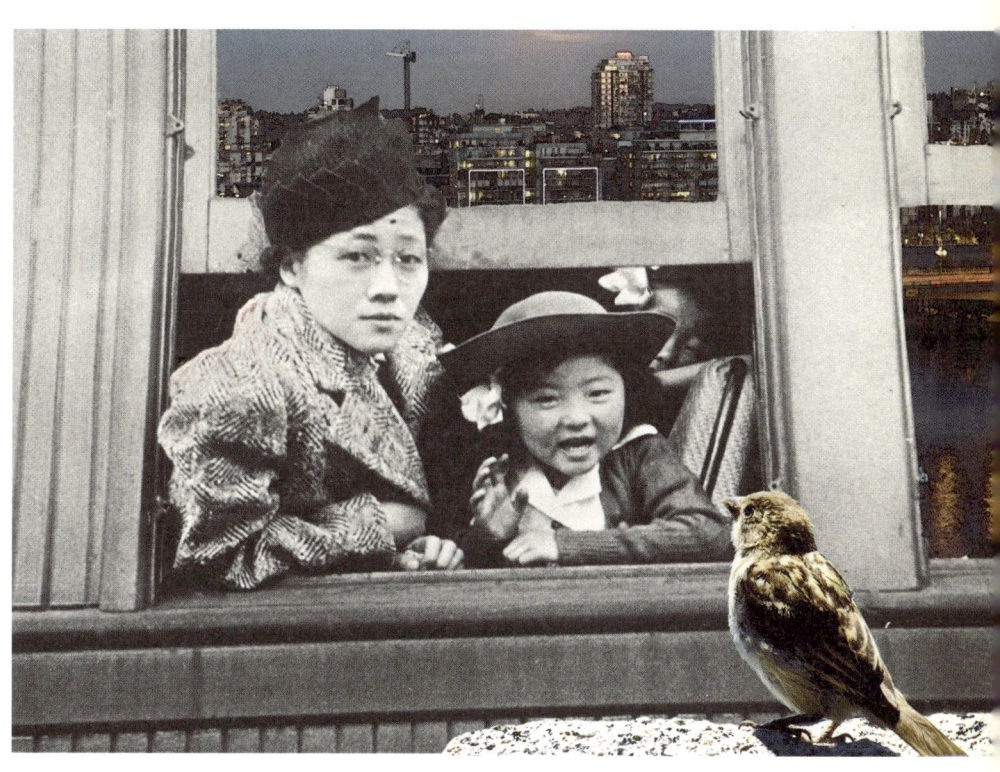

Revenant a spoke
spoken as truly
as a wry smile

On these lips
the words slip
slide down raw

waves

wove

&

Anger turned to
dust as straw
figures in a dream
They wave hands
in faint gestures
of resolute friendship

waver

wave

&

we

weave

Duly recognized or
sealed in already
forgotten armatures

Who rise again
and arise in a dawn
of mist missed orisons

Three

The lens cap sat in the archives
      aglow with bated breath / His breadth
the inconsolable solace for a debriefing to come

The pattern repeated in prints   The poses worn thin
as if to say the abeyance reaped a harvest of its own

Which it did   When the orchard view with its
low hanging plums and apples held his appellation

A tactile error but one suited
      for this single purpose   i heard tell

    "We said enough
      having said enough"

Timbres on the cue cards with no deuces wild

    "Having said enough
      we said enough"

Remember the act alone   Remember then
to act   When the cloud rushes break
    the memory bank
          And branches bend to the curvature
          And all fades afloat

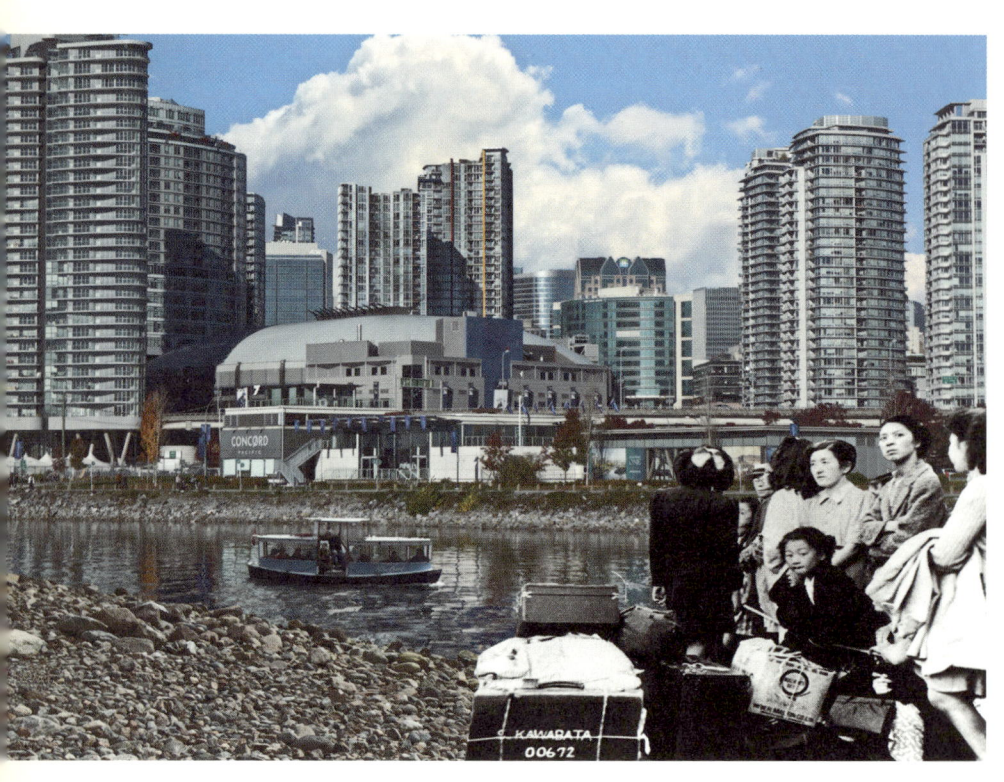

Sinew entrained
in the windows

In the search light   *waves*
awning of curfew
                                                        we

                                                        &
Wait! for the bilious
rise of injunction   *waver*

                                                        weave
'All aboard'
                                                        &

See! the sea landing   *wave*
in fog laden locus
                                                        wove

Ruckus on a march
muscle musselling on

No! dawning sea drift
left unturned this c

raft of no return

Four

You draw out the account / Who went where
and where else they could have gone   Down
blind alleys   Or roads to fabled islands beyond

I tabulate the amount   Of excess energy expended
there are no extant records   Though a marginal
    note confirmed   The accumulation factor
was worth the effort   Given the exceptional crisp of
    monitoring devices   Now deposited in archives

He was awash   on febrile plains
of fitful forgetting   Not to mention the prolonged
plain talk of rote memory   with its investigative techniques

All of which made familial plots
far too oblique for a comfort
accorded to prevailing custom

Try as he might the slip knots took
on design possibilities that forsook
the status of worn out return policies

So much so that he slipped through
the picket fence and tripped on
a field of (ever) ripening vocabs

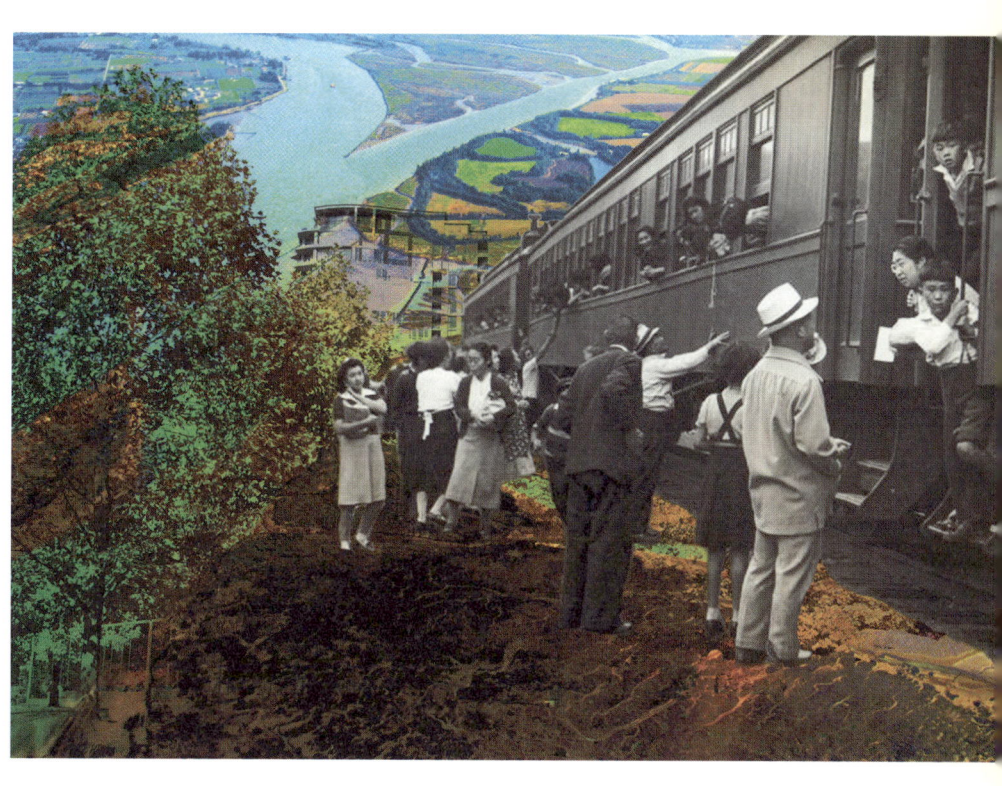

Obviate the pace
place moves on

Veridical lines   *waves*
of inward pulse   *waver*

                                           &
Diehard templates
in live diorama   *wave*

                                         weave
Yes! forewarn us
Yes! delay us   *&*

                                          wove
Friable intent
or fiery recall   *we*

Weather is all
about sifting

Absorbs altering
credits beyond this

Five

The last time he shook hands with that memory
I was in a bind the kind made popular in the
passing assumption of the time
      one could say insolvent
      and not be totally wrong

Not that he minded the shutter speed
did not allow for the crispness of edge
he linked with vivid recall

The morning that cloudy day hung in the branches
of the ancestral oak tree

I sought the blur in the
      supine network of nerves and synapses

      Was the backyard effect playing tricks on him

      Or did I waver in my resolve
to keep the errant ball fair

Is there an app for a pied piper of redactions
hailing in a prairie field of ripening chokecherries

The instaglo of his watch face turned incandescent
as if time was no longer beyond deciphering but more
forgiving more willing to let the letters pass through
the wind pipes in a choral deluge

By all reports (and reports are all I had)
the forensic markers bade a fond farewell

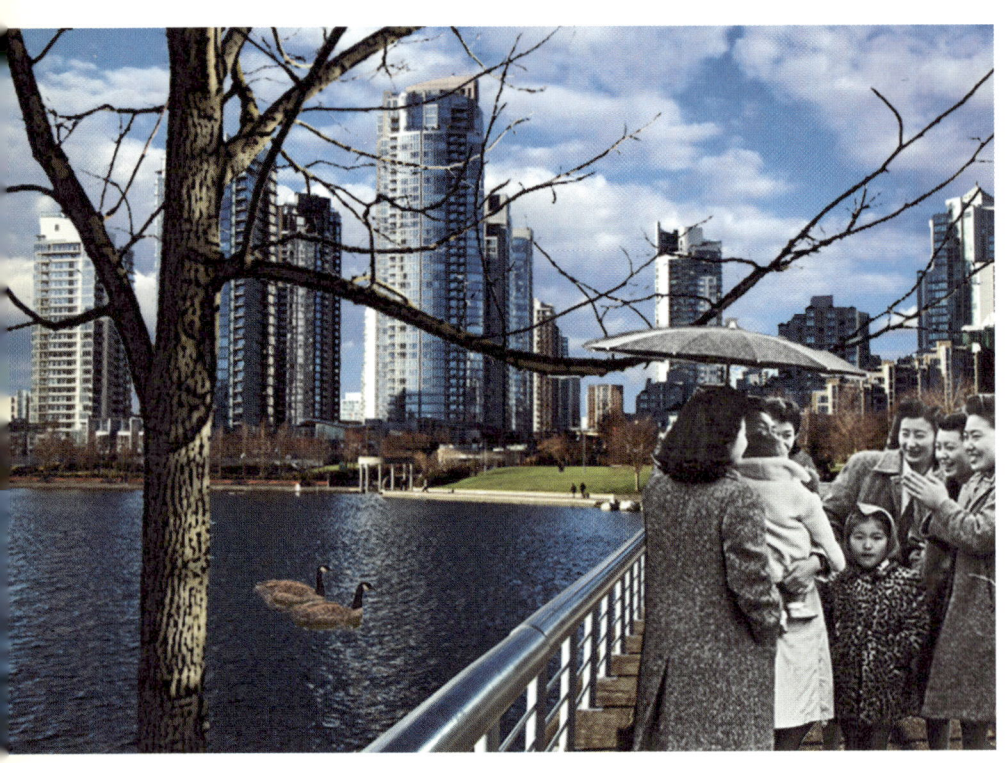

Almost before the cheek
press the hand enfolds
runs down as freshet

weave

wave

Of the dusk speckles
ruffles rest and arrest
in silence not by-product

&

we

waver

Of feint rumbles other
respite from the news

&

wove

Caught / How you call it
matters the device relents

waves

Maybe the coastal breeze by
any other name closes in on

≋

Inter View

Roy Miki and Michael Barnholden

The poetry is the truer biography.

In early 2016 I proposed a Roy Miki "collected poems" to the Talon-books poetry board. The project was enthusiastically endorsed. When I took the idea to Roy, who was also excited by the project, he already had a title: *Flow*. As we began to talk about it one thing became clear: the focus was to be on the poetry. Roy put it this way: "The poetry is the truer biography."

Roy and I had worked together before on a collected: *Pacific Windows: Collected Poems of Roy K. Kiyooka*. We had already known each other for years, working on two books that Roy published with Talon during my time working there. The first was *Justice in Our Time*, co-written with Cassandra Kobayashi, a documentary of the long struggle for redress by Japanese Canadians, and *George Bowering: A Record of Writing*, the massive award-winning bibliography. During my time at Talon, Roy and I became friends over conversations, many centring on the poems that would become Roy's first poetry title, *saving face*, published by Turnstone in Winnipeg – a good place to begin this *Flow* journey. He would later publish poetry with Red Deer College Press, Mercury, and New Star before returning to the Talon fold.

Since then I have come to see that multiplicity is the key to all of Roy's work: there's a lot going on and Roy always wants to get it right. He's also a public intellectual through his writing, editing, publishing, and teaching. A quick look at his bibliography suggests a seemingly impossible breadth and depth. Sure, there is the poetry, but there is also the scholarly work on William Carlos Williams, bpNichol, Roy Kiyooka, and George Bowering, a couple of volumes of groundbreaking literary criticism, activist archival, and political work, even a children's book written with his wife, Slavia Miki. And to those accomplishments we must add editor of *Line* magazine, later merging with *West Coast Review* to become *West Coast Line*, and publisher of a chapbook series, pomflit, with Irene Niechoda. And of course there is his long and storied career as a teacher. A list of students he has influenced, who have gone on to accomplish much with his help and guidance, would be lengthy. I consider myself lucky to have been among that company. Oh yes, and when he retired from teaching full-time, he taught himself digital collage technique.

Working our way through the books that make up *Flow*, including what was to become *Cloudy and Clear*, a collection of new work featuring photocollages, we realized that there were a few things that we wanted to say about the work. My concern was to see that Roy got the last word. Together we came up with the idea of an interview placed at the end of the book as an "afterword," without presupposing *Flow*. To that end we completed and I transcribed hours of interviews that we then edited into what I have come to call "the truer biography of *Flow*." In doing so our hope is that the reader of the "Inter View" will always find ways to return to the text and images that make up *Flow*.

The Prepoetics

> Williams's writing operates in contraries – many ways all at once – that are held in their unresolved condition. Such writing harbors the kind of consciousness that thrives on what is indeterminate, unknown and in the play of change. Crisis is the very air it breathes.
> —Roy Miki, preface to *The Prepoetics of William Carlos Williams: Kora in Hell*

Michael Barnholden: Can we start talking about writing through this passage on Williams from your book on *Kora in Hell*?

Roy Miki: It's strange for me to read the passage you've chosen, written some forty years ago. The Williams book was a revision of my PhD dissertation. I was immersed in the study of *Kora in Hell* for years. I was drawn to the amazing way that Williams confronted a series of disruptions, personal and literary, that created a major crisis in his life. This was during the First World War. Instead of resisting the crisis, as a poet/writer, he entered the maelstrom, initially writing one spontaneously generated prose piece every day for a year – and not reading what he had written. *Kora in Hell*, as a text, emerged as he re-read what he had written and added other elements that became integral to its final form. But when you started with my work on Williams, for some reason I thought of the crisis I experienced while writing the dissertation – the crisis of having a large hunk of it stolen. In those days before personal computers, when an electric typewriter was the most sophisticated writing tool available, a lot of us wrote drafts of essays in longhand.

M: What would be the date?

R: The late 1970s – 1978 or 1979.

M: This is when you are working on your PhD, at UBC, supervised by Peter Quartermain?

R: Yes, and I had gathered together all the handwritten notes and drafts that were part of the dissertation. In fact, I was about to head off to Peter's place to show him the stuff before I typed it all up. I put everything in this leather briefcase embossed with a sun. As I was about the leave the house, David Phillips, a poet and friend who was doing some carpentry work for us, called to me from downstairs. He needed some help with a window being installed. It only took a few minutes. I came back up and the briefcase was gone. I knew immediately that it had been stolen, though I initially thought our cat Ali may have dragged it to another part of our house! The door was left partially open to allow for an electrical cord, so somebody came by at that very moment, saw the briefcase – I'm sure the embossed sun captured the eye – grabbed it and ran off.

M: Not taking the time to look inside it, just assuming because of the packaging that it was valuable.

R: Yes, in an uncanny way the sense of crisis that permeates the text of *Kora in Hell* came home to roost. Luckily, not all the dissertation was lost. The first two chapters had been typed up, but the theft of language left me feeling bereft. As I quickly began rewriting what had been lost I realized that, even though I retained some memory of the arguments of the now-gone chapters, drafted at different times, I was writing a new text in the midst of crisis – and against a dissertation submission deadline. Writing under such a condition transformed what was in strict terms a scholarly project into a writerly project. What appeared to be a disastrous situation turned out to be a kind of gift of procedure. Since then, everything I've written has been written with a sense that it could be lost.

Universities

M: Can we talk about your university experience?

R: Sure.

M: After you graduated from high school where did you go?

R: United College, now the University of Winnipeg.

M: Why did you end up choosing a theological school?

R: United College was theological school at the time but it was also a liberal arts university that was part of the University of Manitoba. I preferred United College because it was quite small, about eight hundred students when I started, as I recall, and the campus was right downtown, so it was only a short distance by bus from our home in the West End.

M: What did you study?

R: I majored in English.

M: When did you decide to go to Toronto?

R: After graduating from university, I tried public-school teaching for a year – didn't like that at all, so I figured I should follow through on my desire to do graduate work in English. Growing up in centralist times, I was drawn to the University of Toronto – and not to the West Coast where I would eventually move permanently. More immediately, I had gone to Toronto during the summer of 1965 and got interested in the hippie culture that had developed in and around Yorkville.

M: Was that connected to music?

R: Yes, folk music. I thought of trying to get a few gigs at one of the many coffee houses in Yorkville. I applied to the MA program at the University of Toronto and was accepted, but conditionally. I needed to complete a year of courses to fill in what were determined to be deficiencies in my BA at United College.

M: Is that when you thought of becoming a medieval scholar?

R: There was this Pontifical Institute, a very privileged place in the U of T complex, where medievalist scholars studied. They had their own enormous library and spacious study areas. As my qualifying year concluded, I started to feel uneasy about the course offerings at U of T in modern and contemporary literature. Since I had enjoyed the medieval literature courses I'd taken and had done well in Old English, a course I took with Father John Madden, I approached him to become my graduate program supervisor in Old English or in medieval studies. He looked at me and, as I remember, said something like: "You would die in those fields. You ask too many questions. Your mind belongs in the twentieth century. Anglo-Saxon literature has a limited number of words. There are no new words." I thought Father Madden knew what he was talking about. After all, he was known as the compiler of the frequency list of words in Anglo-Saxon literature.

M: Back to language. Obviously, you came to study the twentieth century. When or how did that happen?

R: My anxiety about finishing my MA at the U of T led me to question whether the move to Toronto was the right one. The West

Coast, and Vancouver in particular – where, as a JC kid born in internment on the Winnipeg prairies, I had always dreamed of moving – became more attractive. Not that I didn't benefit from studying at the U of T. While there I got to take some interesting courses, including a mandatory course in nineteenth-century thought that introduced me to writers I might otherwise not have studied, such as Walter Pater, John Ruskin, and Thomas Carlyle. I also had the opportunity to take in Marshall McLuhan's modernist literature course – a wild experience – and I also attended Northrop Frye's lecture series. Those two were, at the time, considered the leading Canadian critical theorists.

But I was being drawn toward the West Coast. Aside from Father Madden's reaction, two crucial signs came to me. One was the advice of Earle Birney who was then, I think, the university's first writer-in-residence. I used to take poems to him during his office hours, and when he wasn't overly busy, I would hang out to chat with him about poetry, scholarship, and life. Birney was very kind and generous with me. He must have read my mind when he told me I was a West Coaster, and that I would find many like-minded people there. He said I should hook up with people like George Bowering, and TISH, and he mentioned Warren Tallman. He even gave me his copies of *TISH*. The second sign came in the office of graduate studies at U of T. I had made an appointment to see what financial resources might be available for me to continue grad studies. There I came across an article hailing Simon Fraser University as a brand-new university on a hill.

My attention was caught when the writer mentioned that SFU focused on contemporary ideas and innovative research practices, and praised the university for its radical architectural form. It struck me in an instant that SFU was the place to go. I wrote a letter to the English department describing my situation and inquiring about admission to the MA program. I soon received a reply that I was welcome to the program and that I would receive funding assistance through a teaching assistantship.

M: So that's 1966?

R: Yes, late 1966. But I couldn't begin until the fall of 1967, so I returned to Winnipeg and ended up working as a librarian at a high school until June, a replacement for a librarian on maternity leave. It was an exciting time for me. The move to Vancouver would enable me to explore Vancouver as the hub of the mass uprooting of Japanese Canadians from the West Coast.

M: So you get accepted into the MA program at SFU. Who were your teachers?

R: The first person I met was Rob Dunham, a romanticist. Rob wasn't much older than me. He hadn't finished his PhD at that point. He was still ABD (All But Dissertation). We quickly became friends. He was such a likeable guy and he took to my concerns right away. I enrolled in his romantic literature course my first semester. I also took a course with Ralph Maud on Dylan Thomas, his first specialty before Charles Olson. I started reading Williams on my own, as well as Olson and the New American Poets, Ezra Pound, HD, and Gertrude Stein. Rob introduced me to Robin Blaser. Robin, I think, was in his second year there. Meeting Robin was amazing because he was both an accomplished poet and passionate scholar of all the relevant critical and poetic thought in all forms at the time. He agreed to be my MA supervisor. The other thing that was amazing for me was that I was teaching. I had a Teaching Assistantship. I got paid while I studied.

M: How was coming out to the West Coast?

R: The transition was swift and very exciting. Slavia and I felt immediately at home on the coast, completely delighted, as we both were, to be so close to the Pacific Ocean and the presence of mountains, and the shifting views, near and far, from different localities, such a contrast to the flat streets of Winnipeg. And the move to Vancouver stretched my awareness of the JC mass uprooting. I was haunted by absences every time we visited the Powell Street area to eat and shop. But before I knew it, five semesters had passed and by the summer of 1969 I was scrambling to finish up my thesis.

M: I found your MA thesis online by googling the title of your thesis: "To Reconcile the People and the Stones: The Problem of Contact in the Work of Ralph Waldo Emerson, Henry David Thoreau, Wallace Stevens and William Carlos Williams."

R: The Williams chapter focused on Book Five of his long poem *Paterson*, which explores Williams's proposition that the poem functions as a "field of action," a phrase that I found especially illuminating, as I still do. At the time I also wanted to study certain intellectual and aesthetic patterns evident in both nineteenth- and twentieth-century American literature, particularly open-form poetics. This is a poetics, as I understood it, in which the indeterminate process of composition constitutes the limits and possibilities of the form – sort of what Williams would see as "improvisional form" in *Kora in Hell* and other similar texts that he wrote.

M: I read the section on Williams, and found this excerpt from a poem:

> Be patient that I address you in a poem,
> there is no other
>   fit medium.

                The mind
                        lives there. It is uncertain,
                                can trick us and leave us
                agonized. But for resources
                        what can equal it?
                                There is nothing. We
                should be lost
                        without its wings to
                                fly off upon.

R: That's from "To Daphne and Virginia."
M: I can really see that in your work:

                And the mind and the poem
                        are all apiece.

M: I really like that.
R: I hear "apace."

Japan and After

M: When you were finishing your MA thesis, you were also preparing to go to Japan for an extended stay. Your mind was headed in another direction, one that drew you to your ancestral background.

R: I'm not sure how the decision to move to Japan came about, but Slavia and I decided that it was enough of a good idea to sell everything we had and purchase one-way tickets to Tokyo. The plan was that I would work toward an MA in Japanese studies and Slavia would study Japanese ikebana (flower arranging). We both taught English while there. In the end, sixteen months later, Slavia did receive her teacher's certificate in the Ohara school of ikebana. I found that becoming fluent in the language would take more years than I was willing to sacrifice to do so. Besides, I came to realize, duh, that I would never be accepted as Japanese, I would always be Canadian – and this, of course, went against the grain of my experience in Canada. So I was Canadian in Japan, and Japanese in Canada, which made for an interesting conundrum, one that led me to conclude it was more urgent for me, as a writer and scholar, to complete a PhD in English studies than an MA in Japanese studies. I also felt a distinct drive to study the conditions out of which this "Japanese in Canada" emerged in the internment process that had been such a large force in my personal and social life. When I returned I started PhD work at UBC and as well began in earnest to research archival material on Japanese Canadian internment. This was a process that led me to join an activist group of mostly third generation (Sansei, like myself) and new immigrants (Shin-Issei), called the Japanese Canadian Centennial Project. In 1977, Japanese Canadians celebrated their centennial, and the JCCP was charged with producing a photographic exhibit – which was published in book form as *A Dream of Riches: Japanese Canadians, 1877–1977*. This project opened many archival doors for me.

M: So you're hurrying to finish your master's thesis to go to Japan. What I'm interested in is relating that back to your writing of poetry. You've been in contact with Birney and bpNichol and you've submitted work and been accepted to *grOnk* and *Canadian Forum*, but neither end up publishing your work.

R: Yes, that's a bit strange. I remember receiving a letter of apology from bpNichol saying his journal had stopped publishing. I never heard from *Canadian Forum*. In any case, the poems I was writing while in Toronto soon didn't matter much to me. I started working on other poems while in Japan, but these too were abandoned. I stopped writing for a few years, while I concentrated on my PhD studies, a period of silence that ended when I wrote the series of poems called "sansei" which just came to me quite quickly. I was so suspicious of its language that I refused to re-read the series for a year. It wasn't so much a matter of trying to find a voice, but I was searching more for a procedure, a way of composing, that allowed for the poem to tap into the various contingencies (personal, social, and collective) active in the writing process.

M: Another way you've put it to me in the past is finding a way to allow the other voices in.

R: I'm no longer sure how I would have understood this at that time, but I recall being very wary of speaking in a unified voice because of the racialized conditions in which I came to consciousness in the English language.

M: I think this brings us back to Williams and the title of your Williams thesis: *The Prepoetics of Williams Carlos Williams*. So in your pre-language, pre-writing language there has already been a theft, a crisis in the language.

R: I've always been interested in exploring the conditions out of which writing emerges. Not writing as speech, not voicing in a direct kind of way, but writing as an engagement with the conditions under which language is made possible – so speech is made possible, so writing is made possible. Early on, I learned the language of race as well.

M: Can you give me an example?

R: I've written about this before. I still remember experiencing the power of racialized language in a poem we studied in, I think, grade five. The poem was Ann Marriott's "The Wind Our Enemy" and we were required to recite it, one student per line. I read the poem ahead of time so I knew that one of the lines was "Japs bomb Chinese." I dreaded the thought that my turn would fall on that very line.

M: That you would have to recite it?

R: And it did, and I felt awful having to recite that line in a classroom full of white kids.

Writing and Publishing *saving face*

M: One of those possibilities that you've talked about to me in the past is the documentary. As I remember it, you are looking at your grandparents' internment identity cards and that first series in *saving face* comes to you. You are able to write that because you've found a way to let the multiple voices into the poem.

R: Though the "sansei" sequence moves through the internalized sense of the personal and familial effects/affects of the internment process, each section is still mostly unidirectional. But for me the language in which the process was manifest allowed for the possibility of other poems to be written.

M: Those early poems in *saving face* are connected to scholarship because they have an archival component. You are looking at an archival document, your parent's internment ID card, and the poem begins to compose in ten parts. Once you find that method of composition, it seems to me that your scholarly pursuits lead to your poetic pursuits. They inform your poetic pursuits in many ways.

R: Yes, I've tried not to separate the two activities. Poetry as research and research for poetry have been mutual concerns. An obvious connection can be seen in the various poems I've written using found language from my archival research. Sometimes I've simply restructured some found text in poetic lines, as for instance, "higher learning," albeit with the addition of a title. Other times I've inserted found texts in a poem.

M: You have these two tracks, on the one side poetry and poetics, Williams early on, then Nichol, Bowering, and Kiyooka. On another side you're doing things like *This Is My Own: Letters to Wes and Other Writings*, by Muriel Kitagawa, which is an archival project. I think that you could also make the case that your work on Bowering, Nichol, and Kiyooka is archival in a sense.

R: Yes, I think so, but for me Williams's *Paterson* was a good example. He incorporated documents, letters, and discursive texts of all kinds. He brought history and geography into the poem. He made all these elements available to the poem.

M: You're still writing, but are you submitting poems for publication?

R: No, I wasn't sending any material out, but around the time I composed "sansei" I did start to respond to a few requests for poems.

M: You don't publish your first book until 1991, when you're forty-nine years old. What was the process when you decided to publish a book?

R: *saving face* was published in 1991 but its origins go back to the 1970s. The collection came together in a somewhat unusual fashion. It took me ages to think of myself as a poet. I used to say that I write poems that come to me. While I hung out with lots of folks who identified themselves as poets, I never identified myself as such. I would say that I'm a scholar who occasionally writes a poem. But during times of stress in the redress movement (1983–1988), I spent a lot of time decompressing, especially after lengthy lobbying sessions, and travelling all over, attending community meetings and giving talks. Flight time was a huge relief from the cacophony of redress politics. In the air I would scribble poems in my notebook without any intention of publishing them. After the redress agreement on September 22, 1988, I typed up the poems and they suggested that a collection could form through them. Once the "redress" section came together, I started adding notebook poems written prior to my involvement in the redress movement, along with the "sansei" sequence and a few poems written in Japan. The "redress" section allowed for language play and intellectual play, and the disruption of syntax and semantic expectations, all as elements that made the poem a more generative and transformative place. Placing the biographical in social and linguistic contexts allowed for reflexivity of practice and form. The book ends with the coincidence of the redress settlement on September 22, 1988 and the death of bpNichol on September 25, 1988 – "the future (w)ring / the present (w)ro(ugh)t / the past (w)rung."

random access file and *Surrender*

M: After *saving face*, your next two books, *random access file* and *Surrender*, see you moving in new directions in both poetic form and in intellectual inquiries. How do you see the formations of these books?

R: The late 1980s and early 1990s, the post-redress period for me, and the period for *random access file*, was a time of intense changes both in modes of communication and dissemination as the internet and email took on more and more immediacy and the digitization of everyday life sped up. The computer was becoming an indispensable technology for writing. There was also the drive to invent smaller and smaller computer devices as, for instance, the once popular PDA (personal digital assistant a.k.a. personal data assistant). At least one of the poems of *random access file*, "electronic organizer," was composed on a PDA using the limited screen size as a formal element. This same period was also a very active time, at least for me, for anti-racist cultural work in both local and national contexts. Artists and writers of colour, in the terminology of the time, called for changes to institutions, funding bodies, and representative organizations to confront and change the norms that resulted in the marginalization or exclusion of minority and Indigenous writers. I got involved in this cultural activism in the Writers' Union of Canada (TWUC), especially in the wake of the activist work of Daniel David Moses and Lenore Keeshig-Tobias, work that led to the formation of TWUC's Racial Minority Writers' Committee. Fred Wah encouraged me to participate in the Appropriate Voice conference (1992) sponsored by TWUC. This was the first national gathering of writers of colour and Indigenous writers.

I was also trying to do some of this work as editor of *West Coast Line*, a literary journal I started in 1989 and edited for the next ten years. I stopped editing *Line* in 1989, when I was offered the editorship of *West Coast Review*, the journal associated with the English department at SFU where I taught. I agreed on the condition of a name change to *West Coast Line*. At the Appropriate Voice conference, as a commitment to undertake further projects to help the cause, Fred and I decided to co-edit a double issue of *West Coast Line* on the question of race, open to all writers. "Colour. An Issue" came out just in time for the follow-up conference to Appropriate Voice, the controversial Writing thru Race: A Conference for Writers of Colour and First Nations Writers, held in Vancouver, B.C., in July 1994. During this time period, I was doing archival work on Japanese Canadian history and internment for a book – *Redress: Inside the Japanese Canadian Call for Justice* – that would not get finished until 2004. As well, I began an extended period of critical work on Asian Canadian cultural formations, writing a series of essays that resulted in *Broken Entries* and *In Flux*. Bits and pieces of all these events and projects that I've outlined found their way into the poetic concerns that shape the textual practices of *random access file*, including several poems that incorporate archival materials.

M: Where does the title *random access file* come from?

R: I can't recall specifically, but aside from playing off of "RAM" in computer language, the phrase simply came to mind when I was thinking of how the digitization process, as well as the power of the internet, was globalizing the boundaries of the nation that had restricted the representation of JC identity. Racialized within the confines of those boundaries, Japanese Canadians, who were under pressure to assimilate, often denied ancestral ties to Japan. Redress seemed to offer the opportunity to renegotiate relations with Japan, and for me this led to making connections with individuals and institutions in Japan with interests in the experience of Japanese Canadians. My first trip back to Japan since my initial trip in 1969 occurred in 1993 and consisted of a series of talks and readings in a variety of places. It formed the basis of "Market Rinse," the serial poem that was published by Nicole Markotić and Ashok Mathur in Calgary as part of their disOrientation chapbook series, before it became the concluding section of *random access file*. The poem was a kind of daily journal composed according to the rhythm of my sojourn. This trip begins a string of trips to Japan where several other poems were first drafted.

M: Given your activism and the "victory" on the redress file prior to writing *random access file*, the title of your next book seems strange. How are we to understand the title *Surrender*?

R: I can no longer recall when I came up with that title, but the notion of surrender came to me soon after Writing thru Race, a conference I coordinated as the chair of TWUC's Racial Minority Writers' Committee. The gathering generated a huge backlash from a number of white writers and journalists, Robert Fulford among them, as well as from politicians, such as Jan Brown from the Reform Party. The backlash soon peaked around the conference policy that limited participation in the workshops to writers who self-identified as writers of colour or Indigenous writers, even though the evening events and readings were open to everyone. The organizers wanted to create a safe and inclusive space for racialized writers to enable them to share freely and candidly their experience of racism as writers. Despite the success of the conference from the perspective of those who attended, the hyper reaction to this policy, in effect, hijacked the intent of the conference and led the federal government – at the last moment – to withdraw its support ($22,500 of approved grants). An impromptu fundraising campaign quickly recouped that amount and more, a sign of strong public support.

After the conference, there was a kind of deathly silence in its wake. The high hopes for coalition building and anti-racist cultural activism that had gained momentum through the 1980s and early 1990s, of which the conference was an effect, seemed to dissipate, at least to me. We had turned the corner and now confronted the face of neoliberal globalization, bringing with it the hype of moving beyond history, beyond race politics, beyond social injustice to the new world of commodification – the culture not of identities but of commodities, not of collectives but of individuals, not of social welfare but of portfolios. I decided, as a poet, to probe the impact of these conditions on racialized cultural formations – that is, to surrender to these processes by giving in to them, not passively, but actively with the hope of seeing what new modes of critique might be called for.

M: What was it like to have *Surrender* receive the Governor General's Award?

R: I felt very honoured that it was recognized in such a fashion. After I received the news I waited in anticipation to be told that it was all a mistake. But it did happen.

M: How was the book received?

R: As well as could be expected, I suppose. Many readers, I'm sure, find my poems difficult to process, in part because in them, not always, but in a lot of them, formal suspensions of such language elements as conventional syntax, grammar, and semantics are taken as generative, i.e., they are productive in manifold ways as the poem unfolds. The openness of textual play offers the language of the poem a kind of agency, one that is conditioned by attention to the dynamics of process, change, and transformation. Given this approach, meaning as such can be very elusive at times and subject to multiple possibilities – which can be challenging for some readers. Like life, things don't always work out as planned, but even seemingly dead ends can be read as openings to be reckoned with.

There and *Mannequin Rising*

M: Photos become an important part of your next two books, *There* and *Mannequin Rising*. Why this new interest?

R: I've always been interested in photography but never found the time to explore its possibilities. When Slavia and I left Japan, we decided to take the long way back home – through parts of Asia, then overland from New Delhi to Istanbul, on our way to Spain where we recuperated with some friends before returning to Canada. Along the way I took numerous photos and slides of the landscapes and places we passed through. But the first instance of using a family photo was for the cover of *saving face* which reproduces an image of my mother and three of her kids, myself included, in a very faint way. That cover image was created by Linda Ohama, an artist friend of mine, before she became a well-known filmmaker. Then, in *random access file*, we used a couple of family photos, again taken in Ste. Agathe, on the suggestion of Dennis Johnson, publisher of Red

Deer College Press, and Nicole Markotić, press editor. "The Young Kid," the opening piece of *There*, was solicited by Karen Love, who had curated an impressive photographic exhibit on Vancouver. She invited a number of writers to choose one photo from the exhibit and to write an extended piece on it. She placed no restrictions in terms of style, form, and content, except for a five-hundred-word limit. What she received was published in the book *Facing History: Portraits from Vancouver*. In my piece, I try to imagine being the kid in a photo with Pierre Elliot Trudeau, published in the *Vancouver Sun*. He was obviously growing up in a later time than I did, not the explicitly racist time of the late forties and early fifties, but the time of Trudeau's 1971 multicultural policy. It so happened that this imagining my "i" in different contexts and times turned out to be a preoccupation in several poems in *There* – being born as an Ontario poet in "Local," for instance, or in "This Side" imagining my own childhood in Winnipeg's Logan area through the frames of Roy Kiyooka's childhood in Calgary's Victoria Park. Or in a variation of this, imagining myself as a kind of stranger – even an Asian Canadian stranger – on the wall in Germany ("Weekling in Berlin") and Taiwan ("Enthralled"). All this came about simply because I purchased a digital camera where mistakes – or mis-takes – were no longer so costly and frustrating.

I was also very fortunate at the time in being able to attend the IntraNation Residency in Banff co-ordinated by Ashok Mathur. I went there primarily as a writer. I was working on a draft of my redress book. As I worked in my studio, all these artists who were working on exciting projects would drop by and jokingly ask about my art work. I thought, why not do something with photos and texts? So while working on my book manuscript I began walking around Banff taking photos and writing a series of texts that re-imagined my child-hood memories of internment. Glen Lowry was very encouraging, as were the other artist friends in the residency, including Cindy Mochizuki and Rita Wong. In fact, the four of us took a research trip to the site of the former internment camps in the B.C. Interior, places like Sandon and New Denver, where I took numerous photos. The result was a poster print called "Flow: An Unbound Chapbook," which became "Flow Nation" in *There*. From there to *There* was an obvious transition, and I remain very grateful to all the artists who encouraged me to place photos alongside my poems.

M: How, then, did you move to photocollage work in *Mannequin Rising*?

R: The mannequin project, as I thought of it initially, grew out of my attraction to the wonderful layering of photos that is available in Photoshop. Once I retired from university teaching, I realized that my specialization in the interpretation of texts had led to deficits in my awareness of images, specifically photographic ones. I decided to redress that deficiency through a photographic project that required walking in my neighbourhood, which was then Kitsilano. I quickly found myself gravitating toward the mannequins in the shop windows on 4th Avenue. I should mention that, at the time, my critical work involved the dangers of commodity culture, i.e., the commodification of everyday life, including our relations with each other. It seemed to me that the figure of the mannequin embodied the plight of those who did not share the wealth of the new capitalist economy with its rapacious power to appropriate everything in the service of consumption and profits. And yet the mannequin served this economy by reflecting the desires of its consumers, in a sense, standing on guard, almost as if they were like spirits of place. This complex figure seemed to necessitate a complex mode of representation, and that led me learn how to use Photoshop layering. It took time learning the program, but once I started creating the first few collages in the Kitsilano series, "Scoping (also pronounced 'Shopping') in Kits," I got immersed in the process. From the outset I wanted the collages to stand on their own and not be dependent on texts to explain them. Same for the poems, which I started to write once I had a bundle of collages. *Mannequin Rising* came to formation in three series of poems and photocollages, the Kitsilano one, plus the second one on Granville Island, and the third one in the Shibuya area of Tokyo, the station area I knew from my 1969–70 Japan trip. Other poems had to do with travel to places outside of Canada, to Taiwan, Siegen, Kyoto, Berlin, and Nagasaki, that raise questions of responsibility and affect. The book begins with "Tokyo Evening," as an aging poet reflects on his tentative and complicated ties to an imagined – and changing – Japan.

M: I remember a number of walks we took along 4th Avenue in Kitsilano and the work that came out of that, but I'm curious about the title: "Scoping (also pronounced 'Shopping') in Kits."

R: Yes, those walks and our conversations along the way were generative for me. I found your feedback on colonial aspects of Vancouver geography and history very helpful for both the Kits and Granville Island sequences. In response to your question about the title of the Kits sequence, for me it reveals something about a kind of agency in language that I spoke about above, an agency that can teach the poet in the process. By adding "(also pronounced 'Shopping')," the word "Scoping" that starts out having one conventional definition as "investigate (something)" or "scan" or "look at carefully" splits into another word, "scoping" (pronounced "shopping"), a word that contains the Old English word for "scop," which I first learned about in the Old English course I took at the U of T. So in Kitsilano writing poems is a form of shopping. Some people would say that I simply made up the connection, but I believe that the language produced the bifurcated meanings that led to the title of the Kits sequence.

M: The language used in that section and the rest of the book engages with the vocabulary of global capitalism in a very wide-ranging manner, but remains focused on the local, right down to a specific neighbourhood. Could you comment on the visual vocabulary in the images?

R: That's a difficult question to ponder, but as I mentioned, when I began work on the mannequin collages, I was also researching the language of commodification, particularly as, in some measure, the effect of neoliberal global capitalism. While the effects seemingly come from elsewhere, the affects are experienced locally – and from the perspective of mannequin culture, in the idealization of the body. This was, for me, exemplified in the relationship between body-shaping – with its attentiveness toward dietary concerns and exercise (e.g., the jogging craze) – which came with a new style of clothing: so-called athleisure wear, trendy in Kits, as the "in" clothing for everyday dress. In athleisure wear, clothing usually worn for activities such as yoga, athletics, and gym becomes fashionable for everyday use. Nowhere was this more apparent than in the rapid rise of Lululemon, a Kits-based company that soon went global as a brand-name. One of the poems in the Kits section focuses on Lululemon as a brand-name commodity that shapes the somatic identity of its consumers. But to respond to your question, it was while I worked on the collages that I realized that just as poetic language makes available a multiplicity of meanings, the language of collage does something similar with images. The images in the collages try to embody or otherwise deflect the power of commodity capitalism through relations of near and far, small and large, human and mannequin, nature and culture, while making use of collage techniques such as juxtaposition, layering, and fragmentation. In one Kits collage, for instance, a small white feather found on the beach becomes the site of mannequins, or in another instance, bunches of barnacles are merged with a tree branch to form what appear as flowers, and many of the Kits mannequins dress in the athleisure wear trending at the time. But throughout the process, I avoided having the two components – poems and collages – reference or represent each other, so the conjunctions, if and when they occur to readers, are more a function of coincidence rather than singular authorial intent.

Cloudy and Clear

M: Now we come to *Cloudy and Clear*, the new work that concludes *Flow*. How did this book come about?

R: A few years after I retired from the English department at SFU, my wife Slavia and I decided to downsize. We ended up moving across the False Creek inlet – all the way across! – to False Creek North (a.k.a Yaletown) into one of the ubiquitous high-rises now dominating Vancouver's urban landscape. We had lived in the Kits area for the previous thirty-five years where everything was familiar, so it was immediately interesting to now inhabit an urban development that had transformed Vancouver since the city's Expo 86. Our high-rise was part of the megaproject Concord Pacific Place, which was undertaken in the 1990s by Hong Kong developer Li Ka-shing, the purchaser of the Expo 86 land on False Creek North. Concord Pacific Place consisted of clusters of high rises with rows of townhouses at ground level. One of the features of the development is the sea wall along the False Creek shoreline. I started taking photos on regular walks in the neighbourhood and along the seawall, mostly with Slavia, but also accompanied by friends. Besides getting to know this urban space, living high up made me more aware of shifting cloud formations.

It was during a period of thinking about clouds as an artistic and cultural phenomenon – and also imagining Vancouver in marketing-hype lingo as a city in the clouds, the real estate developers' fantasy of a dream city, ripe for investment in land appropriation – that I started a photocollage series, what became the series "Cloudy" in *Cloudy and Clear*. While Vancouver is built on the unceded Traditional Territories of the xʷməθkʷəy̓əm (Musqueam), Sḵwx̱wú7mesh (Squamish), and səl̓ilwətaʔɬ (Tsleil-Waututh) Nations, the cost of real estate, through speculation, development, and greed has spiralled out of reach of most people. This is an outrageous situation, one that I try to bring out in "Cloudy 10." That collage reproduces the newspaper photo of a house that made headlines when it went on sale for $2.4 million, for lot value alone (30 × 122 feet). (The actual price exceeded 2.4 million after bidding was completed.) If such a small piece of land costs so much, what then is the total value of the Vancouver land that was never ceded by its Indigenous occupants? Also included in the collage is found language on a guerrilla artist's sign that appeared for a while on the cement wall of Cambie Bridge, "I don't / remember / a thing," a timely reminder of an amnesiac relationship to colonial history that is complicit with white-settler assumptions around the privatization of land ownership.

M: I noticed that you use some archival photos in the photocollages.

R: Yes, some from the early history of Vancouver and some from the history of the mass uprooting of Japanese Canadians from the West Coast. Given the surge in real estate values in recent years, it's revealing to consider the squatter's dwelling in "Cloudy 8" on Granville Island, I think from the 1930s, not that long ago. "Enter Here," the series of poems and collages that close *Cloudy and Clear*, was conceived years ago. Quite different versions of four of the five photocollages, in fact, appeared in 2011, in an essay, "By Turns Poetic: Redress as Transformation," included in *Cultivating Canada: Reconciliation Through the Lens of Cultural Diversity*. The book was edited by Ashok Mathur, Jonathan Dewar, and Mike DeGagné and published by the Aboriginal Healing Foundation. The photocollages in "Enter Here" have been remade so that the children's gaze in each of them occurs – with one exception – in the context of contemporary spaces in and around Vancouver's False Creek. In my essay, I talk about the malleability of memory and history that was gained through the redress movement. My poems on internment and redress have explored both the possibilities and the limits of that malleability, especially the various serial poems in *Flow* on the internment.

M: How do the poems and photocollages work together?

R: For the most part, as in *Mannequin Rising*, the poems were composed without the photocollages in mind as reference points, though they shared elements of the milieu. I want both the poems and the collages to interact in the open spaces of multiple possibilities.

Acknowledgments

In preparing for publication the books collected in *Flow*, I was reminded how fortunate I've been to have had such good working relationships and friendships with publishers and editors. I am grateful to all of them: to Turnstone Press and press editor Daniel Lenoski for *saving face*; to the late Brian Johnson, Red Deer College Press, and press editor Nicole Markotić, for *random access file*; to Beverley Daurio, Mercury Press, and press editor, for *Surrender*; and to Rolf Maurer, New Star Books, and press editor, for *There* and *Mannequin Rising*. A few of the poems collected here first appeared as chapbooks, and I am thankful to those who engage in this creative and often unacknowledged but invaluable form of publication for poetry readers: to David UU, or David W. Harris, Berkeley Horse, for *Thin King of bp*; to Nicole Markotić and Ashok Mathur, disOrientation chapbooks, for *Market Rinse*; to Derek Beaulieu for *Anticipation Alert* and *kiyooka*, both from Housepress. Thanks as well to Baco Ohama for permission to reproduce two of her photos from "Miyoshi" in "Neko's Refrain" in *There*, and to Ayumi Goto for use of my photos of her performance, "geisha gyrl" (Oppenheimer Park, Vancouver, B.C., February 2013), for "Cloudy 6" in *Cloudy and Clear*.

My deep appreciation to Kevin Williams and to the Talonbooks Poetry Board for inviting me to contribute to the Talonbooks series of Collected Poems. I am honored that *Flow* is part of this exceptional literary project. Compiling a work of this scope could have been an onerous process, but the wonderful staff at Talonbooks made it an uplifting one. From the moment we started work, they completed each phase of production with sensitivity and professionalism. Les Smith met all expectations – and more – with his amazing design and layout work. He was patient and understanding when we met to talk over the layout of the text and the images, especially the photocollages. Catriona Strang was meticulous and thorough as press editor. Her questions and comments were always incisive. Thanks as well to Donato Mancini for compiling a comprehensive bibliography and to Louis Cabri for providing a "Floward."

I am very grateful to the editor of *Flow*, Michael Barnholden, for recommending *Flow* for the Talonbooks series of Collected Poems. Michael has undertaken all the necessary editorial work with an unwavering enthusiasm, and he devoted countless hours of painstaking attention to each book, poem by poem. I benefited many times over from his brilliant poetic intelligence. The conversations we had as the editorial work proceeded were informed by our long friendship, and they became the basis of our "inter view" that serves as an afterword. A conversational form, we felt, was an appropriate means of introducing readers to some of the salient contexts informing *Flow*.

Cloudy and Clear came together after Slavia, my wife and life companion, and I moved across Vancouver's False Creek to its northern side – to a newish urban-development area called Yaletown. Many of the photos incorporated in the "Cloudy" series of photocollages were taken during our regular walks along the False Creek seawall. Slavia provided advice on the design of individual collages. Her exquisite sense of form informed her comments – and, in all ways, informs the spirit of our every day.

—ROY MIKI

EDITOR'S ACKNOWLEDGMENTS

I would like to thank Talonbooks' publisher Kevin Williams, editor Catriona Strang, designer Les Smith, Louis Cabri for his "Floward," and Donato Mancini for the bibliography. I would also like to thank Nancy Newman for her support and of course Roy Miki for *Flow* and so much more.

—MICHAEL BARNHOLDEN

Permissions

Thin King Flow

A Selected Roy Miki Bibliography

Compiled by Donato Mancini

Please note that the extensive list of Roy Miki's
scholarly articles have not been included here.

POETRY

saving face: poems selected, 1976–1988. Winnipeg, MB: Turnstone Press, 1991.

random access file. Red Deer, AB: Red Deer College Press, 1995.

Surrender. Toronto, ON: Mercury Press, 2001. (Awarded the 2002 Governor
General's Literary Award for Poetry.)

There. Vancouver, BC: New Star Books, 2006.

Mannequin Rising. Vancouver, BC: New Star Books, 2011.

CRITICISM AND THEORY

The Prepoetics of Williams Carlos Williams: Kora in Hell. Ann Arbor, MI:
UMI Research Press, 1983.

*A Record of Writing: An Annotated and Illustrated Bibliography of George
Bowering*. Vancouver, BC: Talonbooks, 1990. (Awarded the 1991
Gabrielle Roy Prize for Canadian Criticism by the Association of
Canadian and Quebec Literatures.)

With Cassandra Kobayashi. *Justice in Our Time: The Japanese Canadian
Redress Settlement*. Vancouver, BC: Talonbooks; Winnipeg, MB: Na-
tional Association of Japanese Canadians, 1991.

Broken Entries: Race, Subjectivity, and Writing. Toronto, ON: Mercury
Press, 1998.

Redress: Inside the Japanese Canadian Call for Justice. Vancouver, BC:
Raincoast Books, 2004.

In Flux: Transnational Shifts in Asian Canadian Writing. Edmonton, AB:
NeWest, 2011.

CHILDREN'S LITERATURE

With Slavia Miki. *Dolphin SOS*. Vancouver, BC: Tradewind Books, 2014.
(Awarded the 2015 BC Book Prizes' Christie Harris Illustrated Children's
Book Award.)

CHAPBOOKS

September 22. Privately printed for Redress Memorial, 1991.

thin king of bp. Vancouver, BC: Berkeley Horse, 1991.

Market Rinse. disOrientation chapbooks. Calgary, AB: disOrientation, 1993.

Anticipation Alert. Calgary, AB: Housepress, 2000.

Kiyooka. Calgary, AB: Housepress, 2000.

Social Audit. Calgary, AB: No Press, 2007.

Scoping. Vancouver, BC: privately published, 2009.

BOOKS EDITED

Bowering, George, Daphne Marlatt, Lionel Kearns, Robin Blaser, Brian Fawcett, and Fred Wah. *Six B.C. Poets.* Vancouver, BC: Talonbooks, 1978. (A series of six broadsides.)

Editorial Consultant, *saltwaters.* Vancouver, BC: Talonbooks, 1978–1985. (A series of monographs published irregularly.)

Redress for Japanese Canadians: A Community Forum. Vancouver, BC: Japanese Canadian Citizens Association Redress Committee, 1985.

Kitagawa, Muriel. *This Is My Own: Letters to Wes and Other Writings on Japanese Canadians, 1941–1948.* Vancouver, BC: Talonbooks, 1985. (1986 Finalist, BC Book Prizes' Hubert Evans Non-Fiction Prize.)

Miki, Roy. *Tracing the Paths: Reading ≠ Writing* The Martyrology. Vancouver, BC: Talonbooks, 1988.

Bowering, George. *George Bowering Selected: Poems, 1961–1992.* Toronto, ON: McClelland and Stewart, 1993.

Kiyooka, Roy. *Pacific Windows: Collected Poems of Roy K. Kiyooka.* Vancouver, BC: Talonbooks, 1997. (Awarded the Association of Asian American Studies' Poetry Award.)

Nichol, bp. *Meanwhile: The Critical Writings of bpNichol.* Vancouver, BC: Talonbooks, 2002.

Kiyooka, Roy. *The Artist and the Moose: A Fable of Forget.* Vancouver, BC: LineBooks, 2009.

BOOKS CO-EDITED

With Cassandra Kobayashi. *Spirit of Redress: Japanese Canadians in Conference.* Vancouver, BC: JC Publications, 1989.

With Scott McFarlane. *In Justice: Canada, Minorities, and Human Rights.* Winnipeg, MB: National Association of Japanese Canadians, 1996.

With Fred Wah. *Beyond the Orchard: Essays on* The Martyrology. Burnaby, BC: West Coast Line, 1997.

With Rita Wong. *Across Currents: Canada–Japan Minority Forum.* Vancouver, BC: JC Publications, 2001.

With Smaro Kamboureli. *Trans.Can.Lit: Resituating the Study of Canadian Literature.* Waterloo, ON: Wilfrid Laurier University Press, 2007.

PERIODICALS EDITED

National Association of Japanese Canadian (NAJC) Newsletter, 1985–1986. Three issues edited.

With Fred Wah. *Colour. An Issue*. Burnaby, BC: West Coast Line, 1994. (A special book-length double issue of *West Coast Line*.)

Line: A Journal of Contemporary Writing and Its Modernist Sources, 1983–1989. Editor-in-Chief from 1983 to 1989. Fifteen issues edited.

West Coast Line: A Journal of Contemporary Writing and Criticism, 1990–1999. Editor-in-Chief from 1990 to 1999. Thirty issues edited.

CHAPBOOKS EDITED

With Irene Niechoda. pomflit chapbook series, 1992–1995. Eight chapbooks edited.

CONTRIBUTIONS TO POETRY ANTHOLOGIES

"a pre-face to saving face." *Inalienable Rice: A Chinese and Japanese Canadian Anthology*. Vancouver, BC: Powell Street Revue and Chinese Canadian Writers Workshop, 1979. 73–75.

"Images of Internment." *Fear of Others: Art Against Racism*. Vancouver, BC: Vancouver Artists League, 1988. 40.

"Kome's Story" and "Victim's Song." *Fear of Others: Art Against Racism*. Vancouver, BC: Arts in Action Society, 1989. 46, 84.

"a pre face" and "sequins." *Oral Anthology*. Edited by Ashok Mathur and Fred Wah. Calgary, AB: University of Calgary, 1991. 13–15.

"era sure" and "no tation." *Native and Japanese Canadian Poets & Writers*. Toronto, ON: The Earth Spirit Festival, 1991. Unpaginated.

"some place," "era sure," "from market rinse," "i've been now." *Border Lines: Contemporary Poems in English*. Edited by J.A. Wainwright, George Elliott Clarke, Ruth Grogan, Victor Li, Robert Ross, and Ann Wallace. Mississauga, ON: Copp Clarke, 1995. 10–14.

"from Market Rinse" and "the rescue." *Premonitions: The Kaya Anthology of New Asian North American Poetry*. Edited by Walter K. Lew. New York: Kaya Production, 1995. 283–89.

"the rescue," "september 22," "in flight, 1/4," and "membrane translate." *Making a Difference: Canadian Multicultural Literature*. Edited by Smaro Kamboureli. Toronto, ON: Oxford University Press, 1996. 212–20.

"The Young Kid." *Facing History: Portraits from Vancouver*. Edited by Karen Love. Vancouver, BC: Presentation House Gallery and Arsenal Pulp Press, 2002. 110–11.

"All Quarters Are Not the Same." *71(+) for GB: An Anthology for George Bowering*. Toronto, ON: Coach House Press, 2005. 93–94.

"fool's scold." *Companions & Horizons: An Anthology of SFU Poetry*. Edited by Stephen Collis. Burnaby, BC: WCL Books, 2005. 174–81.

"make it new," "material recover," "material recovery two," "kiyooka," "fool's scold." *Making a Difference: Canadian Multicultural Literatures in English*. Second Edition. Edited by Smaro Kamboureli. Don Mills, ON: Oxford University Press, 2007. 127–37.

"fool's scold." *The Echoing Years: An Anthology of Contemporary Poetry and Translation from Canada and Ireland*. Edited by John Ennis, Randall Maggs, and Stephanie McKenzie. Waterford, Ireland: Waterford Institute, 2007. 318–21.

"About." *Language for a New Century: Contemporary Poetry from the Middle East, Asia, and Beyond.* Edited by Tina Chang, Nathalie Handal, and Ravi Shankar. New York: W.W. Norton, 2008. 311.

"Early Morning in Taipei." *Rocksalt: An Anthology of Contemporary BC Poetry.* Edited by Mona Fertig and Harold Rhenisch. Salt Spring Island, BC: Mother Tongue, 2008. 158–59.

"There Are Some Days." *A Verse Map of Vancouver.* Edited by George McWhirter. Photography by Derek Von Essen. Vancouver, BC: Anvil Press, 2009. 28.

"Prosthetic Politics," "Tokyo Evening," "From Scoping (also pronounced 'Shopping') in Kits." *Open Text: Canadian Poetry and Poetics in the 21st Century,* Vol. 2. Edited by Roger Farr. North Vancouver, BC: CUE Books, 2009. 67–75.

"Sansei Poem," "Accidental Meeting," "Wa(l)king to New Moon," "[The Train from Narita to Tokyo]," "Watch Signs." *Pulllllllllllllllllllllllll: Poesia Contemporânea Do Canadá.* Edited and translated by John Hevelda, Isabel Patim, and Manuel Portella. Lisboa, Portugal: Antígona, 2010. 177–202.

"attractive," "on the sublime," "make it new." *The Broadview Introduction to Literature: Poetry.* Edited by Lisa Chalykoff, Neta Gordon, and Paul Lumsden. Peterborough, ON: Broadview Press, 2013. 353–57.

BROADSIDES AND OTHER EPHEMERA

"the japanese canadians 100 years" (Broadside Poem). Vancouver, BC: Powell Street Revue, 1977.

"it is a long line" (Poem). *Images of 100 Years: A Slide/Tape History of Japanese Canadians.* Vancouver, BC: Powell Street Revue, 1978.

"Growing Up Asian Canadian" (Talk). Educational video, with curriculum guide. Vancouver, BC: Laurier Institution, 1990.

Native and Japanese Canadian Poets & Writers. Vancouver, BC: The Earth Spirit Festival, 1991. (Note: This pamphlet was prepared for a reading series of Indigenous and Japanese Canadian writers at the Earth Spirit Festival, Harbourfront, Toronto, July 1991.)

"kiyooka in owen sound" (Broadside Poem). *On Edge Reading Series,* Emily Carr School of Art and Design, Vancouver, BC, January 2003.

"Flow: An Unbound Chapbook" (Art Print). Banff IntraNation Residency, May 2004.

"From Scoping (also pronounced 'Shopping') in Kits" (Broadside Poem). Vancouver, BC, May 28, 2008.

"From Scoping (also pronounced 'Shopping') in Kits" (Postcard Insert). *West Coast Line* 40.3, NO. 57 (Spring/Summer 2008).

"For S," "A Recent Trip," "Reel One," "Sojourner," "Eh? Go!," "Lazy Haiku," "Please" (Poems). *pH6: a book of haiku moods.* Vancouver, BC: Powell Street Festival, 2008.

INTERVIEWS BY ROY MIKI

"Roy Kiyooka Interviewed." *Inalienable Rice: A Chinese and Japanese Canadian Anthology.* Vancouver, BC: Powell Street Revue and Chinese Canadian Writers Workshop, 1979.

"Talking West: An Interview with Eli Mandel." *Line*, NO. 1 (Spring 1983): 26–44.

"Self on Self: Robert Kroetsch Interviewed." *Line*, NO. 14 (Fall 1989): 108–42.

"Interruption Is the Form: An Interview with Douglas Barbour on *Story for a Saskatchewan Night*." *Prairie Fire* 3.4 (Winter 1992–93): 18–32.

"Inter-face: Roy Kiyooka's Writing. A Commentary/Interview." *Roy Kiyooka*. Vancouver, BC: Artspeak Gallery and Or Gallery, 1991. 41–54.

INTERVIEWS OF ROY MIKI

Kelly, Paula. "Roy Miki: Writing the Silence." *Word Wrap: The Manitoba Writers' Guild Newsletter*. September 1991: 1–2.

Quinn, Hal. "Legacy of Shame." *Maclean's*, November 18, 1991: 38–39, 45.

"Who's News?" *AQ Magazine*, Simon Fraser University, May 2003: 407.

Fertig, Mona, and Harold Rhenisch. "Poetics Q&A." *Rocksalt: An Anthology of Contemporary BC Poetry*. Edited by Mona Fertig and Harold Rhenisch. Salt Spring Island, BC: Mother Tongue, 2008. 157.

McAllister, Kirsten Emiko. " 'Always Slippage': An Interview on a Collage/Poem Project in Process." *West Coast Line* 42.1, NO. 57 (Spring/ Summer 2008): 148–159.

Beauregard, Guy. "After Redress: A Conversation with Roy Miki." *Canadian Literature* 201 (Summer 2009): 71–86.

McAllister, Kirsten Emiko. "Between the Photograph and the Poem: A Dialogue on Poetic Practice with Roy Miki." *Canadian Journal of Communication* 37.1 (2012): 217–36.

McAllister, Kirsten Emiko. "Between the Photograph and the Poem: A Dialogue on Poetic Practice with Roy Miki." *Tracing the Lines: Reflections on Contemporary Poetics and Cultural Politics in Honour of Roy Miki*. Edited by Maia Joseph, Christine Kim, Larissa Lai, and Christopher Lee. Vancouver, BC: Talonbooks, 2013. 206–26.

Cabri, Louis. "'the coursing of staged crafts': on poetry with Roy Miki." *The Capilano Review* 3.20 (Spring 2013): 8–28.

McAllister, Kirsten Emiko. "Tracing the Lines." *Toward. Some. Air.: Remarks on Poetics* [...] *and Other Practices*. Edited by Fred Wah and Amy De'Ath. Banff, AB: Banff Centre Press, 2015. 95–99.

SECONDARY MATERIALS

West Coast Line 57. Special Issue: Festschrift for Roy Miki 42, NO. 1 (Spring/ Summer 2008).

Joseph, Maia, Christine Kim, Larissa Lai, and Christopher Lee, Editors. *Tracing the Lines: Reflections on Contemporary Poetics and Cultural Politics in Honour of Roy Miki*. Vancouver, BC: Talonbooks, 2012.

JOURNAL AND MAGAZINE ARTICLES

Klobucar, Andrew. "Line Breaks: *West Coast Line*, Past and Present." *Books in Canada* 28, NO. 7 (1999): 14–15.

Budde, Robert. "After Postcolonialism: Migrant Lines and the Politics of Form in Fred Wah, M. Nourbese Philip, and Roy Miki." *Is Canada*

Postcolonial? Unsettling Canadian Literature. Edited by Laura Moss. Waterloo, ON: Wilfrid Laurier University Press, 2003.

Lowry, Glen. "'I missed you in the past tense': An Introduction to the Poetry of Roy Miki." *Ellipse* 70 (2003): 10–19.

Butling, Pauline. "Roy Miki's Editorial Activism." *Open Letter* 12, NO. 3 (2004): 56 et seq.

Dobson, Kit. "Transnational Subjectivities: Roy Miki's *Surrender* and Global Displacements." *Studies in Canadian Literature / Études en littérature canadienne* 32, NO. 2 (2007): 162–72.

Lee, Christopher. "Enacting the Asian Canadian." *Canadian Literature / Littérature canadienne* 199 (2008): 28–44.

Lee, Christopher, Guy Beauregard, Iyko Day, Don Goellnicht, Marie Lo, Glenn Deer, Roy Miki, Rita Wong, and Lily Cho. "Epilogue: A Conversation on Unfinished Projects." *Canadian Literature / Littérature canadienne* 199 (2008): 208–11.

Hart, Jonathan. "Some Reflections on Asian-Canadian Poetry and Culture: Fred Wah, Joy Kogawa, Roy Miki, and Others." *Canadian Review of Comparative Literature / Revue canadienne de littérature comparée* 36, NO. 3 (2009): 310–20.

Lorenzi, Lucia. "Shikata Ga Nai: Mapping Japanese-Canadian Melancholy in the Field of National and Literary Trauma." *West Coast Line* 45, NO. 3 (2011): 100–05.

Cabri, Louis. "the mannequin & the inverse ratio: Roy Miki's *Mannequin Rising.*" *The Capilano Review* 3.20 (Spring 2013): 29-36.

Banwait, Ranbir K. "Ethics, Intention, and Affect: A Proprioceptive Poetics in Roy Miki's *Mannequin Rising.*" *Studies in Canadian Literature / Études en littérature canadienne* 39, NO. 2 (2014): 106–126.

Bates, Catherine. "In Flux: Transnational Shifts in Asian Canadian Writing, by Roy Miki." *British Journal of Canadian Studies* 27, NO. 1 (2014): 122–23.

Markotić, Nicole. "Where the Line Breaks: Disability in the Poetry of Roy Miki and Sharon Thesen." In *Disability in Film and Literature*, 127–41. Jefferson, NC: McFarland and Company, 2016.

Index of Titles and First Lines

Italicized text denotes first lines, regular text denotes poem titles, and CAPITALIZED text denotes section titles. Untitled poems are listed only by first line. Ellipses indicate a continuing line that has been truncated for length in this index. In poems with sections, numbered or not, only the first line of the first section is included.